Knopp, Lisa.
What the River
Carries

of three national treasures—the Mississippi, Platte, and
Missouri rivers. Here we visit places as exotic as Little Egypt
yet as familiar as streams connecting our own backyards
to these great waterways. Knopp asks hard questions about
human interaction—and interference—with these watery
corridors which are largely responsible for American
expansion. Journeying through these pages, we also find tales
of the shell button industry, Indian burial mounds, Mormon
settlement, catastrophic flooding, barge commerce, and
everyday lives of people who work and play along the shores.
What this book carries? Majesty. Knowledge. Inspiration."

—KATHERINE FISCHER, author of *Dreaming the Mississippi*

"A river gathers the countryside, drawing the current of
tributary streams into a single flow, offering passage to
travelers, nurturing all manner of creatures, and eventually,
perhaps by way of larger rivers, delivering its waters to the
sea. Just so, in the hands of a skillful writer like Lisa Knopp,
an essay draws material from a varied terrain of memory,
history, folklore, observation, and reflection, gathering far-
flung sources into a forceful narrative. Linked together, these
narratives trace the ways in which three great rivers have
been used, abused, and partly restored by humans over the
past ten thousand years—a panoramic history that should be
of interest to any reader who's curious about the shaping of
America's interior."

—SCOTT RUSSELL SANDERS, author of *Earth Works* and
A Conservationist Manifesto

WHAT THE
RIVER
CARRIES

WHAT THE RIVER

CARRIES

Encounters with the
Mississippi, Missouri, and Platte

Lisa Knopp

University of Missouri Press

Columbia and London

Copyright © 2012 by
The Curators of the University of Missouri
University of Missouri Press, Columbia, Missouri 65201
Printed and bound in the United States of America
All rights reserved
5 4 3 2 1   16 15 14 13 12

Cataloging-in-Publication data available from the Library of Congress.
ISBN 978-0-8262-1974-9

♾™ This paper meets the requirements of the
American National Standard for Permanence of Paper
for Printed Library Materials, Z39.48, 1984.

Designer: Stephanie Foley
Typesetter: FoleyDesign
Printer and binder: Thompson-Shore, Inc.
Typefaces: Minion and Utopia

For my traveling companions

Contents

Preface

I love rivers. Wide ones, narrow ones, straight ones, winding ones, fast ones, slow ones, single-channeled and braided ones. I love a river's mysterious depths and bottoms, its reflectiveness, its changeability and rhythms—spring thaw, annual rise, low water, winter freeze. I love that a river's rushing waters stir my imagination and connect me with other parts of the region, country, continent, earth. In truth, I've never met a river that I didn't love or grow to love. But three rivers, the Mississippi, the Missouri, and Nebraska's Platte, are especially dear to me. These rivers and the different ways in which I know each of them are the subjects of this book.

I was born and raised just a few blocks from the Mississippi in Burlington, Iowa, and returned to live there twice as an adult. The most essential knowledge about my home stretch of that river came to me when I was a child, through repeated experiences (watching floods come and go; seeing the river almost every day and usually from more than one perspective—bluff top, bridge, boat, and bank) and through stories that my grandparents, parents, brothers, and friends told about it. Consequently, I know a forty-mile stretch of the river in southeastern Iowa and west-central Illinois from the viewpoint of an insider, inhabitant, native, or what the bioregionalist calls a "dweller in the land." Not only is this river landscape filled with personal memories and family history, but it's so integral to my sense of belonging and identity that one of the first things I tell a new acquaintance is that I grew up on the Mississippi. Now when I return to my part of the river, it's as if I'm visiting a beloved family member, with whom I have a deep, rich history. When I explore other parts of the Upper Mississippi, that part of the river between the headwaters at Lake Itasca in Minnesota and Cairo, Illinois, I feel that I'm encountering distant kin: the family resemblance is there, but the long, close relationship is not.

Many times during the three years that I lived in Omaha, and later, during the three years in which I had reason to be in St. Louis several times a month, and more recently, in my rambles in the Midwest and Great Plains, I've come across the Missouri. But because I didn't grow up near it, eat fish drawn from its waters, go to steamboat or catfish festivals on its banks, witness its floods and mayfly swarms, ride in motorboats over its rough or calm waters, or dream about crossing it on bridges that are too high and convoluted or that break mid-journey or that offer smooth passage over beautiful, shining water, I have no attachment to it. Until I began working on this book, the Missouri was merely a familiar stranger, one that I observed but never interacted with. On its banks, I was an outsider, tourist, traveler, or sojourner, marveling at or puzzling over the new, capturing my experiences with a camera and notebook, and then returning to my home near the banks of a different river, which was an even different river than the one that winds its way through my dreams. Most of what I know about the Missouri, I learned from experts and dwellers in the land that have a long and committed relationship with a part of the river, and so my knowledge is largely mediated or secondhand rather than direct and experiential. These guides led me from merely noticing things and surfaces to perceiving connections and meanings. Even so, while exploring the Missouri, I often felt that I was a guest at someone else's family reunion.

Now I live in land watered by the Platte. Here, I've consciously sought to become less of an outsider and more of an insider, which is yet another way of knowing landscape. Over the past twenty years, I've learned about the Platte from books and classes, experts and inhabitants, and have experienced it through extended residence and, most importantly, through my children, for whom the Platte is a first river, a first exterior landscape. Growing to love a landscape is similar to growing to love a person. Both require time and intention, if one is to develop and sustain a love that is deep and committed.

This book is divided into three parts, one for each river. Each part presents that river from various perspectives: what the river was like in its wild state; how travelers, both historical and contemporary, have seen it; how it came by its various names; how First Americans lived near and with it; how those in industry and agriculture have used it; what the river is like after a century or two of human tinkering and engineering; how the culture, politics, and philosophy of the people who live in a watershed have been and continue to be shaped by the river; how the river looks and smells and sounds. The genre I've chosen for exploring my encounters with these rivers is the essay, whose various subgenres and forms allowed me to narrate, report, confess, speculate, reflect, imagine, and expound. In other words, I could speak of these rivers in different voices and from different angles. Within this collection, you'll find travel, autobiographical, and natural-history essays, as well as those that blend the personal and the scholarly. I offer my river stories as but one person's perspective on the complex process of coming to know and love both familiar and foreign places.

Needless to say, a handful of essays can't adequately represent the natural and human history of something as vast and complex as a river. Nor can a handful of essays plumb the subtle and interior process of becoming acquainted with or falling in love with a place. Consider the essays in each section as you do those little morsels on toothpicks that you sample at the grocery store on Saturday mornings. There's just enough of the fresh pineapple or the smoked Gouda cheese for you to experience the taste and texture, aroma and appearance. But there's not enough to fill you. For that, you must buy your own pineapple or wedge of cheese; for that, you must take your own journey into the landscape.

Acknowledgments

I gratefully acknowledge the contributions of the following:

My mother, Patricia Knopp, who answered questions about so many aspects of the Mississippi. Always, she is my first reader.

My son, Ian Knopp, and his good companion, Brandy Kreifel, who took me fishing.

My daughter, Meredith Ramsay, whose vast musical knowledge and expertise was a critical part of my research for "Missouri River Music" and who carefully scrutinized several other essays.

Iowa Representative Thomas Courtney, Molly Edwards-Britton, Rustin Lippincott, Brenda Logan, Liz Murphy, Irene Payson, Ernie Rousek, and the late Marie Carter, who contributed in various ways.

My Modern Familiar Essay students from the fall semester of 2009 at the University of Nebraska-Omaha, who made perceptive comments about an early draft of "Restorations."

Elizabeth Dodd, whose insights and suggestions as an outside reader for the University of Missouri Press made this a far stronger book.

Clair Willcox, Gloria Thomas, Sara Davis, Jennifer Gravley, and all at the University of Missouri Press who saw the project through to the end.

David Boocker, Dean of the College of Arts and Sciences at the University of Nebraska-Omaha, and those members of the English Department who saw to it that I had a lighter teaching load for several semesters so that I could research, travel, write, and revise.

I gratefully acknowledge the attention the following essays received from the editors of the publications where they first appeared:

"Mississippi Harvest." *Big Muddy: A Journal of the Mississippi River Valley,* Spring 2012.

"Catfish Bend." *Natural Bridge,* Fall 2011.

"Painting the River." *Big Muddy: A Journal of the Mississippi River Valley,* Fall/ Winter 2011.

"The Overlook." *NEBRASKAland,* November 2011.

"Missouri River Music." *South Dakota Review,* Winter 2010.

"What the River Carries." *Prairie Schooner,* Winter 2010.

"Restorations." *North Dakota Quarterly,* Fall 2009.

"Nauvoo, the Beautiful Place." *Big Muddy: A Journal of the Mississippi River Valley,* Spring 2010.

"Meanderings." *NEBRASKAland,* August 2010.

"No Other River." *Iowa Review,* August 2009.

"Nine-Mile Prairie." *Michigan Quarterly Review,* Summer 2007.

And I gratefully acknowledge the editors of *The Best American Essays* for honoring two of my essays with Notable Essay citations:

"No Other River." *The Best American Essays 2010,* edited by Christopher Hitchens and Robert Atwan.

"Nine-Mile Prairie." *The Best American Essays 2008,* edited by Adam Gopnik and Robert Atwan.

Part I

The Mississippi

1

Catfish Bend

As a child, I didn't know where the Mississippi River came from or where it went after it flowed past my hometown, Burlington, and my mother's hometown, Keokuk, forty miles downstream. Nor did I know that Iowa's eastern border, as drawn by the Mississippi, could be seen as a misshapen face and neck, with Clinton near the tip of the bulbous nose, the Quad Cities at the nostril, Burlington at the top of the lower lip, and Keokuk on the Adam's apple. Nor did I know anything about those who had lived at my bend of the river before my ancestors arrived there. But I did know how the river smelled, how an abundance of wriggling, gasping, flapping, or snapping creatures lived near or in it, how it shimmered in the sunlight or turned dark when the sky was overcast, how viciously it could flood, and how it oriented me in space, since the river was always east.

I know now that Burlington and Keokuk had their origins in June of 1832, when the U.S. government forced the Sauk, Meskwaki (Fox), and Ho-Chunk (Winnebago) to surrender a strip of land about forty miles wide along the west side of the Mississippi, extending from what would become the Iowa-Missouri state line almost to the Iowa-Minnesota state line. Saukenuk, on the east side of the river eighty-five miles north of Burlington, had been the principal town of the Sauk nation. The several thousand people who lived there had cultivated some eight hundred acres of corn and other vegetables and had caught an abundance of fish near the confluence of the Rock and Mississippi rivers.

In 1832, the United States opened the Black Hawk Purchase to nonnative settlement. The next year, those who settled at the lower-lip-like bend in the river named their village Flint Hills, the English translation of *Sho-quo-quon,* which is what the Meskwaki called the place where they gathered flint for their arrowheads. In 1834, John B. Gray, who purchased the first lot in Flint Hills, renamed the settlement after his home place, Burlington, Vermont. There were other, more evocative names for my hometown, including Porkopolis (in the mid-nineteenth century, Burlington boasted three pork-packing plants), Turd Town (so named because of the contents of the Hawk-Eye Creek, which cut across town to the river), and my favorite, Catfish Bend. The latter is still an honorable name even though in 2007 it was appropriated by a casino that floats not in the river but in a pool of water near the intersection of U.S. Highways 34 and 61.

Catfish was a staple at our house. For most Saturday suppers my mother fried catfish in a flour or cornmeal batter and tossed a salad (potato, pea, cabbage, or macaroni) in a mayonnaise dressing. Cold catfish made a good snack, though my grandfather told me that I shouldn't eat fish alone. "Have crackers or a hunk of bread with it," he advised. Sometimes we went to the Riverview Restaurant in Dallas City, Illinois, a smorgasbord with heaps of fried catfish, or the Eagles Club in Burlington, which my mother judged to have the best catfish that she'd ever eaten and so big that the fish hung over the edge of your plate. Though my father fished, my parents also bought fish at Vice's Fish Market upriver in Oquawka, Illinois. Once, they were there early enough to see the commercial fishermen bring in their catch, quickly kill and clean the fish, and load them onto a truck headed for Chicago, some two hundred miles away. "They'll be served this evening in Chicago's finest restaurants," my mother marveled. Chicago!

When I came home from college for weekend visits and wanted to create distance between myself and a place once called Turd Town, rather than eating my mother's fried catfish, I baked or poached mine, as if it were salmon or halibut—anything but a fish pulled from the old, dirty, and familiar Mississippi.

Nature's wonder: a fish like a cat that sports gracefully sweeping, whiskerlike barbels around its mouth, that rests by day and prowls by night, that gets in brawls with other cats, that slips, felinelike, past obstacles in logjammed water.

My father ran basket traps on the stretch of river between Memorial Auditorium and the railroad bridge. A catfish was lured into one of his baskets by a smelly morsel broken off a cheese brick; wooden slats kept it from swimming back out. To anchor a basket, my father tied a cinderblock to it with about fifty feet of old telephone cord. He marked the locations of his baskets by tying them in his memory to something stable on shore—a dock, tree, or cabin—so he would know where to drag the hook from the boat to snag the baskets and haul them up, hopefully full of slapping, writhing catfish. If my father brought up empty baskets, it may have been because the fish found tastier fare elsewhere. But, too, the baskets may have been vandalized. "Not all folks on the river are honest," my mother says. But often, my dad brought home a mess of flatheads. With its mottled yellow-brown skin, bad underbite, flattened skull between its tiny eyes, and squared-off tail, the flathead was, to my eyes, the ugliest of the catfish.

If my father wanted channel catfish, he went south of town and approached the river from a beach owned by the electric company. There the river bottom was more gravelly than muddy and the water clearer—just the way channel cat like it. My maternal grandparents were also avid fishers, though they preferred ponds and lakes, where they caught perch and crappie. It was with them that I caught my first fish, a bluegill. But in later years, after my grandparents moved to Burlington from Keokuk, my grandfather walked down the hill from his Main Street apartment with his fishing pole and the bait balls that he made from cornmeal and limburger cheese, and he, too, angled for channel catfish. With its streamlined form, deeply forked and pointy-tipped tail, curved and rayed anal fin, and dark freckles on its silvery sides, it was the most beautiful of the catfish.

A survey conducted in 1968 revealed that if there was to be a state fish, most Iowans favored the channel catfish, *Ictalurus punctatus*. The late George L. Marzeck Sr. of West Burlington, a former writer, photographer, and illustrator for *Midwest Outdoors, Field and Stream,* and *Fur, Fish and Game,* spent decades campaigning to get the channel cat officially declared the Iowa state fish. After all, Iowa has a state rock (the geode), a state tree (the oak), a state flower (the wild rose), and a state bird (the eastern goldfinch). Why not a state fish? Marzeck, who signed the lowercase letter *g* in his first name as a stylized fishhook with a small barb on the end, preferred the bass, but because of the catfish's abundance in Iowa's waterways and the desires of the majority, it was the channel catfish that he promoted for the position of honor. "I've had outdoor writers from all over the country tell me, 'I never go through Iowa without stopping for one of your delicious catfish dinners,'" Marzeck told Radio Iowa. "So I says, 'Hey, let's ballyhoo this thing and maybe bring in some more revenue from people passing through.'" Marzeck always said catfish is the tastiest fish you can poke a fork into. "I don't think there's a place in Iowa that serves food that doesn't have catfish on the menu. When you have a church social or any kind of a gathering, what do you serve? Catfish and hush puppies, and coleslaw, maybe."

A joint resolution seeking to designate the catfish as the state fish offered several other reasons why this would be the most logical choice for the position of honor. The catfish not only is native and abundant, but also is found in all ninety-nine Iowa counties and is, in the words of the resolution, "easily recognizable by its slender scale-less body, deeply forked tail, fleshy whiskers, and sharp spines." It's easily and cheaply caught, excellent table fare, the state's most consumed fish, lucrative (Iowa's catfishers spend about $400 million a year in the pursuit), and the most preferred fish among Iowa anglers, reaching trophy size above thirty pounds and providing pole-bending action.

Not all Iowans approved of the idea of making this species a state symbol. In February 2001, the *Burlington Hawk Eye* reported that Garry Thomas, a member of the Burlington City Council and a friend of mine in high school, contended that because the catfish eats dead things, it would damage the state's reputation if it were chosen as state fish. "We should not be portrayed as a scavenger state," Thomas said. "We should not be linked to a fish like this when we're trying to build our image up." Some feel that the bass, with its fierce strikes, its aerial leaps and twists, its top-of-the-food-chain diet, and the specialized equipment that people invest in to catch it, is a more glamorous piscine river dweller. But Marzeck believed that it's the catfish that represents the character of Iowans. "The channel catfish prefers clean, clear water," he pointed out, "but it's tough enough to put up with a lot of crap."

Legislation promoting the catfish was introduced in the Iowa House and Senate several times between 1972 and 2011. Each time it failed. My suspicion is that there are too many men and women in the statehouse who don't spend enough time sitting on a riverbank holding a fishing pole. Despite the defeats, Marzeck continued campaigning with gusto on behalf of the catfish, writing hundreds of letters to state and local officials and giving school presentations at his own expense. Marzeck had been part of a group of six promoting the catfish, but as the fight dragged on, he was the only one left. Even after Marzeck was diagnosed with cancer, he continued his crusade. In a letter to a state senator, Marzeck wrote that "three of my doctors believe my continuing determination to get the channel catfish named the official state fish of Iowa is helping me put on a pretty good battle against my third bout of cancer." Marzeck died September 17, 2006, at age eighty-two without seeing the channel cat receive its due. Though the Iowa Senate passed the proposal in 2008, the demands of other legislation kept the House from voting on it that session.

In a logjam at the bottom of the river near Burlington lives a giant catfish. In the stories we told about the monster, we usually compared him (it was always a "him") to mammals (as big as a dog, sheep, or grizzly bear) or vehicles (as big as a Volkswagen or school bus). Many of the tales about this mossy-backed behemoth were stories of loss or near loss: the disappearance of dogs, pigs, and other domestic animals; broken or lost tackle, arms, and legs; and near drownings. In some stories, the titan fish threatened the lives of those who worked on the bridges. Close encounters with the lunker so spooked the workers that they turned white-headed overnight and found safer jobs away from the river—like on the assembly line at the nuclear-weapons plant west of town. "Maybe every river town has one of these," my mother mused about the giant catfish.

An article in the June 23, 1998, *Hawk Eye* gives the authority of the printed word to the legends. Gene Murray reports that some claim that "Old Moe" is a two to three hundred–pound flathead, though "the wide-eyed commercial fisherman with the huge hole in his trammel net swears to have had him up once and his head would weigh more than that." Murray tells of the time when two young men, one from Iowa, one from Illinois, were determined to pull Old Moe from the river. Since flatheads love carp minnows, the fishers kept "a couple of 25 pounders . . . in the horse tank behind the barn." Since the challengers knew that their regular equipment wasn't worthy of the task at hand, they mail ordered a huge, stainless-steel shark hook with a chain leader. For the mainline, they used two hundred yards of one-thousand-pound-test nylon rappelling rope. "Fearing that no manageable rod would handle the legendary might of Moe," explains Murray, "our heroes opted for a direct connection to the hitch on a four wheel drive pick-up." A crowd gathered; people placed their bets; an announcer narrated the action. Old Moe was fierce. The truck threw sand and gravel into the air as the tires spun. Eventually, Old Moe broke loose and got away. But the pursuit wasn't for naught: the two fishers reeled in a sixty-pound lower jaw.

River people have long been captivated by rumors of leviathan catfish. Perhaps the first written account of a monster catfish was that of the fur trader and explorer Louis Jolliet, who, with Jacques Marquette, a Jesuit missionary, paddled down the Mississippi in 1673 in search of the fabled Northwest Passage to the Orient for the governor of New France. Just north of what is now Alton, Illinois, Jolliet recorded in his journal: "We met from time to time these monstrous fish which struck so violently against our canoes that we took them to be large trees, which threatened to upset us." In *Life on the Mississippi*, Mark Twain says that Indians had warned the two travelers that "the river contained a demon 'whose roar could be heard at a great distance, and who would engulf them in the abyss where he dwelt.'" Twain reports that he had himself seen a Mississippi catfish that weighed 250 pounds and was more than 6 feet long. "If Marquette's fish was the fellow to that one, he had a fair right to think the river's roaring demon was come."

In 1765, over four hundred miles upriver from where Marquette and Jolliet were frightened by monster catfish, Peter Pond, a soldier, fur trader, explorer, and mapmaker in the Old Northwest and the Upper Mississippi, and his crew caught giant catfish. "We put our Hoock and Lines into the Water and Leat them Ly all nite. In the Morning we Perseaved there was fish at the Hoocks," Pond noted in his journal. "They Came Heavey. At Length we hald one ashore that wade a Hundred and four Pounds—a Second that was One Hundred Wate—a third of Seventy-five Pounds." Pond asked his men how many of them it would take to eat the largest fish, the 104-pounder, with "a large flat Head

Sixteen Inches Betwene the Eise." Twelve men skinned it, cut it up, boiled it "in large Coppers," and "Sawed it up." They ate the entire fish, and "Sum of them Drank of the Licker it was Boild in."

My parents' friend Sam catfishes at Lock and Dam No. 18, north of Burlington; the drainage ditch near Iowa Highway 99; the Port of Burlington, a former barge-loading station that is now a State of Iowa Welcome Center; and the beach owned by the electric company. It was at the last that her five-foot, six-inch sister-in-law caught a catfish as tall as she is. Sam's brother waded into the water and wrestled the fish to the bank. A big fish fry followed.

Like Old Moe, these catfish swim in the murky area between fact and legend. But now there are monster catfish whose sizes have been verified with newspaper photographs and documentation through the International Game Fish Association. On May 22, 2005, Tim Pruitt, a factory worker from Fosterburg, Illinois, near Alton, pulled a 124-pound blue catfish, 58 inches long and 44 inches around, from the Mississippi below the Melvin Price Lock and Dam. Pruitt and the fish struggled for more than half an hour. At one point the fish was actually dragging Pruitt's boat. In a widely published photograph, Pruitt, a burly guy, holds a catfish the size of a thirty-four-gallon garbage can across his chest and abdomen. The fish is rather porpoiselike, with its smooth, blue-gray skin, blunt, round nose, slightly humped back, and forked tail. Pruitt donated his catch to the Cabela's store in Kansas City, where it would have lived in a giant aquarium if it hadn't died en route. A fisheries biologist with the Illinois Department of Natural Resources estimated that Pruitt's catch was at least thirty years old. I suspect that this fish inspired river-town legends about a fish as big as an SUV, bridge workers who now drive trucks, and some old fisher who claims to possess a lower jawbone too heavy to lift without help.

It was during the Flood of 2008 that I realized that stories of giant catfish are more than just fish stories. At five o'clock in the morning on June 17, the Mississippi tore a hole more than three hundred yards long in the levee on the Illinois side of the river across from Burlington. The river, carrying cornstalks and other debris, poured into the Gulfport bottoms, moving at about a foot and a half per second. The force of the water pushed the village hall five feet off its foundation. The fast water trapped a man and two dogs in their vehicle on Highway 34. They were rescued by helicopter. Larry Gapen, the Carthage Lake Drainage District pump plant operator, and his dog, Molly, were still at the pump station when the Mississippi burst through the levee. "They came inside and got me and said the levee broke," Gapen told the *Hawk Eye*. "I tried to go out to the road but the water was covering the road so fast there [was] only one way. I told everyone to go to the levee." From that vantage point, Gapen watched the river swallow his house. He left the area by boat.

From Mosquito Park on a bluff above the Mississippi, I saw the sprawling river; the Great River Bridge, which led not from land to land but from water to water; the tops of the trees lining what had been the river's eastern shore; and, instead of the usual village of Gulfport, Highway 34, and fields of corn and soybeans; a vast and sparkling lake. Seventy billion gallons of water covered twenty-eight thousand acres in Henderson County, Illinois. June 18, a levee broke at Meyer, a village of forty to fifty people near Quincy, Illinois, about seventy miles downriver. It was the eleventh levee to fail on the Mississippi since the flooding began. Because a levee breach on one side of the river lessens the severity of the flooding on the other side, the breach at Gulfport saved Burlington (population 26,000); the breach at Meyer saved Canton, Missouri (population 2,550). Levee breaks at Winfield and Foley, Missouri, saved homes and fields in Illinois. The various upriver levee breaks eased the threat in the greater St. Louis area (population 2.8 million). Nonetheless, many river dwellers lost homes and businesses; crops were buried beneath several feet of sand and debris; the toxic water rose halfway up some grain bins; travelers and residents were stranded because of the bridge and highway closings. I had gone home to help sandbag, but with the bridges closed, I couldn't cross to the east side of the river, where help was most needed.

Gulfport still hasn't recovered. Six months after the flood, only two businesses, Sam's Speakeasy and the ADM grain elevator, had reopened. Most houses were so badly damaged that they had to be demolished. In April 2010, almost two years after the flood, only sixty of the two hundred or so people who lived in Gulfport at the time of the flood had returned. But those who have come back are optimistic. They've rebuilt the town hall, are refurbishing the park with grant money from the state, and are seeking $12 million in buyouts and from other sources so they can build the fire department and housing outside of the floodplain. Henderson County is working to rebuild the levee so that it can regain its one hundred–year certification through the Federal Emergency Management Agency's National Flood Insurance Program. In April 2009, voters approved a plan to build a five hundred–year levee that will cost about $37 million.

As I surveyed the submerged towns, farms, highways, and riverfronts during the Flood of 2008, I realized what the monster catfish stories are really about. As a child, I had heard stories about how dangerous and frustrating the river was—not only its floods, but also its low water during droughts, shifts in its course that reworked state and property lines, and its undertows that could pull you under and hold you there, which is why sane people don't swim in the river. But these stories harkened back to earlier times, prior to the 1930s and 1940s, when the U.S. Army Corps of Engineers tamed my stretch of the Mississippi, turning the once free-flowing river into a tightly controlled navigation system, thus providing what the natural river could not: a reliable nine-foot naviga-tional channel to accommodate barge traffic. Now the greatest danger of enter-ing the water isn't the undertow but the chemicals and wastes that it carries and the five hundred–year floods, those roaring and engulfing demons that are increasing in number and severity as the climate changes. To tell and retell stories about the monster catfish that you or someone else glimpsed or almost caught is a way of giving the river's dangers, mystery, beauty, bounty, and per-sistence form and substance, and so of making the river more manageable. To catch a catfish, even if it's too small to keep, is to momentarily master the river.

I now live 320 miles west of the Mississippi, in Lincoln, Nebraska. The catfish in my freezer weren't pulled from the Mississippi by my parents or grandparents or brothers, but from lakes in southeastern Nebraska by my son, Ian. Instead of walking a few blocks to reach the Mississippi, I now have to drive over twenty miles just to see a water flow large enough to be called a river. If I want to see a river deep enough to float a barge, I have to drive over fifty miles.

Though I no longer live at Catfish Bend, several times a week I read in the online edition of my hometown newspaper about the river stages, the area fish-ing reports, the losses of buildings, people, and places that I used to know, and the city's continued movement westward, away from the river. Once or twice a year, I return to Burlington and other Mississippi River towns to do library or archival research about my stretch of the river and to take long riverside strolls. Often, I daydream of owning a rustic little cabin on stilts on the river side of the levee and have, on a couple of occasions, looked at riverfront prop-erty. While I'm no longer part of the daily life at Catfish Bend, because I spent my childhood there, a time when every experience was new and memorable and weighted with significance, a time when everything I knew about the river came to me through the stories of those inhabitants who had a long-lived inti-macy with the place, I know the geography and the human response to it with a depth of love and understanding that I have yet to acquire in my "new" home of twenty years.

In the twenty-some years since I left Catfish Bend, I've acquired the formal knowledge that contextualizes the place I came from. The United States maps that hang in my university and home offices show the entire length of the Mississippi, from Lake Itasca to the Gulf of Mexico, which reminds me where my river comes from and where it goes after it flows past my hometown. When I look at the map, I remember Mississippi River sites that I've explored: the pre-Columbian burial and ceremonial mounds lining the river; the locks and dams; the great cities that prospered because of their proximity to the river; the little towns lost to floods; the wildlife refuges where waterfowl gather; the sites of former fur-trading posts and utopias and mussel-shell ("pearl") button factories; the condominiums, casinos, and shopping malls built perhaps in defiance, perhaps from collective amnesia on the floodplains. Now, when I look at the Upper Mississippi on the map, I remember the points where other rivers—the St. Croix, Yellow, Wisconsin, Rock, Iowa, Skunk, Des Moines, Illinois, Missouri, and Ohio—flow into mine. After these travels over the map, my eyes always come home to rest on the lower-lip-like bend in the river.

Catfish Bend was twice blessed. As Alfred T. Andreas noted in his 1875 *Andreas Illustrated Historical Atlas of the State of Iowa*, the alluvial and prairie soils of Des Moines County made it "one of the best agricultural counties in the state." And just outside our front door was a major transportation corridor that connected the Twin Cities to Burlington to St. Louis to Memphis to New Orleans. In 1868, the Chicago, Burlington, and Quincy Railroad (the CB&Q) entered Burlington when it built a single-track railroad bridge over the Mississippi and established a repair shop, where both my grandfather and father would earn their bread and butter. In August 1872, 147 steamboats passed beneath the Burlington Railroad Bridge. A few decades earlier, flatboats and keelboats weighted with cargo created traffic jams on the river. Now, tows take their time moving petroleum, grain, coal, ammonia, and scrap metal up and down the river; passenger and freight trains pass through Catfish Bend several times a day.

During the latter half of the nineteenth century, Burlington became a booming industrial town, packing pork and milling grain and lumber. The 1911 *Encyclopedia Britannica* reports that in the early twentieth century, my hometown turned local and imported materials into "lumber, furniture, baskets, pearl buttons, cars, carriages and wagons, Corliss engines, waterworks pumps, metallic burial cases, desks, boxes, crackers, flour, pickles and beer." For several decades, Burlington was one of the premier lumber towns on the Upper Mississippi. Several local people prospered as furniture manufacturers, turning huge log rafts from Minnesota and Wisconsin into desks and cabinets and bureaus. In 1871, lumber shipping peaked, the beginning of the end for that industry. A headline in the November 29, 1897, *New York Times* warned, "Western Forests Doomed: Minnesota, Wisconsin, and Northern Michigan Will Soon Be Depleted of Their Timber." In 1915, the last lumber raft stopped at Burlington. Ironically, the Leopold family, who lived on a high bluff above the river and who made a fortune crafting elegant desks, sideboards, and bookcases at the Leopold Desk Company with wood harvested from northern forests, brought forth a child who became one of the world's greatest ecologists and ethicists. In "The Land Ethic," an essay in his book *A Sand County Almanac and Sketches Here and There*, Aldo Leopold calls for a new conception of history. Instead of presenting the past only in terms of human enterprise, instead of merely recounting the wars and industries, the booms and busts, he directs us to understand historical events as "biotic interactions" between the people and the land, with the human as but one member of the "biotic team." Because "the characteristics of the land determine the facts quite as potently as the characteristics of the men who lived on it," Leopold contends, history, properly told, is the story of how people, successfully or unsuccessfully, interacted with the water, weather, soils, fish, plants, and other living creatures.

Stories about catfish and catfishers are one piece of the ecological history of my hometown. So, too, are stories about floods and our response to them. People have long been drawn to the Mississippi because of what it provides: catfish, mussels, waterfowl, water, wood, and energy. But living too close to the river poses dangers. It wasn't until quite recently in the history of human interactions with the Mississippi that people attempted to control it by dredging, straightening, damming, and leveeing. Many continue to see this as the answer to the river's cyclical flooding. Don Kerr, a Warsaw, Illinois, farmer, has drawn local support for his efforts to persuade the government to build a five hundred–year levee along the Upper Mississippi. According to Kerr's calculations, the known losses from the Flood of 2008 to farmers in Hancock and Adams counties in Illinois came to about $80 million, a total that he says doesn't yet include the cost of "about a half-dozen more unknown damages like stress and delayed purchases." Kerr figures that it will cost the government $40 million to raise the levee in his part of the river. A bargain, in Kerr's mind. So, too, for Mark Ford, a commissioner with the Henderson County Drainage District No. 2. In March 2009, Ford told the *Hawk Eye*, "If we can get the levees built up to the five hundred-year elevation, maybe there can be some more development in that bottom ground"—bottomland that recently was under water, debris, and toxic wastes. Because a study done by the U.S. Army Corps of Engineers shows that the cost benefits of the levee don't meet the Corps' one-to-one ratio requirement (i.e., for every dollar spent on levee improvements, there must be at least one dollar's worth of property protected), the plan to raise a five hundred–year levee in western Illinois hasn't received congressional support.

Tall levees offer a false sense of security that encourages risky development in flood-prone areas. When levees fail, as they did at Gulfport, Meyer, Winfield, Foley, and other towns during the Flood of 2008 and at New Orleans during Hurricane Katrina, they do so spectacularly and sometimes catastrophically. Fortunately, a growing number of scientists and public policy makers now see levees as more of a problem than a solution, since they make the river run higher and faster. Wiser land use policies, which limit development near the river, and restoration of the great natural sponges that once lined the river (Iowa, Illinois, and Missouri have allowed over 80 percent of their wetlands to be lost to agriculture or development, making those states the national leaders in the destruction of wetlands) will do far more to minimize the damage from flooding than higher levees. So, too, will limiting the amount of fossil fuels that we burn. The carbon dioxide emitted into the atmosphere by the burning of oil, coal, and natural gas warms the air. Warmer air holds more water vapor than cooler air, which results in heavier, more intense rainfall events. This in turn causes the rivers to flood.

Some cities and larger towns along the Mississippi have been moving away from the river for several decades, though more for economic than environmental reasons. When I was in college during the late 1970s and early 1980s, the factories that had provided so many workers in my hometown with a good living and the money to send their children to college started leaving Burlington for the same reasons they left other midwestern cities and towns. A new mall pulled businesses and eventually the medical center away from what had once been the city's lifeblood: the river. Burlington began a long, slow decline that continues to this day, though the casino, the big-box retailers, and the medical center on the west side of town seem to be holding their own. Even though it's been many years since you could buy a new shirt, get a prescription filled, or watch a movie in downtown Burlington, the people of my hometown will never abandon the riverfront. One of the constants is that there will always be people who want to catch and eat catfish and tell stories about the big one they caught or that got away or that lives at the bottom of the river, too tough and wily to be caught by any of us.

It's been a long time since I've eaten catfish or any other animal flesh. But if I ever fall off the wagon and revert to my old ways, I know what form the indulgence will take. I won't dip the channel catfish in cornmeal batter and fry it. Rather, I'll bake it, seasoned only with a dash of salt, so that nothing will interfere with the flavor of the old, dirty, familiar, magnificent, and uncontrollable Mississippi River.

2

Painting the River

I don't remember where I first saw Henry Lewis's lithograph of Burlington and the Mississippi as they appeared in 1848, when my hometown was a little over one-tenth of its present size. Perhaps it was on display at the public library or the county historical society museum, at the hospital or the depot, or in some old volume of local history. At any rate, the painted image of the soft, quiet hills encircling a bend in the river is one that I've long known.

Lewis presents Catfish Bend from the vantage point of South Hill, where my family lived when I was in middle school and high school. The lowlands below South Hill are broken into farms and pastures where cattle graze. On the low shelf encircling a meander in the river are numerous many-windowed buildings and several churches. In the distance, black smoke rises from a tall smokestack. North Hill, which I remember as a place of Late Victorian–, Italian Villa–, and Queen Anne–style houses, many of which were torn down for the segment of U.S. Highway 34 that cut a wide gash through town in the mid-1970s, is grassy and tree-topped in Lewis's painting. West Hill, the old Swedish neighborhood where my paternal grandmother grew up, is crowned by a tall church steeple. In his journal, Lewis describes my hometown as an amphitheater with the river as the stage and the hills as the tiers of seats. On "stage" in Lewis's day were flatboats, keelboats, log rafts, and steamboats. In my childhood, it was the depot, the railroad tracks near the river, the railroad bridge, MacArthur Bridge (a cantilever truss bridge, since torn down and replaced), barges, water-skiers, and motorboats. Lewis concludes that Burlington was a "fine thriving town, beautifully situated on a gradually rising slope surrounded by very picturesque hills."

Recently, I discovered the context for this painting of Catfish Bend. In 1848, Lewis spent five weeks drifting downriver from the Falls of St. Anthony to St. Louis in a houseboat, sketching what he saw on the shores so that he could make paintings afterward. Shortly thereafter, Charles Rogers, one of Lewis's employees, sketched scenes on the Lower Mississippi, from the Gulf of Mexico to St. Louis. While Lewis failed to create a complete, detailed, and

14

unbiased portrait of the river, as has anyone else who has tried, he did succeed in capturing his impressions of the river as it appeared during the early years of the nation's great westward expansion.

Henry Lewis saw the Mississippi River for the first time in 1835, when he was sixteen years old. He had never seen anything like it either in Newport, England, where he was born and lived until he was ten, or in Boston, where his family lived for a few years before settling in St. Louis. Surely Lewis was impressed by the great river that watered the fast-growing city; that flooded frequently, sometimes violently, as it did in 1844; that drew legions of immigrants to its banks (the population of St. Louis jumped from almost seven thousand in 1830 to seventy-five thousand in 1850, due mostly to the influx of German and Irish immigrants); that was a busy superhighway (1,476 steamboats arrived at the wharf in St. Louis in 1839). By the 1840s, St. Louis, which shipped locally grown hemp, cotton, wheat, corn, and flax to other parts of the country, was surpassed only by New Orleans in river traffic. By the 1850s, St. Louis was the largest U.S. city west of Pittsburgh and the second-largest port, with a commercial tonnage exceeded only by New York City.

In 1836, Lewis took a job building stage sets for an opera house in St. Louis. After work, he may have walked the few blocks separating his workplace from the cobblestone landing, levee, and wharf to witness the great drama occurring within the river: the Illinois shore was caving in, which was widening and deepening the chute between that shore and Bloody Island, so called because of the duels fought there. As the current shifted toward the widening channel, the river deposited silt near the Missouri shore. By 1837, the silt deposits had so accumulated that Bloody Island was a mile long and thick with cottonwood trees. Only a trickle of water flowed between Duncan Island, southwest of Bloody Island, and the Missouri shore, which denied steamboats and other river traffic access to the river south of Market Street. In 1838, Congress funded the construction of two dikes to divert the current from the Illinois shore past Bloody Island and to direct the water toward Duncan's Island and the shoals below St. Louis. In an 1849 lithograph of Front Street, John Caspar Wild shows little of the restored river but quite a bit of riverfront activity: several people on the levee, including a black man pushing a handcart; a long row of buildings, one with an open-air dining room filled with people; a long line of docked steamboats.

At the opera house, Lewis met the artists who painted the stage sets—British drawing rooms and dungeons; mountains, forests, and oceans—and studied their works. Though he had no formal art training and claimed that he couldn't find anyone to teach him, Lewis took up painting. In 1845, he opened a studio that he shared with James F. Wilkins, a formally trained painter who also came from England. Among Lewis's early subjects were the suburban estates of the wealthy and a panoramic view of St. Louis from the Illinois side of the river, which he entitled *Western Metropolis*. On April 6, 1846, Lewis shipped the painting with the following note to the prestigious American Art-Union in New York: "I send you a view of St. Louis the 'Western Metropolis.' This view is taken from the Illinois shore, and you may rely on it being a correct one of our City as I took great pains in making the sketches. . . . The foreground is to a certain extent my own Composition, but it still preserves all the characteristics of the American bottom lands on this river." There are no known copies of this painting, so I have never seen it, but I suspect that it's similar to Lewis's 1848 oil painting of St. Louis, which shows a distant riverfront crowded with white buildings, including the Catholic cathedral, the domed courthouse, and the Planter's Hotel. There are no trees or vegetation in the city. Several steamboats and a large raft with a sail and four passengers seem suspended on the placid surface of the river. In the foreground on Bloody Island are a woman, a man, a covered wagon, and a horse. Though the Union didn't buy *Western Metropolis,* the Mechanics Fair in St. Louis awarded Lewis first prize for the painting.

Throughout the mid-1840s, Lewis received glowing reviews of his work from the local press, and he was in demand locally as a landscape painter. But Lewis wasn't satisfied. He had something grander in mind: he would paint a panorama of the entire Mississippi River.

The word *panorama,* from the Greek *pan* ("all") and *horama* ("view"), refers to a large painting or a connected series of paintings that present a wide, comprehensive view of a landscape or event. During the first half of the nineteenth century, panoramic paintings were all the rage in Europe and the United States.

In Europe, a panorama was mounted on the walls of a rotunda. Viewers sat or stood on a platform that moved them around the still canvas that encircled them, as if they were traveling past the landscape on a train. American audiences, however, wanted to sit still while the scenes moved past them, just as one does in a movie theater. Thus, the enormous canvas of a panorama was fastened between two rollers, and the audience watched as it was gradually and steadily unwound from one roller and spooled onto the other. As the scene glided before the audience's eyes, a stage crew manipulated the lighting to simulate sunrises and sunsets, daylight and darkness; a lecturer delivered a didactic, episodic commentary; and a pianist played. The moving panoramas that Americans preferred could be shown almost anywhere—in theaters, in church halls, on riverboats, and outdoors—so it was a more democratic art form than its European counterpart.

While Europeans wanted to see Old World cityscapes, ancient and contemporary battles, and coronations, Americans craved contemporary landscapes, especially of their own western frontier, which was quickly opening to Euro-American settlement. In *River of Dreams: Imagining the Mississippi before Mark Twain*, Thomas Ruys Smith observes that during the 1840s, a time of aggressive U.S. expansion, the moving panoramas were "emblems of the American belief in progress and expansion" and were strongly associated with manifest destiny, the belief that the United States had the right and the duty to expand from "sea to shining sea."

For a few years in the late 1840s, it was the Mississippi River more than any other subject that sold tickets to panoramas. It offered audiences romanticized scenes of American Indian wars and ceremonies on the wilder upper reaches of the river; tidy, thriving cities, towns, and farms on the rapidly changing middle river; and well-established cities and seemingly peaceful plantations on the lower river. Between 1846 and 1849, six moving panoramas of the Mississippi were exhibited in St. Louis and other cities. The panoramists competed for the public's attention in terms of artistic ability, veracity, accuracy, and, most importantly, size. In 1846, John Banvard claimed that at three miles, his panorama was "by far the Largest Picture ever executed by Man." (Actually, Banvard's canvas was a half mile long.) Two years later, John Rowson Smith claimed that the canvas of his *Leviathan Panorama* was four miles long, also an exaggeration. While none of the Mississippi River panoramas are known to still exist, having been lost, worn out, or cut up and sold, piece by piece, newspaper reports, journal entries, and testimonies by spectators suggest that the most artistic of the Mississippi River panoramas was Henry Lewis's *Great National Work*.

Lewis made two preliminary expeditions to the Upper Mississippi, in 1846 and 1847, to determine which views he wanted to "take" for the first part of his monumental work. On the first journey, he explored the upper river between Fort Snelling in what is now Minnesota and Prairie du Chien, in what is now Wisconsin, making side trips on tributaries of the Mississippi. On the second trip, he had the great good fortune of meeting knowledgeable traveling companions who helped him see what was for him an unfamiliar landscape. In 1847, he explored the valley of the St. Croix River, a tributary of the Mississippi that forms the state line between what are now Minnesota and Wisconsin, with the geologist David Dale Owen, who may have piqued Lewis's interest in geological formations. Lewis also met soldier-artist Captain Seth Eastman, who commanded Fort Snelling, located at the confluence of the Mississippi and Minnesota rivers, then the western reach of U.S. power. Eastman had been assigned to Fort Snelling to do topographic studies of the terrain, which brought him into contact with the Indians. By the time Lewis met Eastman, the captain had made about four hundred sketches, mostly of Sioux and

Chippewa Indians. Lewis purchased seventy-nine of the sketches of Indians and miscellaneous river scenes and based several scenes in his panorama upon them. Lewis remained at Fort Snelling with Eastman, working on sketches of the area, until he returned to St. Louis in November of 1847.

In the spring of 1848, just prior to Lewis's departure for his grand sketching expedition, his project received attention from the *Missouri Republican*:

> It seems that the rich materials of the Upper Mississippi have suggested an enterprize [*sic*] of some considerable magnitude, in which Mr. Lewis, with two other accomplished artists, are about to engage. His is the idea of a gigantic and continuous painting of the Mississippi river, from the Falls of St. Anthony to where it empties into the Gulf of Mexico. It is to be painted on one hundred thousand feet of canvas—and is designed to represent the geological formations along the river, the landscapes, the islands, and, in fact, a truthful view of the river and all the principal objects on its shores the whole distance.

The finished panorama covered seventy-five thousand square feet, with forty-five thousand square feet devoted to the Upper Mississippi and thirty thousand to the Lower Mississippi, so either Lewis scaled back his plans or this reporter erred. The article reports that the "materials" for the project had already been purchased and the sketches of the river around Prairie du Chien "already taken." "From the evidences of energy, taste, and talent which Mr. Lewis has given us in the paintings alluded to . . . we have reason to expect that the contemplated work will prove worthy of the Great West," the article concludes.

At St. Louis on June 14, 1848, Lewis boarded the *Senator*, a side-wheel, wooden-hull steamboat, and chugged 741 miles upriver to Fort Snelling, in what is now St. Paul, the starting point for his journey. Steamboats at the time traveled seven to eight miles per hour and often stopped for the night. At Galena, Illinois, Henry H. Sibley, who would become the first governor of Minnesota, boarded the boat. He spoke at length with Lewis about his experiences as a hunter and a trader with the "Sioux Outfit" of the American Fur Company at Mendota, Minnesota. The voyage took seven days. It was Lewis's third and final trip upriver.

As Lewis ascended the river, the composition of his staff may have been a nagging worry. Shortly before he boarded the *Senator*, his assistant sketcher, Leon Pomerade, resigned and left for New York to begin work on his own Mississippi River panorama. Lewis tried to recruit Samuel B. Stockwell, but he, too, had plans to paint a panorama himself. During the journey upriver, Lewis got word to Henry Skaggs, his business manager in St. Louis, to send Charles Rogers to the Upper Mississippi as soon as possible. Rogers, who had completed sketches for Lewis's panorama of the Lower Mississippi, was working for Stockwell, so there was secrecy surrounding Lewis's efforts to recruit him, but Lewis succeeded. Rogers's role in creating the panorama of the Upper Mississippi was great, and some portions of the painting bear his signature.

At Fort Snelling, Lewis set out to construct a floating studio. Since he couldn't find any carpenters or laborers at the fort, he did the work himself. Lewis secured two of the largest Indian canoes he could find, each fifty feet in length. He attached the two canoes with short beams, forming an eight- by eleven-foot platform on which he built a cabin. Within the cabin he built bunks, where he stored books, weapons, a tent, and food for the long voyage. Lewis christened what he described as this "most odd looking but complete craft" the *Mene-ha-hah,* the Dakota name for the waterfall at St. Anthony, which means "rapid water." Lewis noted that the *Mene-ha-hah* was "admirably adapted to my purpose as it was quite steady and from the top of the cabin, I could sketch with care and see over the country on both sides of the river." Lewis called the *Mene-ha-hah* his "floating curiosity shop," because when he stopped along the river, people gathered to look it over and ask questions.

In addition to Rogers, Lewis's crew included John Powers and Francois Chenevert, who navigated the boat, and John S. "Solitaire" Robb, a correspondent with the *St. Louis Reveille,* who rode along to dispatch reports about the journey in order to promote Lewis's panorama in advance of the actual showing. Lewis, Powers, and Chenevert arrived at Fort Snelling on June 21. Robb arrived on July 1. Rogers would meet the crew at Galena on July 21. Lewis and his crew waited several days for a favorable wind and then, on Monday, July 10, 1848, left the fort in the recently completed *Mene-ha-hah.* Lewis was ready to sketch the scenes that would delight audiences across the United States, Canada, and Europe.

The little boat traveled three to four miles per hour in a regular current, a little faster with a fair wind, and a little slower when the crew had to row against a head wind. The sketching was done from the boat, with Lewis and Rogers viewing scenes either through the open sides or from the flat top of the cabin. I imagine twenty-nine-year-old Lewis, with no wife or children or pressing business concerns in St. Louis to divide his attentions, sitting atop the roof of the *Mene-ha-hah,* sketchbook on his knees, and nothing to obstruct his view as he drifted down the great river. Lewis said that for him and his crew, the five weeks spent on this sketching expedition from Fort Snelling to St. Louis were "the happiest days of our lives."

In 1848, the Upper Mississippi River was still relatively untamed and free flowing, since it hadn't yet been straightened and controlled by the twenty-nine locks and dams and many hundreds of miles of levees. In *Life on the Mississippi,*

Mark Twain tells about the dangers of the wild river to the uninitiated, including rising and falling water, snags, woodpiles near shore, and the treacherous rapids near Keokuk, Iowa, and Rock Island, Illinois, the two main obstacles to navigation on the Upper Mississippi. Lewis mentions the two rapids in his writings, too, and includes sketches of the ones near Rock Island in his panorama. But other than that, he says and shows relatively little about the nature of mid-nineteenth-century river travel.

Lewis does record details about what he found on shore in his journal and in *The Valley of the Mississippi Illustrated,* the book that he would produce several years later about his experience. For instance, at Lake Pepin, a naturally occurring lake in the Mississippi between Minnesota and Wisconsin, the swarms of "the settlers of that region (the *Mosquitos*)" forced the sketching party to move camp. At Little Crow's Village, they encountered rattlesnakes. At Bad Axe, Lewis did the baking since he felt that none of the Indians were capable of it, which caused a late start that day. Near Prairie du Chien, Lewis and his crew etched their names in what he called "The Alter [*sic*] bluff, [because] you can see the pulpit the reading desk and the baptismal font." Near Clinton, Iowa, they holed up in an old cabin during a heavy rain. But before they could enter, Lewis had to scare off the owner's dogs by opening his umbrella in their faces. Near Rock Island and Moline, Illinois, Lewis hunted, though he doesn't say what. In Davenport, Iowa, at the home of Antoine LeClaire, one of the founders of that town, the crew dined with a visitor from St. Louis. At Nauvoo, Illinois, Lewis toured the temple on the bluff and visited Emma Smith Bideman, widow of the Mormon prophet Joseph Smith, who had been assassinated in 1844. Lewis stayed long enough to complete several sketches of the place, which was then practically a ghost town since the non-Mormon neighbors had driven out eighteen thousand of Nauvoo's Mormon residents. Near Clarksville, Missouri, about eighty miles north of St. Louis, Lewis reports that the men were "singing at their oars" and that Rogers was "devouring" Dickens's newest book, *Dombey and Son.* Closer to St. Louis, the crew socialized with James F. Wilkins, the artist with whom Lewis had shared a studio for several years, and George I. Barnett, a St. Louis architect, at the home of a Mr. Poppleton. Lewis recounted his river adventures to them over eggnog. Apparently, Lewis's river journey was as much about crafting and telling stories as it was about sketching and painting scenes.

Because the Mississippi is over 2,300 miles long, Lewis had to be highly selective in his subject matter. How did he decide which of the many thousands of scenes to sketch? Did he select a scene to represent every X number of river miles? Did he choose the settings of representative pieces of American history? Did he decide to sketch far more than he'd ever need and make the final cut later? Did he sketch what was easiest or what was most challenging? Or was it delight that guided him, and if so, whose delight—the audience's or his own? Historian Joseph Earl Arrington writes that Lewis had three principles that guided his scene selection. First, he chose a scene for its grand and picturesque qualities. To that end, Lewis painted imposing bluffs, several with lover's leaps; vast, undulating prairies; the Upper Rapids; the Falls of St. Anthony and Little Falls in what is now Minneapolis; the Piasa Bird, an Indian painting on a limestone bluff near Grafton and Alton, Illinois; a prairie fire; and various river confluences.

Second, Lewis sought incidents that were currently in the national news or were well-known historical events. He painted the scene of the 1832 Battle of Bad Axe, which ended the Black Hawk War; the ruins of the Mormon settlement at Nauvoo, once the second-largest city in Illinois; the Great St. Louis Fire of 1849; the devastating series of earthquakes in 1811 that split the earth at New Madrid, Missouri, and caused the river to rise like a tidal wave; the explosion of the Mississippi Steam Clipper in 1843 at the mouth of the Red River; and the plantation of then-president Zachary Taylor between Vicksburg and Natchez, which he portrays with none of Taylor's hundred-plus slaves visible.

A final and most impelling motive in Lewis's scene selection was to depict thriving settlements and regions with abundant resources in order to draw immigrants. To that end, he presents Savannah, Illinois, a town built on a low shelf of land near the river. Beyond the town he painted trees and steep, tawny bluffs; in the foreground, on an island and on the Iowa shore, dense vegetation. The small steamboat belching black smoke from two towering chimneys connects Savannahians to Galena, St. Louis, and New Orleans. The audience might conclude that this brave little town was conquering the wilderness. "In 1832 there were not more than three or four such small towns above St. Louis," Lewis notes in *The Valley of the Mississippi Illustrated*. "Now there are more than 30, among them a few places of 14,000 and over." He advises readers that "tradesmen, and especially small capitalists, will find more opportunity for advancement in such towns than in the larger cities where more money is required to set up a business because of the competition."

The villages that Lewis depicts are appealing at first glance, and a glance was all the viewer of the panorama got. But if one studies the scenes in *The Valley of the Mississippi Illustrated*, he or she might find the little towns eerie, since they are too tidy, too still, and too empty of people. The few people who do appear in Lewis's portrayal of Savannah are mere dots, dwarfed by the tall bluffs. Where are the crowds that gathered to see the steamboats or the *Mene-ha-hah*? Where are the children playing in the streets or yards or along the water's edge? Where are the people fishing or waiting for the ferries that linked the two shores? What about the inevitable spring rises that inundated towns like Savannah that were built too near the river? Where are the minks, weasels, muskrats, snakes, and turtles that lived and fed near the water's edge; the bison that grazed on the unbroken prairie; the waterfowl, shorebirds, and songbirds that flew, swam, waded, or roosted near the river? John James Audubon would have drawn a very different scene there on the Mississippi Flyway.

I am as interested in what Lewis left out of his drawings as what he put in. Consider his sketch of Fort Madison, a town in southeastern Iowa. Whenever I rode through that town with my grandmother, she would complain that it was the longest little town she'd ever seen. Apparently, Lewis agreed with that assessment, since he used four two-page spreads to capture this sprawling river town—more space than most towns required. On the first left-hand page, signed "V Rogers," is a note that mentions "rafts"; on the first right-hand page, the artist has labeled the Eagle Hotel and the courthouse, notes intended for the lecturer who would narrate the panorama. The town continues onto the second pair of pages. The Madison House, a large hotel built in 1835 to accommodate as many as fifty people, is labeled. At the top of the page is this note: "The old fort with a small garrison was here surrounded—by the Indians—and being closely pressed had to mine [sic] himself out to the bank of the river and left in the night in his boats." Lewis used a pinkish wash for red-brick buildings and a gray wash for stone buildings. The third spread of pages shows the few buildings on the edge of town and on the fourth pair of pages, there are no buildings. Lewis labeled the last as open space awaiting settlement. While in the town portion of the painting, Lewis included the fort that had been abandoned in 1813 and the 1840 Greek Revival courthouse, now Iowa's oldest courthouse in continuous use, he didn't depict the prison, which was conspicuously nestled into the side of a large hill west of town at that time. Built in 1839, it was one of the first prisons established west of the Mississippi. Perhaps the presence of a prison was at odds with the image of the town that Lewis was trying to create for prospective settlers.

Lewis also left out such pivotal events as the reconstruction of the clogged river harbor near St. Louis in the late 1830s; the Great Flood of 1844; slaves working in the hemp fields of Missouri; and the mob murder of abolitionist newspaperman Elijah P. Lovejoy in an Alton warehouse. And, too, there are tantalizing encounters that Lewis couldn't have known about. Perhaps thirteen-year-old Samuel Clemens was one of those who drew near to see Lewis's houseboat when it stopped in Hannibal, and thereafter dreamed of a downriver raft journey.

Parts of the trip must have been intensely pleasurable for Lewis. At Lake Pepin, Robb comments in a letter, he sailed away to pitch the tent, leaving Lewis at the summit of Maiden Rock, "working away with his pencil, completely wrapt up in the beauty of the scene before him." After the crew made camp, cooked and ate dinner, smoked their pipes and went over the events of the day each evening, Lewis observes that they would "turn in and sleep such sleep as is not even dreamt of beneath city shingles." From the top of Mount Trempealeau, "the mountain that steeps in the water" between what are now Winona, Minnesota, and La Crosse, Wisconsin, Lewis explains that he had "a birds eye view of as grand a scene as ever eye rested upon. . . . As I looked I felt how hopeless art was to convey the *soul* of such a scene as this." Of Muscatine, Iowa, he exclaims, "The place was so picturesque that I was induc'd to take three views of it, one from above, one panoramic view and a view over looking it from the bluffs by which it is back'd." Did Lewis ever want to settle down in these places, I wonder, or was it enough just to turn them into art?

On August 5, Lewis and his crew arrived in St. Louis. How good "this glorious city of the west," the point of departure and return, must have looked to them.

Once back in St. Louis, Lewis completed several local sketches, including one of the Jefferson Barracks, where the Sauk chief Black Hawk had been imprisoned. He also sketched several steamboats that he would later insert into the river scenes on the panorama, which reminds us that, like *Western Metropolis*, his river scenes are both representations and fabrications.

On September 11, 1848, six weeks after returning to St. Louis, Lewis moved to Cincinnati for the production of the panorama. He chose this city, where so many other panoramas had been produced, because according to one source, there was a shortage of artists for hire in St. Louis, and according to another, he'd had disagreements with the other scenic artists in his hometown. There was also the fact that in Cincinnati, he could hire such artists as John R. Johnson, who had worked on Stockwell's panorama; Edwin F. Durang, who would become a renowned Philadelphia architect of churches; John Leslie, a scene painter with the National Theater in Cincinnati; and James B. Laidlow, a scene painter from Scotland. So in a city on the Ohio River, Lewis went to work painting the Mississippi.

On September 20, Lewis and his team began transferring the sketches onto the large canvas. The goal was to make it look as if the canvas had been painted by one instead of five artists, with their different and perhaps competing styles, technical proficiencies, and visions. Though they had no choice about the sequencing or procession of scenes, they, or perhaps Lewis alone, decided whether a scene would be bright or dark, which colors would dominate, what to emphasize in each scene (i.e., landscape, buildings, human activity on the river or shore, etc.), and how these scenes would look next to each other. I imagine frequent discussions between the artists, running long into the night.

Audiences viewed the scenes of a panorama quickly, as if they were gliding past the landscape in a boat or train, and so artists didn't have to provide much more than the broad outlines of a scene. Nonetheless, some of Lewis's paintings are remarkably detailed. *The Camp of the Indians*, about a standoff between the Winnebago and U.S. soldiers at Wabashaw's Prairie near present-day Winona, is depicted in neutral colors except for the red of the blankets, loincloths, headdresses, and decorations on the dozens of Winnebago and their thirty-three tepees and ten canoes. The details of the scene in *The Camp of the Troops*—dozens of tents, some so small and distant that I can't count them; several dozen wagons parked in a semicircle; an indistinct but impressive number of soldiers in the distance; several armed guards in the foreground; rugged, mountainlike bluffs in the background; the *Mene-ha-hah,* anchored near the shore; and five American Indians lounging in the foreground—are done in subdued blues, grays, and blue-greens, which contrast with the red blankets that two of the Indians wear. The dominant impression that the viewer of the moving canvas would be left with, Lewis judged, is the contrast between the geometry and industry of the soldier camp and the slapdash arrangement of the smaller, fewer, more closely set tents of the Winnebago.

The painter of a Mississippi River panorama had to find a way to keep all the bluffs, lowlands, islands, and towns from looking alike. Lewis's solution was to create variety through contrasting images from one scene to the next. The lithograph of the gentle, verdant valley of the St. Peter's River (now the Minnesota River) is filled with a soft, blue-pink sky and gently sweeping prairie. On the left is part of a bright blue meander of the low-banked river. In the foreground are two American Indians chatting. One is dressed in red and sits on a rock; one sits on a fallen branch. This pastoral scene is followed by the rocky grandeur of the Little Falls. A dark green scene of Indians hunting deer by moonlight is followed by the bright and violent *Scalping Scene of the Mississippi.* The scene of Galena, viewed not from the river but from a bluff top, allows one to see the many, crowded, gold and brown rooftops of this city, then the busiest river port between St. Paul and St. Louis and the principal city in the lead-mining district of northwestern Illinois. Beyond are the pale blue river and the green-gray bluff on the western shore. This scene is followed by a placid view of the Fever River (now the Galena River): the *Mene-ha-hah* is anchored at the shore; in the right foreground is the sketching party's camp with a table set for five; in the left foreground are red, cone-shaped flowers on the shore and lily pads floating on the water; in the distance is a single house. The point of confluence of the Mississippi and Missouri rivers, a place prone to severe flooding, is a peaceful scene in blues, greens, and yellow-browns, with geese taking off from the water, a couple of rafts, a couple of steamboats, and no human habitations. This is juxtaposed with Lewis's bold red, yellow, and orange painting of the Great St. Louis Fire of May 17, 1849, which killed 3 people and destroyed 430 buildings, 23 steamboats, 9 flatboats, several barges, and 1 floating curiosity shop, the *Mene-ha-hah.*

Viewers of the panorama were probably impressed by the power of humans to remake the river valley as they watched the rough frontier settlements, American Indian villages, and rugged scenery of the upper river give way to the more settled, densely populated places—Galena, Burlington, Quincy, St. Louis—which in turn gave way to the plantations on the lower river and then New Orleans. On the three hundred feet of canvas that Lewis devoted to the Crescent City, he painted the Spanish cathedral, the dome of the St. Charles Hotel, the French Market, the street on the levee, ships, and steamboats.

Lewis and his team finished painting the Upper Mississippi on June 20, 1849, nine months to the day after they began. The canvas for that part of the river was 12 feet high, 3,500 feet long, and covered 45,000 square feet. The canvas for the lower river, which Charles Rogers and others on Lewis's crew worked on from May through August of 1849, covered a little less than half of a mile. Together, the two presented well over a mile of paintings of river scenes.

Lewis's efforts to profit from his Mississippi River sketches were plagued with bad luck. In May of 1849, he exhibited a section of the painting at the Apollo Hall in Cincinnati. Because of the competition from other panoramists, his shows weren't well attended. Likewise he didn't sell many tickets at the June exhibition in Louisville because of a cholera epidemic sweeping the country. In Louisville, Lewis made $429 in ticket sales—hardly enough to cover his payroll, which included $12.50 per week for each of the two carpenters; $6 per week for each of the doorkeepers; $16 per week for the other three assistants; and $20 per week for the lecturer, Charles Gayler. Lewis received nothing for himself or his traveling expenses, which had to be discouraging, given the years of work that went into this production. After the disappointing turnout in Louisville, Lewis returned to Cincinnati to work on the scenes of the Lower Mississippi with Leslie and Rogers. There, on August 18, he displayed the Lower Mississippi panorama for the first time.

The one bright spot on Lewis's tour was in his hometown. He arrived in St. Louis on August 27. Four days later, he arranged a preview for newspaper reporters and for "those who are most familiar with the scenes, and are likely to be the best judges of its fedillty [sic]." The panorama opened to the public on Saturday, September 1, at half past seven in Concert Hall. The admission price for the almost-two-hour program was fifty cents for adults and twenty-five cents for children. The guidebook that accompanied the showing of the Upper Mississippi section of the panorama, *A Description of Lewis' Mammoth Panorama of the Mississippi River, from the Falls of St. Anthony to the City of St. Louis; Containing an Account of the Distances, And Settlements of the Country; the Names and Population of the Various Cities, Towns and Villages on the River, with Historical Remarks, &c. Compiled from Various Authentic*

Sources, was edited by Gayler, the former editor of the *Cincinnati Evening Dispatch*, and sold for ten cents. What impressed many was that unlike other panoramas that only showed one side of the river, Lewis showed both. "By an almost magic power," the *New Era* reported on September 3, Lewis has "drawn before you both banks, and you have, at a single glance, the enchanting and life-like scenery as it appears on both sides." Lewis exhibited the panorama before "very full rooms" in "the city where he first applied pencil to canvas" until September 26. Ticket sales were good. As soon as Lewis's show ended, Leon Pomerade, Lewis's former assistant, began the St. Louis showing of his Mississippi River panorama.

From there, Lewis exhibited his *Great National Work* in several cities and towns in New York, Massachusetts, Maine, and Canada, as well as Chicago, Milwaukee, Detroit, Richmond, Boston, and Washington, DC. He chose this itinerary to avoid appearing in the same cities and at the same times as the other Mississippi River panoramas. He never displayed the canvases of both the upper and the lower river on the same night. Instead, he displayed one view in one town, while his partner, Washington King, displayed the other view in a nearby town. In addition to Gayler, sometimes George Stanley, a man quite knowledgeable about the Mississippi, delivered the lecture, and sometimes Lewis did it himself. Even so, he continued to have problems meeting payroll.

In a July 11, 1849, letter to his brother George, Lewis wrote that by the time he arrived in Bangor, Maine, he was wishing he "could find someone who would buy us out. . . . We have been to every place we can think of in the States, where our exhibition would be likely to pay and we have no alternative but to go abroad." Lewis arrived too late in England, since John Banvard and John Rowson Smith had already shown their Mississippi River panoramas there by the time Lewis began showing his. Ticket sales were better in Holland. But by the time Lewis arrived in Germany, Smith and Samuel A. Hudson had already saturated the market with their Mississippi River scenes. By 1853, the public had lost its appetite for moving panoramas.

That year, Lewis settled in Düsseldorf, Germany, a lively international art center. Apparently, Lewis's move to this city on the Rhine was the result of a long-planned business endeavor with Arnz and Company, the prestigious producer of art books in Düsseldorf. In his journal in 1848, Lewis notes: "Arrangment [*sic*] with Mr Arnst [*sic*] for a work on the Mississippi." This note is followed by a plan outlining what would become the first twenty-four pages of *Das Illustrirte Mississippithal* (*The Valley of the Mississippi Illustrated*). In the early 1850s, several American artists were studying at Düsseldorf's famous art school, Staatliche Kunstakademie Düsseldorf, including Albert Bierstadt and two Missourians, George Caleb Bingham and Charles Wimar. In that fertile climate, Lewis worked on his book, which included excerpts from his journals;

long, unattributed, and in some cases inaccurate quotations from other writers about the geography and history of the Mississippi River; and seventy-eight lithographs.

Numerous problems, or what Lewis called "rascally delays," surrounded the publication. First, Heinrich Arnz, the head of the company, died. Then, in 1854, Arnz and Company was found guilty of fraud and its creditors took over. Though Lewis's book was published in German in twenty installments between 1854 and 1857, the English version was never completed. Bertha Heilbron, who wrote the introduction to the 1967 edition of *The Valley of the Mississippi Illustrated*, says that after the Arnz company failed, an antique book and art dealer bought the remaining copies of Lewis's book and stored them in a warehouse. Eventually, the dealer sold the text as "waste paper" and gave the lithographic plates to students and customers. Few complete copies of the German edition survived. But because of interest from researchers and collectors, a publisher located in Leipzig and Florence reissued *Das Illustrirte Mississippithal* in 1923. Many of the copies of the German edition preserved in libraries were destroyed by World War II bombings. One expert recently estimated that only forty of the copies published by Arnz still exist.

In 1856, Lewis sought a buyer for his panorama. His asking price was $4,000, the equivalent of almost $100,000 in 2010. His one serious offer came from a man he referred to as Hermens or Hermans and whom he described as "a wealthy planter from the island of Java, a Hollander by birth." Hermens, whose intent wasn't to exhibit but to sell the panorama, made a $500 down payment on it. Though Lewis tried to collect on the debt, it appears never to have been paid. Nor was he any more successful at selling his paintings of European landscapes.

But Lewis was lucky in love. In 1859, he married Marie Jones, a British woman who had worked for the Hermens family as a governess. "My life glides on in such [a] quiet stream of tranquil happiness, that my dear wife and myself ask ourselves every day, if we are not too happy!" Lewis wrote to George in 1864. From 1867 to 1884, Lewis served in Düsseldorf as the American consular agent, a position that gave him the steady income that his art could not, so the Lewises lived comfortably. The two were together until Marie died in 1891; Henry died in Düsseldorf in 1904.

After Lewis left the United States, he saw the Mississippi only one more time, when he returned to St. Louis for a wedding in the 1880s. Neither the panorama nor an original English version of *The Valley of the Mississippi Illustrated* has ever been found. Some of Lewis's sketches of his 1848 trip down the Upper Mississippi are part of the collections of the Minnesota and the Missouri historical societies or are owned by descendants of his brothers.

～

Lewis takes us on a fast, smooth trip down the Mississippi River. From the roof of the *Mene-ha-hah,* we see the towns and villages, the cities and camps, the grand bluffs and prairies, all from afar. Lewis's river seems impenetrable: it's a place where reflections waver; it's a place where steamboats, keelboats, and barges slide over the surface. His sky is empty except for clouds and smoke. Lewis offers us a survey, an overview, an outline, the broad view of the entire river valley: it is the work of one just passing by, of one who would soon leave the river, only to return once more and that, decades later.

Nonetheless, Lewis is the great preserver. His scenes of the Mississippi remind us how the cities, towns, and landmarks along the river looked in the 1840s, and I am grateful for that. Many times I have turned to Lewis for an earlier view of one of the places that I am exploring. Yet, I soon tire of his distant views. My eye yearns to engage with the particular and the specific: I want to see the veins in the mayfly's wings; I want to see the creases at the outer corner of the fisherman's eyes.

While I present sweeping vistas as Lewis does, I also offer a closer, more detailed view. I present fewer scenes and unspool them more slowly. On my river journey, we don't just glide over the water, but gaze into it. We collect samples of river water to take back to the lab so we can see what is and isn't in it. We dive to the bottom to feel the bumpy mussel beds. We stop and ask those fishing what's biting and what bait they're using. If the fishing is good, we might throw out a line and stay awhile. On this journey, we aren't content with seeing the decorations on the outside of the temple. Rather, we walk in, look around, and ask for the story of how it was built and destroyed and built again. On this journey, every bridge is worth crossing. Every flood is worth viewing from both the bluff top and the water's edge. The history of purple loosestrife, smallmouth bass, real and imagined river monsters, and those who make wine and cheese for tourists are as worthy of our time and attention as American Indian wars, burning cities, and manifest destiny. I offer a Mississippi River journey that examines, analyzes, reflects, and ponders. I offer a journey that is guided by one who will keep returning to the river long after the voyage is completed, the book written, published, read, and eventually forgotten.

3

Mississippi Harvest

There are buttons everywhere.

On display at the Muscatine History and Industry Museum, formerly the Pearl Button Museum, is a heap of white "pearl" buttons that you can sort by size and quality, just as workers in the button factories once did. Some buttons are utterly plain and functional: round, two- or four-holed, each with an iridescent sheen. But some are fancy, dyed various colors, and shaped like squares, rectangles, triangles, bow ties, diamonds, hearts, or flowers. Some are edged with teeth or scallops or bordered with swirls, waves, or leaves. On the buttons are concave crisscrosses or raised diamonds, ovals, circles, or hexagons. On some buttons, the holes are arranged so as to suggest two eyes and a smiling mouth.

Hanging from the ceiling are large-scale replicas of "button cards," the cardboard rectangles onto which buttons were sewn (nowadays they are attached with wire). One shows a young man, a golfer, wearing a white shirt with four dark buttons sewn down the middle of it and one on each cuff. His necktie blows to his right so one has a full view of the buttons. Hanging next to this is a replica of a button card featuring a stylish, svelte woman in a long, gold dress. Sewn diagonally across the card are four big, white, iridescent buttons. Another replica shows a map of North America. Covering most of Canada are two big letters: "US." In a box across those letters are the words "UNIVERSAL SATISFACTION." Written across the United States–Canada border is "BUTTON, CO." and beneath that "MUSCATINE, IOWA." A set of six glossy white buttons is sewn on either side of the map. At the top of the card is the caption "Who's Got the Button?" with a picture beneath it of six people in button-up shirts who are searching for their buttons. At the bottom of the card is the caption "We've Got the Button" with a picture beneath it of six happy people who have found their buttons.

Also on exhibit are mussel shells from which flat, round disks, or button "blanks," were cut in 1919. Although called "pearl buttons," the buttons were made not from pearls found within mussels, but from their iridescent shells. On some shells, the holes where the blanks were punched are close together and little shell remains. But on others, the waste is apparent: there is more shell than holes. From the early 1900s into the 1920s, the pearl-button industry used an average of 40,000 to 60,000 tons of mussel shells each year, cutting two to thirty blanks from each, depending on the size of the shell and the size of the blank.

A "button shell" provided my first knowledge of Muscatine's unique industry. When I was a child, my great-aunt Pearl ("Pertsie"), who lived ninety miles south of Muscatine in Keokuk, showed me a button shell that she'd been given. It reminded me of rolled-out dough from which sugar cookies had been cut in clean circles. I stuck my fingers through the holes and wore the shell like an awkward, fingerless glove. When I asked her about the shell with the missing pieces, my great-aunt, an assembly-line worker at the Dryden/Sheller Globe rubber company, told me about the many pearl-button factories in Muscatine and the many people in that town, including a friend of hers, who made their living cutting and carding buttons. My great-aunt and great-grandmother bought the pearly buttons to sew onto the shirts and dresses they made. When the garments wore out, they snipped off the buttons and saved them in a jar. Some buttons were probably reused, but most were eventually lost or thrown away. Even though I don't sew, I, too, save buttons in a glass vase on the dresser in my bedroom.

What hadn't been part of my great-aunt's story was where the button shells came from or the ecological costs of the button industry. Once, the most diverse collection of freshwater mussels in the world was found in the Mississippi and other midwestern rivers. But now, 70 percent of the mussel species in Minnesota, Wisconsin, Iowa, Missouri, Illinois, Indiana, and Ohio are extinct, endangered, or in need of special protection. In fact, freshwater mussels are the most imperiled group of animals in all of North America. Many of the shells used by the button industry came from what are now rare mussel species or from species that no one has seen in the Upper Mississippi River for a very long time.

The story of the Muscatine pearl-button industry and how it changed the ecological vitality of the Mississippi River begins in Germany with Johann Boepple (1854–1912). When Boepple was a boy, his father taught him to cut buttons from horn, hooves, bone, and seashells. After young Boepple left his family's village in Germany, he practiced this craft, first in Vienna and then in Hamburg, Germany, where he had his own button factory for eight years. Then two tragedies struck: Boepple's young wife died unexpectedly and in 1879, Germany enacted a new tariff that imposed a heavy duty on imports. Since most of the shells that Boepple used in making buttons were imported from the South Pacific, his business was doomed.

As the founder and pioneer of the American pearl-button industry, Boepple is legendary, and like most legendary people, there are competing versions of parts of his biography. Two different stories explain when and where he first saw a Mississippi River mussel shell. One claims that while Boepple was swimming in the Mississippi (one source says it was the Sangamon, a tributary of the Illinois River), he cut his foot on a mussel shell. When he picked up the object that had caused his wound, he saw that it was a hard shell with a thick, fine layer of mother-of-pearl, much like the ocean shells that he had used in Germany. He realized that he could make buttons from this. The legend doesn't say what type of mussel shell caused the epiphany, but I like to believe that it was one of the "heelsplitters," so named because of a single, wing-shaped extension on the shell.

Another story claims that Boepple saw his first Mississippi River mussel while still in Germany. This story also has different versions. In 1872, William Salter dug mussels either in the Illinois River near Peoria or two hundred miles southwest of Chicago, which places Salter in the Mississippi near Muscatine. Either way, Salter sent some of the shells to Europe to be evaluated for their commercial potential. When Boepple obtained some of them several years later, he saw that they were of as fine a quality as shells from the Pacific. Boepple immigrated to the United States in 1887 or 1888, lived with his sister in Petersburg, near Springfield, Illinois, and worked on farms and railroad-construction crews. His search for the quality mussel shells he had seen eventually led him to Muscatine, a beautiful little city tucked beneath the big nose, belly, or bulge of eastern Iowa. There the Mississippi flows from east to west. Henry Lewis's lithograph of "Muscadine" as it appeared in the late 1840s shows a small town hugging the riverbank, a large bluff rising behind it, several small fishing boats, and a steamboat that overwhelms the view. Mark Twain, who lived there and wrote for the *Muscatine Journal* in the 1850s, claimed that the sunsets that he saw there were unsurpassed on either side of the ocean.

Each version of Boepple's life story leads to the same end: after seeing the excellent shells of the mussels that lived in the Mississippi, Boepple decided to establish a button-making business nearby. He opened a shop in Columbus Junction, Iowa, where he made and sold the buttons and baubles that he cut from mussel shells. But without a lathe, Boepple was limited in what he could do. Two legends explain how he got this essential piece of machinery. One says that he simply borrowed a lathe from a friend. Another says that with scraps of old machinery begged from shop owners and neighbors, he built a foot-powered lathe. Boepple cut blanks, polished them, and sold them to a store in Muscatine. But to start a proper business, he needed investors, so he showed the buttons that he'd made to local businessmen. William Molis, superintendent of the Muscatine Water-works, and I. A. Kerr, a carpenter and builder, provided the capital. Boepple moved his lathe to Muscatine and started the Boepple Button Company, the first freshwater mussel–button factory in the United States. The business grew rapidly.

The outer shell on most mussels is unremarkable: black or brown and rather smooth, though some are touched with yellow or green or are ridged, pimpled, or stippled. But within, the shell is coated with a pearly white and iridescent layer of nacre, or mother-of-pearl, which defends the shell against parasites and debris. If I take the paper clips out of the mussel shell on my desk and rock it in my hand, tiny mineral crystals in the mother-of-pearl break up the light into little bits of shimmering rainbow.

If you've seen an oyster, you know the basic principle of the mussel's body. Enclosed within the hard, nacre-lined shell is the soft, tan body, an oval divided into two halves. The mussel has a circulatory and nervous system, a digestive tract, and gills for breathing, but since it has no head, eyes, or ears, it's hard to tell which end is up. It is a well-muscled creature: with its strong abductor muscles, the mussel opens and closes its shell; with its large, muscular foot that looks rather like a human tongue, it burrows into the substrate and buttons itself to the river bottom. Mussels don't get around much. Instead of pursuing their food, they simply wait for it to come to them.

Most of the time, the mussel lies buried in the river or lake bottom with its shell slightly open and its two strawlike siphons extended. It draws water through the incurrent, or branchial, siphon and pumps it through its body. The mussel's gills extract oxygen and food (microscopic plants, bacteria, and organic particles) from the water; with its fingerlike labial palps, the mussel sweeps the food sticking to its gills into its mouth. Then, the excurrent, or anal, siphon expels filtered water and waste back into the river. A single mussel can filter several gallons of water per day.

Mussels bury themselves in the sediment and, explains Mike Davis, a river ecologist with the Minnesota Department of Natural Resources, become "part of the substrata of the riverbed, stabilizing the river and providing roughness that can be colonized by algae and aquatic insects that eat the algae, and then smaller fish that feed on those insects, and then of course the bigger fish." Davis calls this "a positive feedback loop in the ecosystem." Because mussels filter algae, protozoans, and detritus out of the water with their gills, thus purifying the water, most people find their flesh disagreeable to eat. Tony Brady of the U.S. Fish and Wildlife Service likens eating a Mississippi River mussel to drinking a glass of unfiltered river water. But muskrats, minks, otters, and raccoons don't seem to mind the gamy taste or rubbery texture.

Mussel reproduction is a dicey affair. The male releases sperm into the water and the female downstream captures it in her siphon and fertilizes her eggs with it. The female stores the glochidia, or microscopic larvae, in brood pouches, or marsupia, in her gills. After she expels the glochidia into the river current, the larvae must attach themselves to the gills, skin, or fins of host fish, or they will perish. The successful glochidium becomes encysted and draws nutrients from its host. Depending on the species and the water temperature, this parasitic phase usually lasts from three to six weeks. The fish gets nothing in return, but neither is it harmed by the arrangement.

The metamorphosed juvenile mussel falls to the bottom of the river or lake, preferably where the bottom is sandy or gravelly, stable, and free of silt. There, it burrows in, anchors itself, and matures into an adult. Most species live at least ten years and some, as long as a century. When threatened, the mussel withdraws its siphons, shuts its shell, and makes like a rock.

A confluence of factors established Muscatine as the center of the pearl-button industry. Like many other towns on the Upper Mississippi, Muscatine had a thriving lumber industry from the late 1850s until about 1890. First the lumber companies cut the forests on either side of the Mississippi in Iowa and Illinois. When those forests were exhausted, the companies cut pines in Minnesota and Wisconsin and rafted the rough logs to towns downriver, where workers cut them into boards. When those northern tracts were also depleted, the lumber barons closed the sawmills, lumberyards, and finishing plants in Muscatine and other river towns and cities and moved on to forests in the South and the Pacific Northwest. Consequently, when Boepple began producing buttons in 1890, Muscatine was ripe for a new industry.

The McKinley Tariff of 1890 made imported buttons and the imported raw materials from which they were made too expensive for most consumers and manufacturers. Yet changes in clothing styles—from dresses to shirtwaists and skirts for women, and from pullovers to button-up shirts for men—created a need for even more buttons than the older fashions required. So in 1891 pearl buttons were the rage as both a clothing fastener and a decoration. An advertisement for Boepple's buttons shows a hale, dark-haired, rosy-cheeked young woman with a high, ruffled hat and a many-stranded pearl choker. Her sleeves are decorated with lace and flowers; her ornate, low-cut bodice is lavishly decorated with pearls or pearl buttons. Pearl: the queen of gems, a symbol of purity and perfection, a metaphor for the fine and the rare. Pearl: one of the most popular names for girls born in the United States between 1880 and 1911. With its ready workforce, abandoned buildings, and vast mussel beds, Muscatine was well positioned to meet the nation's desire for inexpensive, pearl-like, American-made buttons.

The first home for Boepple's factory was in the basement of the Davis Cooper Shop. When the business outgrew that space, Boepple relocated to a space above Nester's Blacksmith Shop. Barrels and horseshoes remind us how quickly the technology and lifestyle were changing in the last decade of the nineteenth century. Soon, there would be more cars than horses on the streets. Soon, handmade barrels would be replaced by machine-made containers and pallets. Because Boepple made buttons by hand and oversaw every part of the button-making process in his factory personally, he was always backlogged with orders. His partners, Kerr and Molis, bought a dozen shell-cutting machines to speed up production. But Boepple found the machines, which were designed for cutting ocean shells, useless for cutting river shells. "I repeatedly told these gentlemen if they wanted to make any money they should get the right machinery and do as I said, but never could I get what I wanted when necessary," he recalled years later. Eventually, the partnership dissolved.

In 1897, Congress passed the Dingley Tariff Bill, crafted to support northern manufacturers with even higher duties than the 1890 tariff. Boepple accepted an invitation to consult with those drafting the bill in Washington, DC, about the button industry. After the new tariff went into effect, the number of button-cutting companies in Muscatine grew to fifty-three. Some were cottage industries that only cut blanks; some were large finishing plants that cut, faced, and trimmed buttons. According to the Federal Writers' Project's *Iowa: A Guide to the Hawkeye State*, Boepple "jealously guarded his secrets," kept watchdogs, and even slept in his shop so that no one could steal his process. The stiffest competition, however, came from within: many of the new businesses were started by his former employees.

By the late 1890s, when the button industry wasn't yet a decade old, it had depleted the mussel population in the river near Muscatine. Local "clammers" either moved on to other rivers or found different work. And, too, many of the blank cutters in smaller businesses were using old, ineffective machinery, which ruined what shells they did have. If pearl-button production was to continue, the shell suppliers had to find other sources of mussels and the workers had to have better, faster machines.

But Boepple, a dark-haired man with dark, sad eyes and a big, droopy moustache, continued to make buttons by hand. He found new investors, opened a new factory, and employed over one hundred people. But the new investors were also set on mechanizing. Eventually, Boepple lost his share in the Muscatine business he'd started. He attempted to establish a button factory twenty miles away in Davenport and worked for a while as an independent shell buyer. In 1909, he accepted a position with the U.S. Bureau of Fisheries at its Fairport Fish Hatchery, just a few miles upriver from Muscatine, where he participated in research on how to propagate mussels. Ironically, or fittingly, in 1911 while a contentious strike by the pearl-button workers festered in Muscatine, Boepple stepped on a mussel shell while working in an Indiana river. This foot injury wasn't as auspicious as the first. On January 30, 1912, he died of blood poisoning at Bellevue Hospital in Muscatine. At the mayor's request, Muscatine businesses closed during Boepple's funeral.

In the first few decades of the twentieth century, Boepple's legacy was apparent along the Mississippi River at pearl-button factories in many towns, including Wabasha, Minnesota; Guttenberg, Davenport, Muscatine, Montrose, and Keokuk, Iowa; Andalusia, Kampsville, and Cairo, Illinois; and La Grange and Canton, Missouri. And his legacy continues. Muscatine is still known as the Pearl City. In 2006, the city installed in its Riverside Park a twenty-three-foot bronze sculpture of a "clammer" holding a clamming fork, the long handles gracefully curved and strangely beautiful, high above his head. *Mississippi Harvest,* it's called.

Prior to 1890, mussels were so abundant and the beds so vast that the bottom of the river seemed paved with cobblestones as it hosted the world's most diverse collection of freshwater mussels. In the 1890s, people came from all over the country to harvest mussels and sell them to the button factories. The U.S. Fish and Wildlife Service's "History of Mussel Harvest on the River" compares the hunt for freshwater pearls on the Upper Mississippi River during the 1890s to the California gold rush of 1849 in its intensity. In the 1890s, there were thousands of clamming boats on the Mississippi, entire mussel beds were picked clean, and millions of mussels were killed.

In the late nineteenth and early twentieth centuries, there were three methods of harvesting mussels. The most primitive was wading into shallow water and collecting the mussels by hand. "Toe-digging" or "pollywogging" was fine if you didn't need very many mussels. A more sophisticated method was using a long-handled clamming fork or tongs to scoop the mussels from the bottom of the river. Most sophisticated was "brailing," a method invented in 1897, based upon the seine-and-brail method of fishing, by which one lowered a net vertically into the water and when it was full, pulled it up with ropes and pulleys or a pole—the brail. The mussel brailer built an eight-foot-long frame of wood or metal pipe with twenty, thirty, or more lines of various lengths hanging from the frame. To the end of the line, he attached small grappling, or "crowfoot," hooks. He lowered the crowfoot drag bar in front of his johnboat and drew it across a mussel bed. In response to this threat, the mussel clamped its shell shut—on one of the hooks. When the brail was heavy with mussels, the clammer pulled it out of the water, stood it on the side of the boat, and removed the mussels.

Back at camp, women and children killed the mussels by cooking them in boiling water in tanks or cauldrons. Once the shells cooled, they pried them open, cleaned out the soft, cooked bodies, and sorted the shimmering shells by size and species. The shells were hauled by wagon, train, truck, or barge to the factories; the meat was thrown back into the river or fed to hogs. Among the most desirable species for buttons were ebonyshell, washboard, threeridge, mucket, pimpleback, elephantear, fat pocketbook, winged maple leaf, yellow sandshell, and Higgins' eye mussels.In the early years of the industry, clammers sold the shells by the pound. But as demand increased, they sold them by the ton. In 1897, one ton of mussel shells netted about $12 (now about $300). In 1899, a clammer earned about $10 a week, twice what a laborer earned. Occasionally a clammer would find a pearl formed inside a mussel shell. Finding a large "slug," which was a pearl shaped like a tooth or a big piece of puffed-rice cereal, brought a nice bonus. Finding a round pearl was like hitting the jackpot, since it brought what now would be several thousand dollars. Most clammers loved the freedom of living and working on the river. But at the end of the season, most returned to the din and darkness and seemingly endless repetition of work in the button factories.

When John and Nicholas Barry visited a button-making factory located near their father's plumbing business in Muscatine in 1898, they decided that they could design a faster and more efficient button-making machine. What they invented were two automatic machines: one for "facing" or cutting patterns in the buttons and one for drilling holes in them. In 1904, they further streamlined the process with the "double automatic," a single machine that both cut and drilled. This invention transformed the pearl-button industry. One double automatic could face and drill the blanks produced by seven cutting machines, over 21,600 buttons per day, at a quarter of the cost of the older method. In 1903, the Barrys sold their pearl-button factory to Henry Umlandt, who renamed it the Automatic Button Company. In 1905 Muscatine button makers turned out 1.5 billion buttons, well over one-third of the world's button production.

During the industry's peak from 1913 to 1919, almost half of Muscatine's population of about sixteen thousand was employed in some aspect of button making, from clamming to designing, manufacturing, marketing, or record keeping. The factory jobs were clustered around several operations. The most skilled and highly paid was that of the button cutter, who used a revolving saw to cut as many blanks as possible from a single half shell. The cutter dropped the blanks into a bucket, which another worker, usually a boy, toted to the grinders, who removed the rough outer side of the shell (the "bark") and ground the blanks to a uniform thickness. At the finishing machines, workers carved out the center, drilled holes, and trimmed the edges. Buttons were fed into this machine by hand, one at a time. Next, workers polished the buttons by tumbling them for a day and a half in a churn filled with water and powdered pumice. Then, they washed and dyed the buttons, dried them in sawdust, and moved them onto the sorting tables. Finally, women and girls sorted the buttons according to quality, color, and luster, sewed them onto cards by hand or machine, and packed them in boxes for shipping.

Only men could be button cutters, the highest-paid job in the factory. Women did most of the other jobs, earning about half of what the cutters earned. Many workers were paid by the piece rather than by the hour. In the early years of the industry, the work week was fifty-four to seventy-two hours long. In the absence of health and safety regulations, button making was dangerous work. Workers used blades and grinders and worked near shaft-powered belts. The shell dust caused eye and respiratory problems, workers stood or sat hunched over for long shifts, and the water in which the shells soaked so that they were easier to cut was often a stagnant, bacteria-filled brew. And the workforce included children.

In 1910, about one thousand Muscatine button workers formed the Button Workers Protective Union #12854, affiliated with the American Federation of Labor. Any button maker over the age of fourteen, male or female, whether employed making buttons at home or in a factory, could join the union. What the workers wanted were fairer counting and weighing practices and a revision in how they were paid for piecework. In response, the majority of Muscatine's forty-three button factories and cutting shops ceased production on February 25, 1911, and locked out 2,500 workers, an action that management claimed was a reasoned response to overproduction. The strike, which lasted fifteen months, was dramatic. The factories hired strikebreakers and armed guards to protect them. A striking worker shot and killed a policeman, the police attacked and beat a number of the strikers, and someone set what the *New York Times* called an "incendiary fire" at the Automatic Button Company. The police hired men from Chicago and St. Louis to help quell the violence, and the governor sent three companies of state militia to maintain order. "Many heads were broke following the arrival of the Deputy Sheriffs," the *New York Times* reported. Pearl McGill, a sixteen-year-old button worker in Muscatine and union secretary, raised money for the striking workers with rousing speeches, which she gave in Chicago, New York, Boston, St. Louis, and other cities. Union membership swelled. In May 1912, labor and management agreed to end the strike with all employees returned to their positions and no discrimination against union members on management's part. While workers had endured many months without paychecks to buy food, fuel, shoes, and medicine, the button companies weren't adversely affected by the strike.

～

A 1906 photograph in the Oscar Grossheim Collection at the Musser Public Library in Muscatine shows five clamming boats with crowfoot drag bars parked near the riverbank, with one or a few people in each boat. On the shore are half a dozen shacks, a big white tent, and eight people. Houses with gracious porches, brick chimneys, and dormer windows are perched atop the bluff. What you might miss if you weren't looking carefully is that the shore between the water's edge and the shacks is blanketed, drifted, mounded with many thousands of mussel shells. Likewise, in a photo from the U.S. Fish and Wildlife Service, circa 1911, about forty children and men are posed on the side of a mussel shell mountain, so high that the top edge of the photograph lops off the peak. The wonder to me isn't that the pearl-button industry in Muscatine eventually ended, but that given this excess, it continued as long as it did.

By 1900, the mussel beds near Muscatine had been decimated. During a three-year period, clammers took 10,000 tons of mussel shell from a 1½-mile-long, 300-yard-wide bed near New Boston, Illinois, about twenty miles downriver from Muscatine. After they'd exterminated the mussels in that bed, they moved on. In 1909, there were 2,600 clamming boats on the Mississippi. In 1911, there were so few mussels that the number of boats had dropped to 400. Clammers moved on to other parts of the Upper Mississippi and its tributaries in Minnesota, Wisconsin, Missouri, and Illinois. By 1920, shell tonnage harvested from those regions was also declining sharply. For instance, between 1914 and 1929, the annual mussel harvest from Lake Pepin, a section of the Mississippi between Minnesota and Wisconsin, dropped from over 3,000 tons to just 150 tons as the mussels were killed off. Then clammers moved to many other rivers, including the Fox, Wabash, Ohio, White, Arkansas, and Tennessee. In the 1930s, button manufacturers advertised that their buttons were made from mussel shells pulled from rivers in nineteen states.

Ebonyshell (*Fusconaia ebena*) was the most coveted species for pearl-button making. In fact, clammers were paid more for the ebonyshell's thick, inflated shell, with its high quality, white, lustrous, mother-of-pearl lining, than any other. Also desirable were yellow sandshell, whose white nacre was tinged with cream or salmon, and pistolgrip, a pustule-covered shell shaped like a pistol handle. Today the ebonyshell is endangered in Iowa, Ohio, and Wisconsin; both the yellow sandshell and the pistolgrip are endangered in Iowa and threatened in Wisconsin.

The depleted mussel beds were of such concern to the button manufacturers that they asked for assistance from the U.S. Fish Commission (now the U.S. Fish and Wildlife Service). In 1908, Congress established the Fairport Fish Hatchery eight miles east of Muscatine on land donated by the Association of Button Manufacturers. Congress's goal wasn't to save imperiled species, but to preserve an industry that employed thousands and made millions. From

1909 until his death in 1912, John Boepple was one of the researchers at the hatchery.

I wonder what the factory owners, the clammers, the assembly-line workers, and others who profited from mussel-shell buttons thought of the decimated mussel beds? Did they assume that they would rebound and the harvest would continue? Did they ever wonder what would happen to other aquatic organisms when mussel populations declined or crashed? Did they believe that some other material, natural or human-made, would replace the shells so that the double automatics, sales, and paychecks would continue without interruption? Or were they so preoccupied with rumors of war in Europe, the polio outbreak in Iowa, the long button workers' strike in Muscatine, the sinking of the Titanic, and all those people coming from Mexico to Muscatine to pick fruit and vegetables and to build the railroads, that none of these questions occurred to them?

Changes in the river also contributed to the diminishment or disappearance of the mussel beds. Because mussels are filter feeders, contaminants from agriculture and industry accumulate in their tissues and sicken or kill them. Pollutants also sicken or kill the fish that host the mussels' glochidia. No fish hosts, no mussels.

Mussels need free-flowing water for reproduction and feeding. The U.S. Army Corps of Engineers' system of locks and dams on the Upper Mississippi turned rivers into navigation pools with stabilized water levels. This altered flow regimes, water depth, and water temperature. Dams and impoundments reduced the velocity of the current and its ability to carry sediments, causing silt, sand, and clay to drop out of the water column and settle on the river bottom, burying and suffocating mussels in some places. Locks and dams also affect the migration of host fish. After Lock and Dam No. 19 at Keokuk began operating in 1913, some fish and mussel species were not seen again north of the dam. One of these fish, the skipjack herring, whose upstream migration was blocked by the dam, is the only known host of ebonyshell and elephantear mussels. No fish hosts, no mussels.

Freshwater mussels are now the most threatened and endangered group of animals in all of North America. Filter-feeding mussels prevent or limit those bacteriological or algal infestations that endanger the well-being of entire aquatic ecosystems. Because this important work is largely unseen and unsung, for most people saving mussels isn't as urgent or as glamorous as saving polar bears, right whales, California condors, or Karner blue butterflies.

In 1946, Muscatine celebrated the fiftieth anniversary of the button industry. In preparation for the celebration, the employees at each of the pearl-button factories voted for a queen candidate to represent that company in the competition for the title of Button Queen. Though he did not attend the ceremony, Ronald Reagan chose the queen and sent a representative from Warner Brothers Studios to announce his pick. On July 4, the winner was named and crowned at a coronation ceremony. When Helen Burke of the Automatic Button Company heard that she had won, she fainted. After she revived, she took her place of honor, seated inside the opened, yet still hinged, valves of a giant replica mussel shell on the button-industry float in the July Fourth parade. The other queen candidates, one each from Iowa Pearl Button, Hawkeye Pearl Button, Perkins Button, McKee Button, Muscatine Pearl Works, and Weber Button, sat on the lower level of the float in long white dresses.

In 1946, the pearl-button industry was a dying star. Several of the major factories closed during the 1930s and 1940s, including U.S. Button. In 1946, there were only seven button factories left in Muscatine and one in Washington, Iowa. What caused this reduction was the shortage of freshwater mussels and the availability of a viable substitute: plastics. Some factories had been experimenting with plastic buttons since the 1920s. But it was the government's research with plastics during World War II that created a higher-quality material and technology. Manufacturers found that plastics were cheap, easy to work with (the double automatics were adapted to cut blanks from sheets of plastic), and better able to withstand washing machines and the new detergents than mussel-shell buttons. Most important, plastic doesn't run out or die off.

In 1955, Weber and Sons Button Company made its first acrylic button. Two years later, it switched to polyester. J & K Button, owned by William Umlandt and Barry Hahn, was the first factory to make only plastic buttons. "I've always stood up for the pearl button," Umlandt said, "but I've got to say, and with great regret, that the plastic button is a better button." By 1957, McKee Button Company had switched to plastics as well. There are three button companies remaining in Muscatine today, Weber & Sons, McKee, and J & K, and all three manufacture polyester buttons. The combined workforce of the three is less than a hundred employees. Instead of truckloads of wet and smelly shells being transported to Muscatine from far rivers, polyester syrup arrives in clean, tidy tubs.

About the same time as pearl buttons were being phased out, a new use for mussel shells developed. In 1893, Kokichi Mikimoto, a Japanese oyster farmer, was awarded a patent for culturing round pearls through the process of surgically implanting a bead, or nucleus, made from mussel shell into an oyster. In response, the oyster secretes a nacreous coating around the irritant: a pearl. Since it took a ton of shells to produce a mere forty to sixty pounds of pearl nuclei, mussel shells for Japan's cultured-pearl industry became a major export for states along the Mississippi River by 1960. At its zenith in 1993, the industry exported almost seven thousand tons of shells. In the mid-1990s, the mussel-shell market collapsed when the Chinese developed beadless, or tissue-nucleated, pearls, produced from a tissue graft rather than a shell bead.

During the mid- and late 1970s, when I lived in Iowa City, I frequently took the Trailways bus home to Burlington, forty miles downriver from Muscatine. The bus followed Highway 22 into Muscatine and, before heading south on Highway 61, wound through downtown to the bus depot. We'd pass the old brick buildings near the river, much like the old brick factories and warehouses in other Mississippi River towns, except that in Muscatine, they once housed button factories. I remembered Great-aunt Pertsie's story about thousands of workers streaming in and out of the factories at the beginnings and ends of shifts; the machines within rattling and roaring; glistening mussel shells entering the factories at the loading-dock doors and exiting by those same doors as the iridescent disks that would hold up trousers or fasten shirts and blouses, pajamas, coats, and rompers. I regretted that this part of Muscatine was a shadow of what it once had been. But at that time, I didn't know what the pearl-button industry had done to the river.

Since the turn of the new millennium, various wildlife and environmental agencies have been working to restore mussel populations in the Upper Mississippi River. A species of special concern is the Higgins' eye pearlymussel (*Lampsilis higginsii*), listed as a federally endangered species since 1976. The outer shell of this beautiful mussel is smooth, yellowish brown or olive, with green rays; the inner shell is silvery-white, iridescent and touched with cream, pink, or salmon. The Higgins' eye was once common, but like so many other mussel species, its numbers were decimated by the pearl-button industry, and its prospects for recovery were further compromised by the locks and dams and the rising levels of chemicals, sewage, and toxic metals in the river. Added to these is a new threat: the invasion of the Upper Mississippi by Eurasian zebra mussels. These interlopers, carried in the ballast water of transatlantic ships, were first found in Lake St. Clair near Detroit. From there, they rapidly spread throughout the Great Lakes and connected waterways. In 1991, they were found in the Upper Mississippi. Populations of native mussels have been particularly hard hit by zebra mussel infestations since zebra mussels so encrust the shells of native mussels that they can't travel, burrow, open and close their shells, eat, or breathe.

To save the Higgins' eye, experts extract microscopic glochidia from brooding females and inoculate host fish with them. They place the larvae-infested fish in cages in the river until the larvae transform into juveniles and fall off. Then scientists harvest the juvenile mussels and plant them in the river.

One of the reintroduction sites is Pool No. 16, which extends from Lock and Dam No. 16, near Muscatine, to Lock and Dam No. 15, near Davenport.

In October 2003, scientists found substantial numbers of juvenile and adult Higgins' eye mussels in this area. Four years later, the Mussel Coordination Team, a coalition of eleven federal, state, and private agencies led by the U.S. Army Corps of Engineers, bolstered the strength of that population by taking 4,700 Minnesota-raised "sub-adults," two- and three-year-olds, and releasing them into Pool No. 16 not far from the Fairport Biological Station, where John Boepple once worked. Divers marked the shells with a dot of black glue and placed the mussels near a rope that they anchored to the riverbed so researchers could find the marked mussels again. For many years to come, scientists will monitor the survival and growth rate of the mussels and the mussel bed.

The harvest they hope for is one of numbers. They hope for a viable population of Higgins' eye mussels, *viable* meaning at least five hundred individuals that can successfully reproduce. They hope to count growth rings on the shells for many years to come. They hope to find many thousands of glochidia hitching rides on fish to other parts of the river, beyond the scope of their study, where the juveniles will fall to the river bottom and live long, productive lives. They hope the numbers will reveal that the river has become healthier, since mussels filter the water, making the river cleaner for all who use it—catfish, diving and dabbling ducks, water celery, dragonflies, eagles, algae, water snakes, common map and smooth soft-shell turtles, and people. They hope that when the numbers are in, Higgins' eye and other native mussels will be so abundant that once again, the river bottom will appear to be paved with cobblestones.

4

Nauvoo, the Beautiful Place

Nauvoo, Illinois, is encircled by a horseshoe bend in the Mississippi River in a part of western Illinois that some call "Forgottonia." This town of about 1,100 people, 270 miles southwest of Chicago and 190 miles north of St. Louis, can only be reached by a two-lane state highway or by boat. Yet, since the turn of the century, Nauvoo has drawn as many as 1.5 million visitors per year.

The town has a remarkable past. In the 1840s, it was one of the twenty largest cities in the United States, rivaling Chicago in size and economic importance. During the nineteenth century, it was the site of two utopias: one Mormon, one Icarian. In Nauvoo, Joseph Smith, founder of the Church of Jesus Christ of Latter-day Saints (LDS) and the Community of Christ, received 133 divine revelations, including those calling for polygamy, baptism of the dead, and the construction of a grand temple on the bluff above the Mississippi there. In Nauvoo, Etienne Cabet, the founder of Icaria, a French socialist experiment, sought to create a society free of poverty, ignorance, and injustice. The French, Swiss, Liechtensteiners, and Germans who immigrated to Nauvoo made it the first grape-growing and wine-making locale in Illinois. Until World War I, Nauvoo was known as the most German-speaking town in the state. Any one of these facts could be developed into a narrative that would provide healthy summer tourism, even for a town that isn't directly on the way to anywhere. But one narrative dominates, almost to the exclusion of all others.

In 1999, Gorden B. Hinckley, president of the LDS Church, announced that the Nauvoo Temple, built in the 1840s and destroyed by arson and tornado, would be rebuilt on its original location. That year, the number of tourists to Nauvoo doubled. Most were Mormons. Thousands of LDS volunteers poured into Nauvoo to work at the temple open houses. Some of the tourists and volunteers liked what they saw and returned as LDS missionaries to lead tours of the historical sites or as temple workers to perform or assist with ordinances. Some returned as students with Brigham Young University's Semester at Nauvoo. And some returned to buy property and live there. Most non-Mormon residents of Nauvoo are conflicted about this surge of interest in their home. They welcome the growth, but question the effect of Mormon tourism. Others would just as soon forgo the crowds, the tourist dollars, and the new residents and regain their quiet little town. When I told my parents that I was planning to write about Nauvoo, they expressed regret over how it had changed. "You won't recognize it," they said. "Now everything is Mormon."

"Mormon tourism has brought a lot of money to that town," I said. "It's keeping it alive."

"But at what price?" my mother asked.

On December 29, 2005, I visited Nauvoo for the first time in over a decade. I drove from my home in Lincoln, Nebraska, across southern Iowa, and crossed the Mississippi at Burlington, thirty miles upriver from Nauvoo. From there, I drove south on Illinois State Highway 96, the Great River Road, and passed through one dispiriting little town after another—Gulfport, Carman, Lomax, Dallas City, Pontoosuc, Niota—each with a stagnant or declining population, each with empty buildings and little or nothing open on a Thursday morning, except, perhaps, a convenience store. When I arrived in Nauvoo, the first thing that I noticed was the new temple: a five-story, 54,000-square-foot, Greek Revival, limestone box perched atop the bluff. Each of the temple's thirty pilasters is adorned with sunstones, moonstones, and starstones, which represent the "three degrees of glory" in Mormon afterlife. Those qualified to enter the temple do so through a triple-arched portico. A spire holds a golden figure of the angel Moroni 165 feet above the earth. The temple is hideously beautiful—or beautifully hideous—and disproportionately large for such a small town.

The second thing I noticed was people. The shops and restaurants on Mulholland Street, the main street through the business district, were open though quiet in the post-Christmas lull. Grandpa John's Café, where I ate lunch, was packed. In front of the gleaming temple, a beautiful, dark-haired bride laughed as her groom picked her up in his arms and spun her in a circle, her white dress and veil billowing. A handful of people snapped pictures. Even on a cold, gray morning with the tourist season months away, Nauvoo was clean, bright, and alive.

At the LDS Visitors' Center, the staff were preparing to meet with reporters from area newspapers about the release of a new movie commemorating the 200th anniversary of Joseph Smith's birth. So for the most part, I was alone with the exhibits. I studied the topographical map of Nauvoo in 1845, impressed that such a large and sophisticated city arose there almost overnight. I was taken aback by a white, white statue of Joseph Smith kneeling during a vision while a youthful and European-looking God and Jesus stood on air in front of him. I marveled at the sunstone, which once topped a pilaster on the original temple, and the curious, human face that it bore. I watched a film about the Mormon pioneers in Nauvoo that emphasized external threats but made little mention of the dissension within. After touring the visitors' center, one might conclude that Nauvoo history began in 1839 with the arrival of the Mormons and ended in 1846 with their expulsion.

To understand the controversies swirling in Nauvoo around tourism, indeed about how Nauvoo's history will be presented and understood, one must know something of the history of both the town and those who built it.

The first people to live near the bluff and peninsula that would become Nauvoo were mound-building American Indians, who may have arrived as early as 200 BC. In historic times, the Illinois tribe dominated the area, but in the early seventeenth century, they were displaced by the Sauk and Meskwaki, who in turn had been displaced from their original home in the St. Lawrence River Valley by other tribes. The Sauk and Meskwaki grew corn and hunted near the banks of the Mississippi. Though the Treaty of 1804 transferred Sauk lands to the U.S. government, they were permitted to hunt near their former home. In 1805, the United States established an agricultural school and trading post in the area. In 1824, James White, a retired Army captain, bought land on the peninsula from the federal government. White traded with the Sauk and ran a "lightering" business, which transferred freight from steamboats onto flatboats or wagons and carried the cargo by water or land so that the steamboats could pass over the Des Moines Rapids—eleven miles of dangerous limestone rocks in the river—and then reloaded the cargo onto the steamboats. In 1830, a post office was established for the town of Venus, population sixty-two. Later that decade, two towns were platted on the peninsula: Commerce and Commerce City; the population of the latter may have reached two hundred before it crashed in the financial panic of 1837. Two years later, five thousand Mormons settled on the "Flats," the low half circle of land jutting into the Mississippi.

The Mormons were followers of Joseph Smith Jr. (1805–1844), whom Jon Krakauer describes as "one of the most remarkable figures to ever have breathed American air." When he was a teenager, Smith received *The Book of Mormon: Another Testament of Jesus Christ*, the doctrinal foundation of the LDS and the Community of Christ churches, from the angel Moroni, son of the prophet Mormon. This book tells the story of Israelites who came to America about 600 BC and of Christ's visit to this continent following his resurrection.

After attending revivals in upstate New York during the winter of 1828–1829, Smith tried to discern which of the many churches to join. Two "personages," who identified themselves as God the Father and Jesus Christ, appeared to him and said, "They are all abominations in my sight. None of them are good."

Consequently, on April 4, 1830, Smith started his own church. According to Krakauer, this new religion offered "a kinder, gentler alternative to Calvinism," then the dominant type of Christianity, which taught that people were inherently evil and that God was inherently vengeful. Smith rejected the idea of original sin, insisting that God's chosen, the Mormons, were virtuous people living in a wicked world. Moreover, they could become gods, just as God had once been human. Also contributing to the success of Smith's religion was its materialism: the church taught that earthly wealth reflected spiritual standing. Thus, Mormonism not only approved of but encouraged prosperity and consumption. It was a quintessentially American religion.

For the next couple of decades, Smith and his followers sought a home. But wherever they went, they met with disapproval, sometimes outright violence. People who initially welcomed the Mormons became hostile once they saw how quickly and completely their new neighbors established social, economic, and political dominion. Mormons believed that theirs was the one true religion and that all others were wrong, which is not an uncommon position for the adherents of any religion, but the Mormons went so far as to call themselves "Saints" and non-Mormons "Gentiles." Smith had a vision that charged him to lead the Saints from Palmyra, New York, to Kirtland, Ohio. In 1838, seven years after they arrived there, the Mormons were forced to leave. Just months after their arrival in northwestern Missouri, where an entire county, Caldwell, was set aside for their use, the governor issued an "extermination order" against them. What led Missourians to war with the Mormons was that they planned to build a Zion in Missouri that would draw converts from all over the world and that Mormons, though not abolitionists, refused to own slaves.

Following the Mormon War of 1838, Smith's followers fled Missouri and gathered in Quincy, Illinois, fifty-three miles downriver from Nauvoo. Dr. Isaac Galland, an agent for the New York Land Company, sold land to Mormon leaders on both sides of the river in what is now Lee County, Iowa, and Hancock County, Illinois, for two dollars per acre, nothing down, no interest, with payments to be made over twenty years. Galland told Smith that the Mormons would receive warm hospitality in the territory of Iowa and the state of Illinois.

In May 1839, Joseph and Emma Smith, their children, and his parents moved into James White's "plantation" on the Flats. Smith renamed the town Nauvoo, a Hebrew word meaning "beautiful place" or "beautifully situated," from Isaiah 52:7 ("How beautiful upon the mountains are the feet of him who brings good news"), about the suffering servant turned victorious and the triumphant return of God's people to Zion, references that Smith probably applied both to himself and to the Zion that he and his Saints were building on the Mississippi. At Smith's beckoning, converts from Europe, Canada, and the United States and its territories poured into Nauvoo. Epidemics of malaria, typhoid fever, and typhus were common and deadly until the settlers dug a ditch at the base of the bluffs and drained the swampy peninsula. That ditch still drains water in Nauvoo State Park today. By 1840, they had built about 250 block houses in the Flats. By 1845, Nauvoo had between 15,000 and 20,000 residents, a couple thousand homes, a half-completed temple on the bluff, and lush gardens. Nauvoo, the beautiful place.

In Nauvoo, the charismatic Smith established a theocracy in which he was mayor, chief magistrate, lieutenant general of the Nauvoo Militia, newspaper editor, real estate promoter, grocer, and in 1844, U.S. presidential candidate. Religiously, Nauvoo was significant because Smith received his revelations there about baptism by proxy for dead relatives, rebaptisms, endowments of spiritual powers to initiates to the priesthood, second anointings, and plural marriages (Smith may have had dozens of wives). And in Nauvoo, Smith received divine orders to build a fit dwelling place for the Lord. When Josiah Quincy, who would become the mayor of Boston in 1846, visited Nauvoo just weeks before Smith's death, "General Smith," as Quincy called him, took him to see the temple construction. To Quincy, the temple was "wonderful" though "indescribable," since it was "like something Smith had seen in a vision [and] certainly cannot be compared to any ecclesiastical building which may be discerned by the natural eyesight." Smith told Quincy that each of "the monolithic pillars" cost three thousand dollars. The baptistery in the basement was "centered in a mighty tank, surrounded by twelve wooden oxen of colossal size." Quincy judged that "the City of Nauvoo, with its wide streets, sloping gracefully to the farms enclosed on the prairie, seemed to be a better temple to Him who prospers the work of industrious hands than the grotesque structure on the hill, with all its queer carvings of suns and moons."

As in Ohio and Missouri, the Saints and their beliefs rubbed their neighbors the wrong way and the Gentiles retaliated. Orville F. Berry, an attorney in Carthage, the Hancock County seat, identified the two chief sources of such local resentment toward the Mormons. One was conflict over the treatment of criminals. When a county official arrested a Mormon for breaking the law, Smith's court would issue a writ of habeas corpus, which would release the accused from the custody of the civil court. The other was restricted freedom of the press. On June 7, 1844, the first and only issue of *The Expositor,* a newspaper founded by disfellowshipped Mormons, divulged Smith's secret teachings on polygamy and the plurality of gods. Smith and the Nauvoo City Council ordered the city marshal to destroy the press and burn all remaining copies of the newspaper, a violation of the First Amendment. On June 12, Thomas C. Sharp, a judge and the editor of the *Carthage Gazette* and the *Warsaw Signal,* prophesied that "war and extermination" were inevitable for the "infernal devils," as he called his Mormon neighbors. Sharp's chief complaint was that the Mormons voted as a bloc, throwing any Hancock County election in their favor. Sharp called for his readers to respond "with powder and ball." Berry and Sharp offer valid explanations for a reasoned opposition to the Mormon majority. But the ferocious hatred that many locals felt was caused by something more visceral: jealousy over the Mormons' material success and aversion to their otherness.

Joseph Smith and his brother Hyrum were arrested on charges of treason but were soon released after a Mormon tribunal issued them a writ of habeas corpus. Then a non-Mormon justice in Nauvoo exonerated the brothers of charges against them. Threats of violence against the Mormons increased. On June 18, Smith called up his militia and declared a state of martial law. Even though Smith knew that he and his brother would be "massacred," the two men turned themselves in, were arrested on charges of treason, and were put in the Carthage Jail in the care of a local militia company, the Carthage Greys. The Warsaw Dragoons, another local militia company, stormed the jail, overcame the Greys, who did little to resist, and began shooting. Five men, including Sharp, were acquitted of the June 27, 1844, murders of the Smiths. The prophet's death wasn't enough to quell the violence. In the months that followed, vigilantes burned the houses and crops of Mormon settlers, beat the men, and harassed the women and children.

In January 1845, the state legislature repealed Nauvoo's charter and ordered the Mormons to leave. The Saints sold their properties for a fraction of what they were worth and built wagons to carry them far from Nauvoo. During their final months there, work on the temple continued at a feverish pace. Once special rooms in the temple attic were completed and furnished in November 1845, "the secret temple work" (such as the blessing of endowment, the sealing of plural wives, and adoptions by church leaders of men in the priesthood and their families) continued day and night until February 1846. Then thousands of Mormons walked down Parley Street, the "Street of Tears," and walked across the frozen Mississippi into Iowa. Eventually, they settled in Utah, far from Gentiles and U.S. laws. A few, such as Joseph Smith's wife, Emma, their children, and his mother, Lucy, remained behind, as well as those who would complete the work on the temple. At the Battle of Nauvoo the following September, an armed force drove out most of the remaining Mormons. Church officials sold the temple. In 1848, arsonists torched it, fearing that if the temple was still there, the Mormons would return.

In the May 2005 issue of the LDS youth publication *New Era*, Janet Thomas states, "After the Church members left to go west, Nauvoo faded into a small farming community." Though Thomas's statement provides a fitting end to the story of Mormons in Nauvoo, it's not historically accurate.

In 1849, the Icarians, under the leadership of Etienne Cabet, bought the Mormon structures, including what remained of the temple, and attempted to build their utopia there. The Icarians, who came from France, Germany, and Switzerland, sought to create an egalitarian community with no social classes, money, private property, poverty, or competition. The communal, French-speaking Icarians may have seemed as odd to the people of Hancock County as the Mormons. But there were far fewer of them (though two thousand passed through Icaria, never more than five hundred lived there at one time), and unlike their predecessors, they lacked what Krakauer calls an attitude of "divine entitlement." Cabet and his followers were converting the fire-damaged temple into a lecture and dining hall when a tornado toppled two walls and damaged a third. For safety reasons, Cabet ordered that the remaining walls be demolished. On the temple lot, the Icarians built a boarding school for their children, a communal dining hall, press, infirmary, pharmacy, and a library, purportedly the state's largest at the time. After Cabet lost his reelection bid for president of the colony in 1856, the group broke into two factions, one of which moved to St. Louis, the other to Corning, Iowa. By 1857, most Icarians had left Nauvoo.

Legend has it that viticulture began in Nauvoo in the 1830s, when the Catholic priest Johannes Alleman planted grape roots there. In the early 1850s, John Bauer, the son of a Bavarian winegrower, and John Tanner from Switzerland introduced winegrowing to Nauvoo. One of the earliest wineries there belonged to Alois Rheinberger from Liechtenstein. But it was the descendants of the Icarians who made Nauvoo one of the foremost grape-growing and wine-making regions in the center of the country. Emile Baxter, who joined the Icarians in 1855 and remained in Nauvoo after the colony disbanded, kept an eight-acre vineyard and in 1857, established a winery. Baxter died in 1895, but his sons continued his work as Baxter Brothers. During Prohibition, they sold fruit instead of wine; following the repeal of the Eighteenth Amendment, theirs was the first Illinois winery to reopen. When Emile's son Cecil died in 1947, his was the only winery in the state. In 1987, Kelly Logan, Emile Baxter's great-great-grandson, bought the business, now called Baxter's Vineyards and Winery.

In addition to wine making, Nauvoo's other principal industry was cheese making. In the 1930s, Oscar Rohde, a professor at Iowa State University, created a recipe for blue cheese that used cow rather than goat milk. Rohde bought the building that had once housed the Schenk Brewery and converted it into a cheese factory. This was an ideal place, since the limestone caves in the bluff beneath the former brewery provided the constant temperature needed to properly age the cheese. In 1937, the Nauvoo Blue Cheese Factory opened. This factory eventually became the United States' second-largest producer of blue cheese, the winner of several international awards, and Nauvoo's largest employer.

To celebrate its two unique industries, each Labor Day since 1937 Nauvoo has hosted a grape festival that includes an annual pageant, "The Wedding of the Wine and the Cheese," which is also staged in Rochefort, France. When my father was a child, his family went to the festival each year to watch the parade and to picnic in Nauvoo State Park. As a member of the Keokuk High School band, my mother marched in the Grape Festival parade several years.My childhood memories of Nauvoo are of going there with my paternal grandmother to buy apples and grapes or going to the Hotel Nauvoo, a restaurant in a spacious house built on the bluff during the Mormon era, with Great-aunt Pertsie or my parents. Homemade bricks from Joseph Smith's General Store, some bearing finger indentations, were used to repair a wall in the hotel in 1879. And my father made wine from Nauvoo grape juice.

The people and the community of Nauvoo have not faded since the Mormon exodus; nor are they defined only by farming.

Because the earth is thickly layered with the sacred and temporal stories of different groups of people, the meaning and interpretation of a single place has become increasingly complicated. It's as if all the world were Jerusalem, where one historical site, say, the Temple Mount, Haram al-Shariff, a raised platform in the Old City, is sacred to the followers of three religions for different yet overlapping reasons. The Temple Mount is sacred for Jews because it was the site of the first and the second temple, and it's the spot where Abraham offered his son as a sacrifice to Yahweh. It's significant for Christians because it's the site of the second temptation, where Satan asked Jesus to throw himself down from the pinnacle of the temple so angels could catch him, thus proving his Messiahship. Haram al-Shariff, Islam's third-holiest site after Mecca and Medina, is sacred to Muslims because of its association with Abraham, David, and Solomon and more importantly, because from there, Muhammad ascended into heaven. One site, three histories and meanings. The control of this site, under Muslim authority since the twelfth century, is hotly contested.

What privileges one historical narrative and the associations of one group of people over those of others? Mormon history dominates in Nauvoo for several reasons. One is the sheer size of the community that lived there in the 1840s. For the past 160 years, Nauvoo's population has remained but a fraction of what it was during the Mormon years. Another reason is that with over six million members in the United States, the LDS Church, the nation's fourth-largest denomination, and the Community of Christ, formerly the Reorganized Church of Jesus Christ of the Latterday Saints, with 130,000 members in the United States, are alive and well. The Icarian movement, however, never had a wide following and was dissolved in 1898. While Nauvoo had an American Indian and German American past, the stories of these groups are memorialized and celebrated in many other midwestern places. But Nauvoo, the site of a Mormon utopia, the holy city, the New Jerusalem, the City of Joseph, is unique. Also contributing to the success of Mormons at promoting their history in Nauvoo is that they are judged cultic or heretical by evangelical Christians and sexist, racist, and homophobic by progressives. An outcast status goes far in creating group unity and resolve. And the LDS Church is wealthy enough to invest $30 million in a new temple in Forgottonia.

Efforts to develop Nauvoo into a site that would draw tourists and pilgrims began early in the twentieth century. In 1903, the LDS Church bought the Carthage Jail, then a private residence. In 1909, the Reorganized Church of Jesus Christ of the Latter-day Saints (RLDS), began acquiring and restoring the Joseph Smith historic sites. In 1937, the LDS Church purchased part of the temple lot and the building that once housed their newspaper, *The Times and Seasons*. In 1938, it restored the Carthage Jail and continued to purchase portions of the temple block as they became available.

Nauvoo Restoration, Inc. (NRI), the nonprofit foundation that has restored the buildings on the Flats to something close to their former condition, had its beginnings in the 1920s, when J. LeRoy Kimball, who was attending college in Chicago, went to Nauvoo to see the house in which his great-grandparents had lived. Kimball's grandfather, Heber C. Kimball, had been Brigham Young's first counselor and one of the twelve original apostles. In 1954, J. LeRoy Kimball, then a Salt Lake City physician, bought and began renovating his ancestors' home. In 1962, he established NRI, with himself as president. The new organization went to work excavating the site of the temple and several other Mormon buildings. In 1971, the LDS Church opened a visitors' center in Nauvoo. In 1982, NRI, then run by the LDS Church, dedicated sixteen nineteenth-century buildings that it had restored on the Flats. At that time, Nauvoo averaged 200,000 to 250,000 tourists per year, mostly a mix of visitors from Illinois, Iowa, and Missouri and Mormons from Utah. I toured the buildings in the late 1970s, in the mid-1990s, and again in 2005. On my second visit, I stood in the Browning House and Gun Shop crowded with Saints pilgrimaging from New York to Utah and the Mormon historical sites between and listened to the family stories they told each other about this gun shop, the artifacts within, and Nauvoo in general. For them, it was a highly charged landscape, the site of sacred, familial, and corporate history. They, too, loved Nauvoo.

In 1998, the LDS Church bought St. Mary's 1874 priory and 1957 girls' boarding school, both of which occupied the former temple site, from the Sisters of St. Benedict. In 1999, LDS president Gordon B. Hinckley announced that the Church would reconstruct the Nauvoo Temple on the original site.

The City of Nauvoo and the LDS Church reached an agreement under which the latter would provide a city planner for two years and pay the City almost $471,000 up front for infrastructure. Now, the "Williamsburg of the Midwest" includes almost forty restored historic buildings and the thirty-million-dollar temple, all tax exempt since they are church properties.

While most other small towns on the Upper Mississippi River are losing population, Nauvoo's rose from 1,063 in 2000 to 1,155 in 2005, an 8.7 percent increase. But these numbers don't tell the whole story. The Mormon population of Nauvoo rose from 178 in 1999 to about 900 in 2004, and continues to grow. In other words, Mormons are moving in and non-Mormons are moving out.

Some of Nauvoo's non-Mormon residents are resentful of these changes. Just prior to the opening of the temple, Colleen Ralson, then director of the Christian Visitors' Center in Nauvoo, told the *San Francisco Chronicle* that "many feel that the Mormons will reoccupy the town." She pointed to the fact that the LDS bought the hardware store and turned it into an LDS bookstore and that Nauvoo's largest motel is Mormon owned. Ralson also didn't like the way Mormons act. "It's their attitude, their arrogance: 'This is my town—I will do what I please.'" Jane Langford, owner and editor of Nauvoo's weekly newspaper, the *New Independent,* told MSNBC about a "master plan" that involves the LDS Church raising property prices in Nauvoo until longtime residents are forced out. "I think it's been thought out for years and I think that they will get control of the City Council and the School Board within five years." Langford told *Time* magazine that the Mormons "want to take back Nauvoo, and since they can't do it with guns, they are doing it with money." What these women are really saying about the return of the Mormons is that they are afraid of being overpowered by people whom they see as too different and of losing their homes and businesses through economics or reconstruction—just as many in Hancock County felt in the 1840s.

Real estate prices in Nauvoo are high for that part of Illinois. According to City-Data.com, the estimated median value of a house or condominium in Nauvoo in 2009 was $130,360. Fifteen miles away in Carthage, the county seat (population 2,455), it was $82,283. Seven miles from Nauvoo in Fort Madison, Iowa (population 10,884), it was $68,585. *Time* reported that in 2000, a house in the Flats that not so long ago would have sold for $20,000 now goes for $250,000. Just as property values have risen sharply, so, too, have property taxes. While Rustin Lippincott, Nauvoo's exuberant director of tourism from 2004 to 2008, dismissed the conspiracy theories, he acknowledged the effect of real estate prices. "Everything goes up with real estate," Lippincott said. "A working class family can't come to Nauvoo." Consequently, Nauvoo's director of tourism lived in Fort Madison. Lippincott said that for the most part, the only people who can afford to move to Nauvoo are those who have sold a house in another, costlier part of the country and see real estate prices in Nauvoo as "dirt cheap."

Brenda Logan and her husband, Kelly Logan, the great-great-grandson of Emile Baxter, own Baxter's Vineyards and Winery on Parley Street, the Street of Tears, the oldest vineyard and winery in continuous operation in Illinois. The Logans also own Carol's Pies, Treasures Gift Shop, and Nauvoo Cheese, Inc. Kelly, the viticulturist, and Brenda, the winemaker, produce three to five thousand gallons of wine per year from their fourteen-acre vineyard. The rising prices of real estate following the rebuilding of the temple trouble Brenda Logan. Until then, Nauvoo had been a bedroom community, with Nauvooans commuting to jobs in Quincy, Keokuk, Fort Madison, and Burlington. But now, people are leaving to live in less costly towns such as Hamilton, Illinois, about ten miles downriver. Older residents, who long complained about the influx of Mormons, are selling their houses to the newcomers at inflated prices and moving away with the profit. Young people leave town as they always have, but the difference is that now, because of the temple crowds, they're not returning in their thirties and forties as they used to.

One might think that the higher taxes and real estate prices would be offset by tourist income, but that isn't the case. Brenda Logan says that the Mormons who come to Nauvoo are on a religious pilgrimage in search of their history and religion. Some are affluent, but most are not. They may sleep twenty people to a single hotel room and buy food at the grocery store rather than patronizing local restaurants. Some have the expectation that everything should be free for them. Nauvoo could work, Logan says, if the tourists were more willing to put money into the community in the form of restaurant meals and souvenirs.

Lippincott was sympathetic about Mormon interest in Nauvoo. "The LDS want to come back and remember their history. Many of their doctrines got started here. They want to be good neighbors and reinvigorate their history at whatever costs. They're willing to pay the high prices."

But what about the nonmonetary cost of this reinvigoration? What struck me about the LDS missionaries that I spoke to was how little interest they had in Nauvoo beyond its Mormon history, or in what their presence had done to the town in terms of economic stability and communal history and identity. When I told them that I had grown up in Burlington, that my mother's people came from Keokuk and Montrose, and that I'd long been familiar with Nauvoo, they did not respond with expressions of commonality, as I expected. Perhaps they couldn't imagine or acknowledge that Nauvoo is dear to or home to others. Or perhaps they've never forgiven us for the bloodshed and bigotry that their ancestors encountered there.

When the LDS Church knocked down St. Mary's Priory and Academy and the blue cheese factory, two Nauvoo landmarks, many locals thought that the LDS members were trying to erase everyone's history but their own. It may appear that way, Lippincott said, but that's not the case. Some of the nuns at St. Mary's told him that with the rising cost of education, declining enrollments, and the worsening condition of the building, it was just too expensive to keep the school open. St. Mary's was once the most prominent building in Nauvoo, and its large auditorium was frequently used for local events. In years past, the school was where "troubled girls" were sent for education and discipline. When I was a teenager, "She went to Nauvoo" was all we had to say to communicate a girl's reputation. When the deal with the LDS Church was being worked out, some local residents tried to pool their money to buy the convent so that the LDS couldn't, but the package the LDS officials offered the Benedictines was better. After the LDS Church bought the priory and academy, they razed them so that people would have an unobstructed view of the planned new temple.

The removal of the cheese factory is a similar story. ConAgra Foods of Omaha purchased Nauvoo Blue Cheese in an effort to buy out its competition. Then ConAgra sold the company to the conglomerate Saputo, Inc. of Montreal. Production at the factory ceased in 2003, terminating the employment of sixty-five workers. Saputo only wanted the Nauvoo Blue Cheese trademarked name, so the empty building went on the market for $1 million. No one in town needed such a large building, and because it contained mold and asbestos, it could never again be used for food production. "A terrible building. An eyesore," Lippincott says. "The LDS Church was the only viable entity." The Church bought it, knocked it down, and planted grass. What Lippincott emphasizes is that the LDS Church repurchased property that had once been theirs.

Repurchased, the prefix *re-* meaning "again, anew, back, or backward." The LDS had "bought again" land that had been theirs before they were driven from it by their Mormon-hating neighbors. In Nauvoo, the LDS members were recovering, recapturing, regaining, repossessing, reclaiming, and returning to.

Nauvoo's "drawing card," says Brenda Logan, is the LDS sites. The Icarians, the winery, the river, and the Hotel Nauvoo complement it. But LDS tourism can't stand alone. It needs a town to provide infrastructure—roads, sewers, police force, fire and rescue equipment. In other words, Mormon tourism needs Nauvoo. And since Nauvoo hasn't the industry or other types of tourism to sustain itself, it needs the Mormons. *Reciprocation:* "to give or feel something mutually or in return."

Before I left Nauvoo on my most recent visit, I toured the Joseph Smith homestead. This had long been my favorite part of Nauvoo since it was positioned on the outer cusp of the peninsula, just feet from the river, offering a wide view of the river and Montrose. Bald eagles, their white heads bright against the gray sky, soared overhead. Hundreds of Canada geese stood on the ice, honking. Cardinals, red-bellied woodpeckers, nuthatches, sparrows, and other backyard birds flitted in the trees.

The Smith Homestead, the oldest building in Hancock County, had been a two-room log cabin, one room up and one room down, where Joseph and Emma Smith, their children, and Joseph's parents had lived. To this, the Smiths added two rooms up, two down, and a spring house to store perishable food. When I visited the homestead in the late 1970s, the river had been closer. But in 2005, the Smiths' yard was set back farther from the river, and scruffy wetlands lay between them.

The homestead at the edge of the peninsula and the grand mansion a little further inland to which the family moved in 1843 are the sites of competing narratives. Following Smith's death in 1844, a controversy developed as to who should succeed him as church president. Some believed that Smith had designated his eldest son, Joseph Smith III, to be his successor. Yet Joseph III was only eleven at the time of his father's death, much too young to lead a church. Some wanted James Strang or Granville Hedrick or Sidney Rigdon or one of the many others who claimed to be the rightful heir at the helm. While most eventually followed Brigham Young, the head of the Quorum of the Twelve Apostles that formed shortly after Smith's death and went west to found a new home for the Church, dozens of sects with other leaders would name Smith and his Nauvoo revelations as foundational, as their religious point of origin in the world.

After her husband's murder, Emma Smith and Brigham Young had bitter disagreements over her rejection of polygamy and how to untangle what was church property from what Emma believed was her husband's inheritance for his children. After Young and his followers began their trek to what is now Utah, Emma, her children, and Joseph's mother, Lucy, remained behind in the almost-empty town. In 1847, Emma married Major Lewis C. Bidamon, a non-Mormon. They lived in the mansion and attended the Methodist Church. In 1860, Joseph III accepted a call to lead a newly organized church. In 1872, the church that he headed added "Reorganized" to its name to distinguish it from the Utah Latter-day Saints, who at that time were practicing polygamy. In 1909, the RLDS began acquiring the Smith historic sites in Nauvoo.

During my 2005 visit, after touring the LDS Visitors' Center, the Cultural Hall, and the Scovill Bakery, where missionaries delivered well-rehearsed speeches and led tightly controlled tours, I decided to continue my explorations without an official guide. But the only way to gain access to the homestead, Smith's general store, hotel, and the mansion, was through a tour. I walked south on Main and east on Parley to the Community of Christ's Joseph Smith Historic Center, where I paid for a tour.

My guide, a woman named Irene, answered my questions with depth and ease, and she didn't proselytize. Her story of Smith and his followers revealed an understanding of geography and economics that extended beyond Mormon Nauvoo. At the same time, she delved more deeply into the story of Nauvoo than anyone or anything I'd seen or heard that day. She said that during Smith's time there, Lumber Street ran between Water Street and the river, which meant that there had been an entire block of land between the homestead and the water's edge. Then, there had been a wooded island in the middle of the river and a treacherous, eleven-mile stretch of shallow water and rocky riverbed between the confluence of the Des Moines and Mississippi rivers near Keokuk and the head of the rapids at Nauvoo and Montrose.

Irene posited that some of the hostility that the Mormons experienced was economically inspired. Thomas Sharp, the editor of the *Warsaw Signal* and one of the men who shot Smith, not only was fearful of a Mormon political majority but also wanted the businesses that served the steamboats to be centered in Warsaw rather than Nauvoo. As a result, Sharp fomented animosity toward the Mormons in his newspaper column.

After the Mormons left, there were several significant changes in the river. In 1877, the federal government dug the Des Moines Rapids Canal so that travelers no longer had to lighter to pass over the rapids. When Lock and Dam No. 19 at Keokuk began operating in 1913, it brought the river closer to the Smith homestead. This created confusion as to where the Smith family graves were located. After the martyrdom, Joseph's and Hyrum's bodies had been taken from Carthage to Nauvoo for a wake and burial. Given the anti-Mormon sentiments of some of the locals, Emma and church officials feared that the Smith brothers' bodies would not be safe in the ground, so they hid them between the basement walls of the Nauvoo House, the Smiths' hotel that was not completed, and provided decoys—sand-filled coffins—for the funeral. When construction of the Nauvoo House resumed in 1845, Emma secretly buried the bodies beneath the spring house southwest of the homestead. Emma, who died in 1879, was never sure of the exact location of her husband's and brother-in-law's graves. By 1928, the dam had caused the river water to back up to the point where it seemed that the graves might be in danger. That year, Frederick Madison Smith, president of the RLDS Church, hired a surveyor to locate the unmarked graves of his grandfather and great-uncle so they could be given a proper burial. After the surveyor found the bodies, they were moved a few feet. Now the graves of Joseph, Emma, and Hyrum are marked with a single slab of gray granite. The Smiths' parents and one brother are also buried near the homestead.

Irene said that in the 1950s, the U.S. Army Corps of Engineers built a berm around Smith's hotel, which is now used as a hostel for Community of Christ youth retreats. Nonetheless, when the river floods, water laps at the hotel foundation. Irene said that when she arrived in Nauvoo in 1997, the river had been closer. Now, because of silt deposition, it's farther away. The Corps won't dredge the channel because of objections by farmers.

I looked out over the swampy, silty area. It should be filled with cattails, reed canarygrass, rushes, and sedges and host to a rich diversity of wildlife. But it's not. Now it's well established with purple loosestrife. Like many of our most noxious weeds, purple loosestrife is native to Eurasia and thrives on disturbed soil—like that near a river or lake that has recently flooded. Loosestrife forms such dense, impenetrable stands that with the exception of bees and butterflies, who like the nectar, and red-winged blackbirds, who nest in the branches but won't eat the seeds, it edges out native plants and animals. Efforts to control or eradicate the weed by cutting, pulling, digging, or poisoning are largely unsuccessful.

Irene regretted the plant's invasive, competitive nature, yet she said she found it beautiful in the early summer, when the silty area is nothing but purple blossoms. I could imagine how the peninsula would look in June: a blue sky, gray-brown water, burbling red-winged blackbirds, and a field of waving purple wands. But the image of the vast purple swatch made me uneasy, since it pointed to something beyond itself. Perhaps it told a story of displacement, of the Illinois Indians being displaced by the Sauk and Meskwaki, who in turn were displaced by Galland, White, and the early residents of Venus and Commerce, who in turn were displaced by the Mormons, who in turn were displaced by their "Gentile" neighbors and immigrants from other countries, who in turn are being displaced by Mormons, returning to reclaim what had been theirs some 160 years ago. Then I imagined this jut of land as it should be: not dominated by a single plant that crowds out all of the others, but a rich, diverse place of bulrushes, cattails, reeds, bitterns, rails, ducks, geese, hawks, wrens, turtles, muskrats, frogs, toads, and other creatures, each appearing in its season, each an integral part of the ecosystem of this beautiful place.

5

Mound Builders

For the past couple of years, my mother had been telling me that she wanted to go along on one of my writing-related research trips. The first few times we talked about taking such a jaunt together, our plans never left the wishful-thinking stage. But then I thought, "Why not?" The last time we'd taken a trip together—the kind in which you're gone for more than a few days, see new places, camp or stay in motels, eat in restaurants, and spend so long in the car that you get on each other's nerves and share more deeply than you can in phone chats and at family gatherings—was when I was a teenager. What would it be like for us to travel together now? Given the way time was piling up behind us, I didn't want to wait any longer to find out.

While there were many places on the Mississippi, Missouri, and Platte that I needed to visit or revisit, it was Effigy Mounds National Monument in far northeastern Iowa that seemed to be calling us. There on the floodplain and the high bluffs above the Mississippi, prehistoric American Indians had shaped the earth into mounds. Some mounds were rounded like scoops of ice cream; some were shaped in the forms of birds, mammals, amphibians, and reptiles. While these animal-shaped "effigy" mounds had been common in what is now southwestern Wisconsin, northwestern Illinois, northeastern Iowa, and southeastern Minnesota, most were eventually destroyed for farms, roads, and settlements. But within the 2,556 acres of Effigy Mounds National Monument, the National Park Service is protecting 206 known mounds, including 175 linear and conical mounds (cigars and upside-down bowls, to my eyes) and 31 effigy mounds (lumbering bears and birds in flight), and researchers keep finding new ones there, the most recent being a panther-shaped mound.

When my father died in 2006, I found myself drawn to this story in the land about how grieving people in the distant past memorialized their dead. Several months after we buried my father's remains at Catfish Bend, my daughter, Meredith, and I drove to the monument and explored the mounds and nearby river. I tried to write about the experience but because I hadn't been able to find the deep story, I eventually abandoned the essay. A return trip is what I needed if I was to finish it. Because there was snow on the ground when Meredith and I were at the monument, we weren't able to hike the rugged, south-unit bluff during that visit and see the Ten Marching Bears mound formation atop it. This time, I was determined to see the parade.

October was the perfect time for our trip. Mom loves autumn, and during the first weekend of October, this northern place wasn't far from peak color. Because Dad's birthday was on the twelfth, his death on the twenty-fourth, and his memorial service on the twenty-seventh, October was a hard month. A trip to the mounds would give us a good October memory.

My mother flew to Nebraska from her home in Ohio, spent a day with her grandchildren, and then, on a gorgeous Saturday morning, we set out across Iowa. Mom, an Iowa Hawkeyes fan, enjoyed seeing people whizzing past on the interstate on their way to the football game in Iowa City, their black and gold car flags fluttering. When she saw the many hundreds of wind turbines bristling the west-central Iowa landscape, she was deeply impressed. I knew the statistics: while Iowa has the tenth-best wind resources in the country, it's the second-largest producer of wind energy in the country, topped only by Texas, a much larger state. And, Iowa is number one in the use of wind-generated electricity. "I'm just so proud of Iowa for doing this," Mom said as she watched the low, spinning stars.

On the long drive, we had plenty of time to talk and plenty of subjects for our conversation—politics, of course; memories of Dad; how much livelier Mom's life was now that she had a "manfriend" ("Don't call him my 'boyfriend,'" she said. "That sounds like we're in high school."); and my growing sense that it was time for me to leave Nebraska, my home for over twenty years, and settle someplace with soft wooded hills, tall bluffs, wide rivers, and a record of electing Democrats for the presidency. I also shared with her what I'd read about the provenance of the effigy mounds.

In the seventeenth, eighteenth, and nineteenth centuries, the European Americans who passed through or settled in the area of the mounds couldn't imagine that the ancestors of the American Indians they encountered, people diminished by wars, forced removals, and foreign food, drink, and diseases, had created these remarkable earthworks. When questioned about the origin of the mounds, the native peoples were reported as saying that they didn't know where they had come from, which many interpreted as further evidence that the mounds were not raised by indigenous peoples.

For the better part of the eighteenth and nineteenth centuries, both the learned and the unlearned explained the discrepancy between the ancient mounds and the "degenerated" state of the native peoples they observed by assuming that there had been two groups of people in ancient America: one civilized, enlightened, and productive; one savage and depraved. The former, variously identified as Vikings, Hindus, people from the lost continent of Atlantis, and the descendants of the lost tribes of Israel (the latter theory was promoted in *The Book of Mormon*), built the mounds and disappeared, perhaps conquered by the American Indians who lived in the vicinity of the mounds. Many European Americans were attracted to this myth of foreign mound builders because it justified their government's Indian-removal policies. Since the ancestors of the contemporary Indians had destroyed the mound builders, they had to be punished. Since the ancient mound builders had come from Europe or the Near East, the contemporary Indians had to be removed so that European Americans could reclaim what had once been theirs. And too, ancient, foreign mound builders provided the youthful United States with a glorious, sophisticated past, like that of Rome, Athens, or Jerusalem.

It was Cyrus Thomas, an Illinois minister turned entomologist, botanist, and archeologist, who was largely responsible for debunking the Lost Race hypothesis. Initially, Thomas supported the hypothesis. But after hundreds of mound excavations in Wisconsin, he concluded that the mound build-ers were the ancestors of the contemporary Winnebago, Mohawk, Huron, Sioux, and Algonquin. Throughout the twentieth century, researchers found ample evidence to support Thomas's theory. In 2001 and 2004, skeletal remains and funerary objects on display or archived at the monument were repatriated to the likely descendants of the mound builders, including the Iowa, Otoe-Missouria, Sac and Meskwaki, Dakota, and Winnebago. While scientists like Thomas and curious locals used to dig into the mounds and take the valuable objects within, now researchers can study the contents of the mounds through the use of ground-penetrating radar surveys, magne-tometers, and other nondestructive methods. Most of the mounds that my mother and I would be exploring at the monument were intact, just as their makers left them.

Mom was relieved to hear this. When she and dad were dating, they and another couple had visited the Dixon Mounds at Lewiston, Illinois. "It was so depressing to see a heap of skeletons on display. That place was sacred to people and should have been left alone. I felt the same way when I saw the contents of the holes that archeologists uncovered at Petra in Jordan. Some had been used for trash, which gave up all kinds of information about the people's everyday lives. But there were also pits where the ancestors had been buried, right within the dwelling. Leave the dead alone," she said defiantly.

It was a good seven hours or so to Prairie du Chien, Wisconsin, directly across the river from the monument. If we couldn't get there in one day, we planned to spend the night in Dubuque or Guttenberg, both on the Iowa side of the Mississippi. Mom hadn't seen the river since Dad's memorial service; I hadn't seen my river since I'd been in the St. Louis area the previous June—too long. Both Dubuque and Guttenberg offered spectacular views of the bluffs and river. Mom remembered an old, beautiful hotel that she thought might be in Guttenberg—if it still existed, if it ever existed—and once, Dad had hunted pheasants there. Midafternoon, she called motels in Guttenberg. But that weekend, this little town was host to a wedding/motorcycle convention, and there wasn't a single motel room left. We speculated about the type of evening we might have had if there had been one room left, we'd taken it, and then had to listen to old guys and their Harleys all night.

As we drove down the big hill into Dubuque on U.S. Highway 20, we got our first glimpse of the river: gray-green and sparkling, with the graceful Julian Dubuque Bridge arching above it. In Henry Lewis's 1848 painting of Dubuque, many buildings are crowded in the lowlands near the river; the hills beyond were too steep for either houses or farming. Now the bluffs are filled with houses and churches with tall steeples. Before heading to the waterfront, we stopped at the Dubuque Welcome Center and asked the woman behind the counter about motels. No rooms left in Dubuque, she said. Both Clark and Loras colleges were celebrating homecoming that weekend. She checked her computer and made phone calls. There were rooms in Platteville, Wisconsin, if we didn't mind driving twenty miles. Rather than walking along the riverfront, we set out across southwestern Wisconsin.

This beautiful country—winding roads, tall wooded hills, river valleys that deeply dissect the bedrock—is the Driftless Area, a land shaped by absence. In most of the Upper Midwest, the most recent glacier, the Wisconsin, had scraped and leveled the land and filled in the low spots with clay, gravel, sand, silt, and rocks ("drift"). But the glacier had skirted this area, leaving the landscape untouched. As the lobes of the glacier covered the surrounding area, many plants and animals found refuge here. I had read about one Ice Age relict, the endangered Iowa Pleistocene land snail, a creature with a brown or greenish shell about one-quarter of an inch in diameter, tightly coiled and domed, which is found only in the Driftless region in parts of Iowa and Illinois. This tiny, camouflaged snail had gone unnoticed by humans until 1955. What other relicts might be hidden from us in this large and rugged landscape?

Mom was trying to read the map but couldn't see the highway numbers. I gave her the pair of reading glasses I keep in the car. She positioned them on top of her own glasses. Even so, she had trouble reading the highway numbers. "Is this a five or what?" She held the map up to my face.

"Mom, I'm driving! Besides, I can't see that without my glasses."

She looked at me through the double lenses, her blue eyes large from the magnification. We started laughing. "We're just a couple of old ladies who can't see, aren't we?" she said.

Well, yes. The thought troubled me. Two old ladies, but a generation apart.

The next morning, we set out from Platteville for the mounds. The farms along U.S. Highways 61 and 18 were nestled into the sides of the hardwood- and pine-covered hills. The round hills reminded me of exceptionally large burial mounds. I snapped blurry pictures of them through the car window. The trees in low places were in standing water from the heavy rains that had caused the Wisconsin and Trempealeau rivers to jump their banks. Campaign signs for longtime Wisconsin senator Russ Feingold and Tea Partier Ron Johnson were as common as corn. The towns along the highway were either small or very small. Could I live in such a beautiful but sparsely populated place?

On our drive to Platteville, we'd heard the first part of *Prairie Home Companion;* Sunday morning, we listened to the remainder of the program. As we passed through Lancaster, Fennimore, Mount Ida, and Mount Hope, we sang along with Garrison Keillor and the Guy's All-Star Shoe Band: "Harvest Moon," "Love Lifted Me," "I Love to Tell the Story." We quickly learned the chorus to "The Methodist Blues." What will we do if Garrison Keillor ever retires?

I complimented Mom on all the changes she'd made in recent years. "That took courage," I said.

She agreed. "I'm a lot younger than I used to be."

It was true. Five and ten years ago, I often felt sad talking to my mother since she seem so absorbed in her own matters and so disinterested in my children and me. We lose our parents by degree, I'd reasoned. But a couple years after my father's death from cancer, a cancer my family lived with for ten years, Mom joined a church, a book club, and a lunch group, and started dating. She stopped cutting her faded, though still red, hair, which now falls halfway down her back. "I had to do something so I wouldn't look like all the other old ladies at church with their short, gray hair," she explained. Because of the physical demands of caring for my father through the latter stages of his illness and her grief over his death, followed by surgeries to replace both knees, to remove a cancerous tumor from her breast, and to repair a fracture in her neck, my mother is much slimmer and more mobile than she was in her sixties. Now she is alert, engaged, and interesting. At seventy-five, she *is* younger than she was in her sixties.

"I'm learning a lot about you on this trip," she said nonchalantly.

"Like what?"

"We'll, it's a lot like traveling with your father."

This was not what I wanted to hear. "Examples?"

"The way you hug the shoulder when a semi passes. Joe did that, too." She paused. "The way you tap the acceleration pedal, rather than applying steady pressure. It's not a smooth ride at all. The first time Joe's mother rode with me, she complimented me on the smooth ride. 'Joe jerks the car like this,' your grandmother said." Mom laughed as she imitated her mother-in-law's jerky, forward and backward movements.

"Other ways?"

"That text message you sent me at 5:15 this morning telling me not to take a shower or be noisy because you were going to go back to bed. That wasn't necessary. Dad was always telling me things I already knew." Yes, I suppose that text message had been unnecessary, but I hadn't slept well and the walls between the adjoining rooms were thin. Her shower and hair dryer would have awakened me.

"Anything else?"

"At Dixon Mounds, your dad was so mad because the mounds were further away than he'd expected. He was impossible, griping about how much gas we'd gone through, all puffed up like a rooster. You're like that, too, when things don't go your way."

I was taken aback. "I know about this, and I'm working on it. Really. Anything else?"

"I'm thinking."

I knew of other similarities. Like my father, I fall silent when my mother talks too much, since she runs down more quickly if no one is responding. And there are my ritualistic behaviors that give me a sense of security and control when I act them out. Returning home to check that the iron is unplugged before heading out on a trip. Needing to pee, no matter how inconvenient, before beginning anything even mildly eventful. I observed both of those behaviors in my father and can't seem to stop them in myself.

"You're probably thinking of us checking the oven and stove three times before going to bed."

"Well, yes." She paused. "I remember when we lived on Lower West Avenue Road. Dad had to open and shut the garage door every night before he went to bed. One time I watched him. He opened the garage door, stepped out, looked both ways, and came back in. I think that looking both ways was part of it."

"Then he had to check the stove three times."

She nodded.

"Yeh, that's magical thinking. He did that to protect us from harm."

We fell silent. A few minutes later, Mom reached over and patted my arm.

I was learning a lot about my mother on this trip. How much coffee she drinks, for one thing. How brave she is in demanding the type of life she wants. How proud she is to have been a high school and community college biology teacher for most of her adult life. How many events she remembers that I have forgotten or didn't know about because I was no longer living at home when they happened. She told the story about the death of our beloved German shepherd from cancer. At the vet's office, Max cried and cried—everyone could hear him—until Mom and my brother John took him to the car. Then, he was calm and quiet. At home, they made him a bed in the living room and he died there shortly thereafter. "Max was very obviously relieved to be at home," Mom said. "He seemed to die contentedly." When Dad came home, he wrapped Max in a blanket, put him on a sled and pulled him down the driveway, up the road and over the ditch to the far side of the creek. There, Dad buried him near Swamper, the coonhound, Belle, the beagle, and the previous owner's dog.

"Was it hard to leave the pets when you moved?"

"Oh, yes," she shook her head from side to side for emphasis. "That's why I had Konrad cremated. I'm taking him wherever I go." Konrad, my parents' last German shepherd, also died of cancer. "If I'd cremated Max, he'd still be with me."

Mom had cremated my father and buried his ashes at Aspen Grove Cemetery. I was conflicted as to whether Dad would rather have his ashes there or in an urn on a shelf in someone's living room. When I was in elementary school, my grandmother, father, brother Jamie, and I often visited the cemetery on Sunday afternoons. We'd drive the narrow, twisty, shady paths, looking at the military graves, Babyland, Potter's Field, the mausoleums, the swans on the pond, and the graves of people Dad and Grandma had known. Then we'd get out and walk to the Knopp and Freiberg graves. Jamie and I ran around and climbed on tombstones while Dad and Grandma arranged flowers, positioned wreaths, cleaned up the graves, and reminisced. Sometimes, Dad's brother and sister-in-law or one of his aunts would also visit the graves and we'd have an impromptu family reunion. Given the importance Dad's family placed on tending the graves of the dead, I supposed that my father would like to have people visit his grave on Sunday afternoons. While his brother and sister-in-law do visit, his wife, children, and grandchildren all live too far away. Perhaps it *would* be better to have Dad's ashes on a shelf in my living room.

Eventually, our conversation drifted to views of the afterlife. We marveled that some think of the afterlife as something like a great coffee shop in the sky where they'll meet their friends and family, and never again have to work or pay bills.

"What do you think it's like after we die?" Mom asked.

"I have no idea. Our bodies and brains will be gone, so we won't experience things the way we do now. I hope that our spirits just merge into God's. I think that would be wonderful but like nothing we can imagine."

"Is it so bad to hope that there's nothing after we die—it's just over?"

"Not at all," I said. "But I suppose if nothing persists after we die, then tending the physical remains and our memories of the dead is even more important." Either way, I felt I needed to return to Catfish Bend and tend to my father's grave.

Highway 18 took us into Prairie du Chien, the Dog Prairie. This had been the great rendezvous site for French traders, American Indians, and trappers in the 1600s, which makes it the oldest town on the Upper Mississippi. We crossed the side channel near the Wisconsin shore and then the main channel via the Marquette-Joliet Bridge. At the foot of the bridge on the Iowa side is the little town of Marquette, nestled into the side of the bluff. There, we turned north onto Highway 76, part of the Great River Road, which hugs the tall bluff. "Two thousand years for every half-inch," Mom remarked. "Rock of Ages," I said. Here hikers scale bluffs as tall as five hundred feet and follow trails that skirt deep ravines. Louis Jolliet called these cliffs "mountains."

When Meredith and I had visited the monument in March of 2007, there had been just a few other cars in the parking lot and we'd seen only two other hikers on the trails. But this was the Annual Hawk Watch Weekend, and the lot was almost full. People were gathered around the displays about raptors and arts and crafts outside the visitors' center. Hawk-watchers sat on lawn chairs near their telescopes. The day's activities included a puppet show for children, a program about recent efforts to reintroduce ospreys in Iowa, and a program called "Big Owls Hoot, Little Owls Toot." I photographed Mom standing next to a big, messy eagle's nest on display. She wore a cream-colored sweater and her new, purple-framed glasses. Her face, softly wrinkled, faded, and fallen, bears little resemblance to the bright, firm, and vibrant image of her that I carry in my mind. True to form, Mom refused to smile for the camera. In this photo, it's my own face twenty-some years hence that I see grimly gazing back at me. Inside the visitors' center, we strolled past displays on the history of Iowa Indians, arrowheads, food sources, pottery, and the development of the national monument. We marveled at the crude elegance or elegant crudeness of the ancient pots suspended by hangers in a glass case. Like the effigy mounds, these, too, were earthen extensions of the landscape.

Upon his retirement at age seventy-three, Ellison Orr, a local man who had worked as a farmer, teacher, surveyor, county clerk of courts, and manager of the Waukon telephone company, became a "dedicated amateur archeologist," according to one of the display placards. In the 1930s, Orr began locating, mapping, and excavating village sites, burials, and mound groups in northeastern Iowa. He excavated and cataloged what remained of the Great Bear Mound. In the gift shop, I bought a postcard with Orr's 1910 map of the Pleasant Ridge Mound Group, the Ten Marching Bears. Orr's map shows the ten cookie-cutter bears marching single file, head to tail, downriver. Two birds facing the river lead the formation; another bird soars near a kink in the queue as if it's a parade official keeping the cubs in line. Two linear mounds bring up the rear. Each of the effigies on Orr's map is drawn in red. Swirling gold lines show varying elevations. The Military Road built in 1840 to connect Fort Crawford (Prairie du Chien) and Fort Atkinson (near the Iowa-Minnesota state line) is a gray line that curls around the bears. The background is cream.

Just outside of the visitors' center, at the base of the north bluff, are three earthen domes, smooth and grassy lumps, none of which are taller than me. They are conspicuous and unnatural: protuberances like these do not arise on a floodplain on their own. The nearby sign explains that each of these conical mounds, constructed during the Middle Woodland Period, about 2,100 to 1,400 years ago, houses skeletons that were disassembled and the bones laid together in compact piles, or bundles. One mound contains about a dozen bundle burials. Also in the mounds are exotic grave goods: a breastplate hammered from copper from Michigan's Upper Peninsula; shells from the Gulf Coast; ceremonial obsidian points from the Rocky Mountains; flint from the Knife River in what is now North Dakota. Apparently, the mound builders were a people who traveled in order to trade—or traded in order to travel. Another mound contains an altar and bones charred during a cremation, evidence of a ritual burial. Apparently, the mound builders were a ceremonial people. Yet another mound is a reconstruction, since the original was destroyed by the building of a road that allowed loggers to climb the north bluff and cut timber. Now the former logging road is the well-mulched hiking trail that leads to Eagle Point, Fire Point, Big and Little Bear Mounds, and beyond.

"I am so glad these mounds haven't been disturbed," Mom said.

I was glad to be back in these oak- and hickory-covered bluffs near the Wisconsin, Yellow, and Mississippi rivers. Inexplicably, it felt familiar and homey to be trekking in this landscape that I'd seen only once before.

There were no handrails on the lower reaches of the trail, so I offered Mom my arm. But she insisted on making the ascent on her own. As we climbed and rested, climbed and rested, I told her what I'd read about the origin of the effigy mounds. The experts still aren't sure why, between the years of roughly 500 and 1300 AD and mostly in this small, bluffy, river-laced region of the Upper Midwest, the inhabitants sculpted the creature-shaped mounds. While effigy mounds were constructed by many American Indian cultures, those living in Wisconsin and this part of Iowa built more than any other group. The creation of the emblematic mounds may have been a new idea that occurred to an individual or the group or it may have been an idea or custom carried into the area by outsiders. Or the shapes may have been modifications of old ritual forms: a turtle instead of a circular mound, a lizard instead of a linear mound. Perhaps the circles and lines were effigies too, say, mussels and slugs, though we don't recognize them as such. Or perhaps, and this is the theory that I find most tantalizing, something about this wrinkled landscape evoked this particular creative response in the inhabitants.

While most effigy mounds contain human burials, some don't. The animal-shaped mounds contain far fewer artifacts than the conical and linear mounds, suggesting a decline in long-distance trade, a modification in how people viewed their journey in the afterlife, or a shift in their reasons for making the mounds. What the experts are fairly certain about is that the mound groups were used primarily as ceremonial centers and occasionally for social, religious, political, and economic purposes. In other words, the effigy mounds were a gathering place, the fixed point, the hub, the nexus, the center of the world. Everything else was located in relation to them.

Perhaps the river dwellers stopped building effigy mounds because they'd settled into more permanent villages and spent more time cultivating corn than hunting and gathering. Perhaps they stopped because they turned their creative energies to pottery, shaping the earth into thin-walled globular vessels tempered with crushed shells and designed by incising hawks and falcons into the wet clay with blunt tools. While the river dwellers continued building linear and especially conical mounds into the early seventeenth century, there is no evidence that they ever again shaped the earth into birds and bears, panthers and turtles.

The climb up the bluff was more difficult than I remembered. A gray-headed couple in their late fifties or so passed us on the trail. Five minutes later, they returned. "Too steep for us!" the man offered. "I don't feel as bad," Mom said. "I just burned off twenty-five candy corns," a little girl told her parents as they, too, passed. Many on the trail complimented a woman who was ascending the bluff with a toddler on her back. Several hikers were using trekking poles and hiking sticks to add thrust to their ascent. The photo of Ellison Orr in the visitors' center shows him clutching a big walking stick. Apparently, he also found the ascent challenging.

Mom was wheezing, so she sat down on a chairlike rock in the bluff. I left her there so I could see what the rest of the trail and the view from the top were like. I followed the path around the bluff and looked up to see a long, zigzagging handrail ahead. By the time I reached the top of the bluff, I was winded and my head was pounding. I followed the trail to Eagle Point for a quick view of the river. Signs with a drawing of a tumbling man and flying rocks warned me away from the edge of the cliff. This was the view I'd been longing for: the south bluff; a crescent of land bearing a railroad track across the Yellow River; the island-filled Mississippi. Gray squirrels leapt from branch to branch, hundreds of feet above the floodplain. I loved that the land here was higher and older than that surrounding it and that it was a pucker in the fabric, where various habitats met and mixed. I was grateful that this landscape, sought out for military posts and roads, the lumber industry, cropland, homesteads, and towns, was now protected by the federal government and so belonged to all of us.

When I came back down the bluff, my heart leapt. My mother wasn't where I had left her. She had climbed farther; she was coming to meet me. Once again, I was struck by her determination.

"It's really a long way to the top," I said. Now I was wheezing. I wanted Mom to see the view from Fire Point, but I was worried that the climb would be too much for her. Because I needed to return to the bluff top to take notes and photographs, she decided to return to the visitors' center. We walked down the bluff, stopping along the way to look at the flora—American bladdernut, with its lovely, inflated papery pods; prickly gooseberry ("Do you remember that gooseberry pie that Jane Watson's mother made us?" Mom asked); and shagbark hickory, my father's favorite, a tree that I rarely see in Nebraska. This landscape supports astonishing diversity since here, forest and prairie meet, creating a patchwork of microhabitats: small remnant tallgrass or "goat" prairies; burr oak savannas; wooded slopes (basswood and sugar maple on the northern slopes; oaks and hickories on the southern slopes); wetlands; swamps; and backwaters. Anthropologists call it an extremely "food-rich" environment. If you had to overwinter in the Upper Midwest in a time before there were grocery stores, restaurants, and grain surpluses, this would be the place to do it.

Mom got her book from the car and we walked back to the busy visitors' center, where she settled into the couch to read.

After I scaled the bluff again, I stopped at Eagle Point to catch my breath. Prairie du Chien is set upon a floodplain terrace. Close by is St. Feriole Island, the original site of Prairie du Chien. South of there, the Wisconsin River flows into the Mississippi. Just south of where I stood, the Yellow River flows into the Mississippi. Both shores of the flooded Mississippi were dotted with cabins and summerhouses. When Henry Lewis and his sketching party passed by here in the summer of 1848, they climbed what he called the Altar Bluff at Prairie du Chien, so called because in this bluff, you could see a pulpit, reading desk, and baptismal font. There, somewhere on the opposite shore, Lewis and his crew etched their names.

A riskier exploration of the bluff would have revealed the mysterious karst terrain, with its caves, disappearing and underground streams, blind valleys, sinkholes, springs, and cold streams. On the north side of the river bluffs in the Driftless region are cold-air talus slopes, places where cold-air seeps keep the rocky, north-facing slopes cool enough to support what to me is utterly exotic: a boreal ecosystem, with ferns, mosses, liverworts, balsam firs, Canada yews, yellow birches, the Iowa Pleistocene land snail, and the threatened northern wild monkshood, a kind of buttercup with blue, hood-shaped flowers.

At Fire Point, it wasn't the view of the river that drew my attention but a procession of conical mounds unfurling toward the northwest as far as I could see. "Out of respect please do not walk on the mounds," a nearby sign said. But that was exactly what I wanted to do: walk on the mounds. I also wanted to lie prostrate on one, feeling the curve against my heart and belly, and then roll over and feel the curve against my spine. Another sign, with a message entitled "A Glimpse into the Past," conjectured that these mounds were built about 1,500 years ago by the Hopewell Indians, who lived in the Ohio and lower Illinois River valleys before they spread out across the Upper Midwest. Because the Hopewell placed exotic, lavish items in their mounds, they are described as having "flamboyant" mortuary practices.

When building a conical mound, the earth shapers scraped aside the leafy humus, gouged out a square-shaped pit, and positioned within it the remains of a several people, one on top of another. They buried with the dead long copper beads that look like cinnamon sticks and a copper breastplate about the size of my hand from wrist to middle knuckles. They tucked beneath the right arm of one woman found buried face up, with her arms folded, a bundle of bird-bone needles used for sewing. The mound builders heaped basketloads of soil over the bodies and the grave goods and then piled rocks on the mound: an earthen breast. They tossed mussel shells and limestone pebbles atop the pile and heaped more earth over the mound until everything was covered. "One final—and possibly ceremonial—act remained," the sign said. In the last layer of earth, the mourners sprinkled a mixture of cremation ashes and baked red clay that they'd carried up the bluff from the river. A millennium or two later, these sumptuous mounds still stand as a graceful and enduring dialogue between humans and the earth. On the trail near the mound, I picked up a piece of rust-stained limestone. The sharp edge formed an overhang; in the jagged side was a cave. I dropped the miniature bluff into my pocket.

I followed the trail through the woods to the Great Bear Mound and the Little Bear Mound. Great Bear is 138 by 65 feet, which makes it the largest effigy at the monument and the largest existing bear mound in the world. It's easy to understand why the ancient residents of these bluffs and rivers were so drawn to bears. Like humans, bears can stand upright on two legs; are intelligent; can be fierce or timid; bring forth young that are bald, toothless, and helpless; prey but rarely are preyed upon. Bears, with their long hibernations, are masters of winter survival, surely impressing people who, even in such a food-rich environment, were cold, hungry, and fearful during the long, deep winters.

Because of Great Bear's low profile (it's only three and a half feet tall) and soft, round edges, its shape is not distinct. The form had been easier for me to see when there was snow on the ground at my last visit, but this time it was just a weedy lump. The nearby sign said that while most bear effigies are left-side up, this bear is right-side up and facing the river. What I had identified as a foot was actually the head. How did the experts decide this was a bear instead of a bison or just an oddly shaped mound? A small group of people were circling the lump, trying to discern the form. "They need a viewing platform," one woman commented. "If we could look down on this, we might be able to see that it's a bear."

Extending from Great Bear's head is an arc comprised of seven conical and three linear mounds. The horns on this crescent point away from the river. Extending from the center of the crescent toward the river is a long linear mound and another effigy, an unnamed bear. South of this configuration is Little Bear. This thousand-year-old mound, eighty by forty feet, isn't even hip high. Between Little Bear and the edge of the bluff is one conical mound after another, the continuation of the procession of mounds I'd first seen at Fire Point. I counted nineteen of them. Chain of Pearls, they're called. The last one, near Little Bear's rump, appears larger than the others. It's the period at the end of the sentence. If I saw this constellation from above, I might see it as a bear on a leash or a bear attached to the river by an umbilical cord. The creators conceived of the mounds as belonging together and of being read together. Perhaps they saw this chain of burial mounds as an earthly link with the great life-filled, life-giving river and its creator.

Paul Radin, an anthropologist with the Bureau of Ethnology and author of *The Winnebago Tribe* (1923), believed that the effigy mounds were the work of the Winnebago alone. Radin's informants, Winnebago who had been removed from Wisconsin to Nebraska, told him that the clans were divided into three groups, one headed by the thunderbird, one by the bear, and one by the water spirit. Radin related the three common types of effigy mounds to the three-part division of the natural world: sky, earth, and water.

In the 1970s, Robert L. Hall, an anthropologist at the University of Illinois–Chicago, saw a link between the shapes of the effigies and the manner in which the tribes that had lived near the mounds depicted the powerful spirits that resided in the upper and lower worlds of their cosmologies. The upper-world, or sky, mounds, for instance, were represented by bird effigies (hawks, falcons, thunderbirds) or human-bird effigies (horned heads; wings that could be arms; split tails that look like legs), as well as conical and linear mounds. These mounds were usually built on lofty bluffs in the Mississippi River Valley in southwestern Wisconsin and northeastern Iowa. The lower-world was divided into water and earth, with the former represented by water spirits (long-tailed creatures that resemble panthers, turtles, or lizards) and the latter by bears. Water-spirit mounds were concentrated in eastern Wisconsin, a low-lying place of lakes, swamps, marshes, and springs. Bear mounds were more common in central and western Wisconsin and northeastern Iowa. Interspersed between upper- and lower-world mounds were linear mounds.

Because the mound builders often placed forms from opposing or complementary groups together, such as birds from the upper-world and bears from the lower-world, Luther College anthropologist R. Clark Mallam proposed in 1980 that the three types of mounds represented the three natural realms that provide the resources that people need in order to survive. They were built "to symbolize and ritually maintain balance and harmony with the natural world." Consequently, atop the monument's south bluff are soaring birds and marching bears. Sky and earth. At the very heart of this essay in the earth was the act of achieving balance, poise, equilibrium.

In the late spring, the effigy-mound builders who had been dispersed during the winter came together and raised mounds so they could worship and bury their dead. A group-integration exercise, Mallam calls it, meaning that the process was more significant than the final product. In other words, these mounds are verbs as well as nouns, and their construction not only eased the sting of loss, but also cemented social networks.

As I paused near the String of Pearls, it wasn't the distant mound builders I was thinking of. Rather, I was imagining a different memorial service for my father. In my mind's eye, I saw family and friends gathering at Catfish Bend shortly after Dad's death. We would gouge out a place in the earth with pitchforks, shovels, and trowels where we would lay the body or ashes of our father, husband, brother, friend, and coworker. Into what shape would we form his mound? That of the muskrats he'd trapped as a child? That of the CB&Q and Burlington Northern locomotives that he'd worked on for forty-one years? Something abstract or geometrical, a rhomboid, perhaps, with its unequal sides and oblique angles, to represent a man whose quirks and imbalances I learned to tolerate and eventually love, and many of which I now carry within me? Or would his mound be yet another piece in a pattern determined long ago, before the deaths of his grandparents, parents, aunts, uncles, brothers, cousins, and grandson, also buried at Aspen Grove Cemetery? This pattern, our own chain of pearls or falling dominoes or migrating birds winging their way up or down the Mississippi Flyway, would balance the forces: light and dark, summer and winter, scarcity and plenty, arrivals and departures.

After we shaped the mound, we'd tenderly place Dad's emaciated body or his ashes and bone fragments in his earthen cradle and cover it with the dirt that we'd removed as well as that that we carried in buckets and wheelbarrows up the hill from the creek bed. How satisfying it would be to handle the soil in which his bones would rest, decay, and mix. What cherished possessions would we place in the mound with him? His gold railroader's watch, since he was always so acutely aware of the time? Photographs of him when he was in the Army in Korea or working on the railroad or playing with his grandkids? The black lunch bucket that he carried to work? A flat, ribbed nut within the bony husk of the shagbark hickory? After we built my father's mound at the center of the world, we'd pray for his safe passage and for wholeness and harmony for the living. Then we'd admire our handmade memorial, our flamboyant mortuary practices, drink a toast, and have a picnic. Such ceremonies would transform Aspen Grove Cemetery from a place of cold stone and plastic factory- or shop-made memorials into a soft landscape shaped by human hands and filled with personalized remembrances.

I could have kept walking farther into the woods, but my mother's absence tugged at me. The point of this trip was to spend time with her as well as to finish my research. Before descending the bluff, I stopped at Eagle Point for a final view of the river from this height. On my first visit to the monument, Meredith and I had watched eagles land on branches or slabs of ice in the wide, gray river. This time, I watched a turkey vulture soar on a thermal with splayed wing feathers.

Four years had passed since Dad left us. Four years? It seemed like it had been so much longer since I'd seen his face. Four years? Surely it hadn't been that long since I'd heard the timbre of his voice. Since 775 miles had separated us, my father and I had seen each other only once or twice a year in his final years. When he died, it was hard to believe that he was gone, really gone, since it wasn't a daily presence that I was missing. In fact, for several months after he died, I felt that if I dialed his telephone number, he just might pick up. Then I could gather tips from him on how to grow sweet potatoes or tell him some good news—my new house, Ian's new job, Meredith's scholarship—or inquire how he carried on after his mother's death from cancer when he was forty-three, something I never thought to ask about when he was alive.

When I came to the Effigy Mounds National Monument in 2007, Meredith was a junior in high school and glad to have a place to go for spring break, even if it was with her mother. Last spring break, I didn't see her at all since she went on a university-sponsored hiking trip to Arches National Monument and the Grand Canyon. Always, Ian is so busy with work and friends or hunting and fishing that it's too seldom that we spend an afternoon together, hiking, fishing, or just hanging out. How many years will pass before my children will take an excursion with me like the trip I took to the monument with my mother?

My first journey to the mounds had been about commemorating the dead. But this journey concerned the living: my long relationships with my mother and the river. But it was time for us to go. The Ten Marching Bears on the south unit bluff would have to wait for another day. We had yet to stand on the bluff at Guttenberg, take pictures of the islands in the river and the barges parked along the shore, search for an old motel, and get close enough to smell and touch the river, and see what stories it offered up.

6

What the River Carries

State Lines

The first bridge to connect Hamilton, Illinois, and Keokuk, Iowa, was a wrought-iron drawbridge that opened to wagon, buggy, and train traffic in 1871. Even though the placement of the piers and the near presence of the treacherous Des Moines Rapids made this, in the opinion of the U.S. Army Corps of Engineers, "the worst bridge for the passage of [lumber] rafts, and one of the worst for the passage of steamboats, on the Mississippi River," the bridge stood until 1915, when a new one was built on the old pillars.

Not long after the first bridge opened, a dispute arose between Iowa and Illinois as to how much each state could tax the owners of the bridge. Iowa claimed the right to tax to the middle of the river. Illinois claimed the right to tax to the navigation or commercial channel, which at that time and place ran closer to the Iowa than the Illinois bank. The Keokuk and Hamilton Bridge Company complained that because of these different opinions about the location of the state line, it was paying double taxes for 716 feet of the bridge. Was the border at the river's midpoint or at the thalweg, the part of the channel with the greatest depth and fastest flow? The answer to this question had far-reaching implications since the two states shared nine other Mississippi River bridges.

In *State of Iowa v. State of Illinois*, 147 U.S. 1 (1893), the U.S. Supreme Court ruled that "all the recognized treatises on international law of modern times" identify the middle of the stream channel as "the true boundary" between adjoining states. When there are several channels, the boundary is to be drawn in the middle of the principal one. Between Keokuk and Hamilton, the steamboat channel was 880 feet from the Iowa shore and 2,162 feet from the Illinois shore, which meant that Illinois was justified in taxing most of the bridge. Yet, when Justice Stephen Field, who delivered the court's opinion, wrote that the navigational channel "varies from side to side of the river, sometimes being next to the Illinois shore and then next to the Iowa shore, and at most points in the river shifting from place to place as the sands of its bed are changed by the current of the water," he was telling the two parties that when the state line is drawn by water, it is a moving thing.

But shifts in a river channel are seldom followed by changes on the map or in jurisdiction. Until the mid-nineteenth century, the Mississippi made a sharp turn to the west and then to the east at a point about halfway between St. Louis and Cape Girardeau, Missouri. On the peninsula within the meander, land firmly attached to Illinois, French settlers built the town of Kaskaskia, which became a bustling commercial center and the capitol of the territory and later the state of Illinois. But in 1844, the river began shifting its course. During the Flood of 1881, the river abandoned its channel and captured the former valley of the Kaskaskia River. This cut off the big meander and turned the area into an island. Today the terribly flood-prone Kaskaskia Island is separated from Missouri only by what appears to be a creek but is, in fact, the old river channel, and the town can be reached only by boat or by a bridge from St. Mary, Missouri. The river's thalweg flows on the east instead of the west side of the island, making this soggy piece of land the only part of Illinois that lies west of the Mississippi.

Nonetheless, Illinois has fought and won numerous court battles with Missouri so that it can ignore where the river draws the line and keep the 2,300 acres of prime bottomland on its tax rolls.

Oxygen

Depending on where they live on the river, mayfly nymphs emerge from the water between April and August. They break the nymphal skin, unfurl elegant, many-veined, transparent wings, and molt again. Then they take to the sky and head toward the shore in swarms so large and dense that the National Weather Service's Doppler radar records the phenomenon. When I was a child, we called them Mormon flies, a name that harkens back to 1846, when waves, legions, swarms of Mormon refugees, perhaps as many as twenty-five thousand, escaped their persecutors by crossing the Mississippi in boats or ferries or walking on the frozen water from Nauvoo, Illinois, to Montrose, Iowa, where my mother's mother's people lived.

The order name *Ephemeroptera* announces the short-lived, transient, fleeting nature of the mayfly. What is ephemeral about this aquatic insect is that in its winged, adult form, it lives only a few hours to a few days. The adults mate; each female lays as many as eight thousand eggs over the water; then the adult flies die. Fish, birds, bats, frogs, snakes, and other river dwellers feast on the live or freshly dead bodies. No sooner have the mayflies emerged than the riverfront is littered with their corpses, piled into drifts on bridges and heaped beneath electric lights, crunching and squishing beneath our feet. It is good and fitting, at times like this, to remember that the "stink bugs" carry tons of phosphorous and nitrogen out of the water and back onto the land. These nutrients lower oxygen levels in the water and are responsible, at least in part, for the Gulf of Mexico's "dead zone."

Compared to the winged adult's brief and messy existence, the mayfly nymph or larva is particularly long lived. For a few weeks to a few years, it lives in a U-shaped burrow dug in the sediments at the bottom of the river. Unlike the adult mayfly, which breathes air, the nymph depends upon dissolved oxygen (DO), microscopic bubbles of oxygen gas in the water, which it absorbs through its gills.

Oxygen enters the river water by diffusion and by the aeration caused by wind and waves or by water tumbling over riffles and rapids, falls and dams. But the most important sources of DO are phytoplankton and aquatic plants. Through photosynthesis, they release oxygen into the water. Organic wastes—such as untreated or partially treated sewage; animal droppings; leaves; grass clippings; algae blooms; fertilizer runoff (i.e., phosphorous and nitrogen); and dead plants, pigs, and people—deplete the DO, since the bacteria that break down these wastes consume oxygen. Too little dissolved oxygen is as harmful as too much.

Mayfly nymphs can alter their behavior and metabolism to accommodate some changes in the DO levels. The nymph has ten abdominal segments, the sides of which are lined with feathery gills. In sufficient levels of DO, the nymph flutters its gills to create a current, which increases the flow of fresher, more-oxygenated water across its tracheal gills. It fans and rests, fans and rests. If the amount of DO in the water decreases, the nymph compensates by increasing the average number of gill movements per second, followed by briefer periods of rest before the next round of rapid fanning: the mayfly's equivalent of panting.

When the DO levels drop, pollution-sensitive organisms—including mayfly, stonefly, and caddis fly nymphs, beetle larvae, mud puppies, pike, and small-mouthed bass—either move or die. The number of pollution- and turbidity-tolerant sludge or sewage worms, blackfly larvae, leeches, curly-leaf pondweeds, and various types of carp increases. What results is a less ecologically complex, a more polluted, breathless, and hungrier river.

Commodities

Just before the Iowa River enters the Mississippi, it takes a hairpin turn north. Nestled in the crook of the bend is Oakville, Iowa, population 439. When a nearby levee broke on June 14, 2008, the flooding was so extensive that news reports declared that the town was gone for good. Of the 35,000 to perhaps as many as 45,000 swine in the Oakville area, all but about 1,000 were evacuated. After the levee broke, the remaining hogs and the feces from their flooded confinement buildings entered the Mississippi. Most of the hogs drowned. Some were stranded on roofs. Some swam to the levee, but when the sheriff's deputies saw that their hooves were cutting the plastic wrapping on the slopes, they shot them. The decaying carcasses and feces entered a river already toxic with diesel fuel, fertilizer, pesticides, chemical waste from industry, chemicals from flooded garages and basements, garbage, and—because of flood damage to water treatment plants—raw human wastes.

Evidence

Dead bodies turn up in the river with regularity. Despite the presence of lover's leaps up and down the river (in *Life on the Mississippi*, Twain says that there are fifty), murder is more often the cause than suicide. One of the more heinous and high-profile cases occurred in 1983, when two anglers found the torso of Joyce Klindt lodged against a riverbank near Bettendorf, Iowa, her intestines floating nearby. Klindt's chiropractor husband, James, had thrown her in the river after chopping her up with a chain saw. More typical, however, are the people who were shot or hit over the head and then thrown, dumped, or pushed into the water. For the murderer, it must be a relief to watch the body sink, the evidence out of sight, food for carp, catfish, and other bottom feeders. But the fishers, who are usually the ones to find the bodies and report their presence to the police, are left with memories of swollen, wrinkled, and discolored corpses and the stench of putrefaction.

Some bodies in the river are there accidentally. My great-grandfather slipped and fell down a bluff in Burlington into the river and drowned. People assumed that it was the strong drink that he couldn't leave alone that had caused him to lose his footing and his fight with the river. His is yet another story about the awful Mississippi that gives and takes life and then offers up the dead.

Sediment

In a rather shallow part of the river, where the bottom of the channel is hard and gravelly or rocky, the male smallmouth bass vigorously sweeps the area with his tail fin until he has scooped a depression a few inches deep in the center and a few feet in diameter. Then he goes in search of a female. To guide her back to the nest, he gently nudges and nips at her pale, yellow-white belly. At the nest, the pair of red-eyed bronzebacks swim in a circle, with him frequently nipping at her operculum, the bony covering protecting her gills. Finally, near the center of the nest, she releases her eggs and he his milt. After fertilization is complete, he drives her away. The eggs settle to the bottom and stick to the rocks and gravel that the father bass has cleared of silt. He may court other females, ultimately filling his nest with as many as twenty thousand eggs. As he circles the full nest, he frequently lowers his snout so he can inspect his offspring by sight or smell. Four to ten days later, the eggs hatch. Until the young are ready to disperse, he guards them from predators.

What the father bass can't guard his young against is silt: fine-grained particles of soil or rock that are carried in and by the water. Some fish—catfish and bullheads, for instance—don't mind turbidity, since they locate their food through smell. But the smallmouth bass, native to the Upper Mississippi, is a sight, or clear-water, predator: it must be able to see the crayfish, frogs, insects, and other fish that it preys upon. If the water is too murky, it can't find its food. Likewise, the juvenile smallmouth can't find the crayfish, clams, snails, worms, and mayfly nymphs it feeds upon when they're covered by sediment. In the absence of food, fewer of the young reach adulthood. The smallmouth bass is an indicator species. When it fails to thrive, something is wrong with the water.

For many millennia, silt in the Upper and Middle Mississippi was, for the most part, the result of natural erosion from riverbanks. Before the construction of the twenty-nine dams between Minneapolis and St. Louis, the water flowed fast enough that the sediments were carried along rather than settling. During low water, they were exposed to the air, which allowed the organic part to decompose, thus reducing the volume of the dregs once the water rose again.

Now the chief causes of sedimentation are human activities that strip the land of vegetation and allow storm water to carry the eroded soil to the river. There are ways to stop or slow this process, including taking highly erodible land out of production; no-tilling or strip-tilling; terracing and contour planting; building retention walls and ponds; using erosion-control mats and silt or filter fences; and restoring wetlands, which collect and filter sediment in runoff water. Yet, far too few farmers, builders, and homeowners are taking the time and expense of implementing such abatements.

The suspended sediments that drop out of the water column and settle onto the river bottom affect more than just the bass: they bury mussel beds; clog the gills of aquatic animals and insects; smother fish eggs, including those of such rare fish as pallid sturgeon and paddlefish; reduce the amount of dissolved oxygen in the water; and reduce the amount of sunlight that reaches plants living in deeper waters.

The smallmouth bass may be able to keep silt from settling on the eggs he's fertilized, but he can't clear the water so that he and his young can find their food.

Sunken Treasures

The *War Eagle*, a side-wheel riverboat that was 255 feet long and had 46 staterooms and costly furniture set on elegant velvet carpets, was reputedly one of the finest on the river. The ship served various purposes until 1866, when it was purchased by the La Crosse and St. Paul Packet Company to transport passengers, mail, and freight from La Crosse, Wisconsin, to St. Paul, Minnesota, with stops along the way.

On the night of May 14, 1870, the *War Eagle* docked at the Milwaukee Road Railroad Depot in La Crosse. Passengers boarded and the crew loaded mail and freight, including unprocessed lead from the mines at Galena and barrels of Danforth's Non-explosive Petroleum Fluid, a lamp oil. Some of the barrels were leaking, so the ship's carpenter tightened the hoops. As he worked, his lantern tipped over and the fuel from the leaking barrels caught fire. Soon the ship, warehouses, depot, train cars, grain elevator, a barge, and other steamboats were ablaze. The *War Eagle* burned to the waterline and sank. Since the ship's records burned, no one knows exactly how many people died, though most sources report either five or seven.

Some of the immigrants on board had carried all of their worldly possessions with them. Lost were trunks from the Old Country filled with family Bibles, embroidered shirts, hand-carved whistles, the only photograph of the old folks, sausage-stuffers, wedding gowns, and fiddles. Also lost were the burned remains of the ship's furnishings and the possessions of those traveling for pleasure or business: jewelry boxes, silverware, goblets, chamber pots, china-head dolls, pocket watches, spyglasses, canned goods, pans, and mail—at a time when people spread the news through handwritten letters. For decades, these treasures lay at the bottom of the river. When the drought of 1931 caused the water level to drop enough that the upper part of the *War Eagle* was exposed, people entered the shallow water and looted the artifacts. When the rains returned, the water rose, once again covering the ship. In the early 1960s, scuba divers brought up artifacts, many of which are now the property of the La Crosse Historical Society.

There was so much on the river that could destroy a steamboat. Not only could a wooden ship be ignited by grease fires in the galley, smoking passengers and crew, sparks from the tall, fire-breathing iron chimneys, boiler explosions, and tipped-over lanterns, but encounters with snags, ice, bridges, or other boats could tear its hull. Steamboat wrecks were so common and the loss of cargo so costly that early in his career James Buchanan Eads, the builder of the St. Louis (now the Eads) Bridge, invented and patented a double-hulled boat with derricks that could lift steamboats out of the water and an airtight diving bell that supplied oxygen to divers as they walked on the bottom of the river salvaging freight. Eads made a fortune on his invention.

In 2002, *National Geographic* reported that there are seven to eight hundred documented wrecked steamboats embedded in Mississippi mud. Yet, because riverbeds are what Eads described as "a moving mass," forever shifting, forever moving south, because objects on the river bottom roll and toss in the currents, because sediments can quickly bury anything, and because floods lift and carry and deposit things, the contents of these wrecks and those treasures that people intentionally throw or accidentally drop into the river (wedding rings, cell phones, messages in bottles, bottles of whiskey, cameras, arrowheads, rods and reels, pickup trucks, illegal drugs, war medals, toe shoes, trophies, diaries, keys, and chain saws) are not where we left them.

Reflections

You have always believed that what bounces off the surface of the water is an exact but upside-down image of the real thing near the river. But on this day, you look again and again at the cottonwood tree several feet upstream from where you stand and at the wavering tree in the water before you, until finally you realize that the tree in the water is smaller and farther away than the actual tree on the bank. You notice that the leaves on the reflected tree aren't green but a darkness that suggests green; that the leaves are in double motion, fluttering in the breeze and rippling in the water; and that when reflected in the water, the sky, actually cerulean, lightly salted with wispy white clouds that give it depth and dimension, isn't blue but a silver-blue glossiness. The really surprising discovery, though, is that the water shows you a forked extension, not a branch but a broken place that once held a branch on the underside of the cottonwood. It corresponds to nothing that you can see on the actual tree from where you now stand.

And you thought that you knew this river.

Politics

Perfluorochemicals (PFCs) and the various PFC derivatives (PFBA, PFPeA, PFHxA, PFHpA, PFOA, PFNA, PFDA, PFUnA, PFDoA, PFTA, PFBS, PFHxS, PFOS, PFOSA, to name but a few) are human-made compounds of carbon and fluorine, remarkable for their thermal stability and indestructibility. Because of this durability, PFCs are responsible for such wonder products as Teflon, Stainmaster, Gore-Tex, Scotchguard, aqueous film-forming foam (AFFF) for firefighters, and coating for photographic film. Because of this durability, PFCs may be the most dangerous compounds ever invented. Unlike many other toxic chemicals, PFCs are extremely resistant to breakdown through biodegradation by microorganisms or removal or degradation through wastewater treatment. Consequently, these chemicals are, in the words of Dr. Fardin Oliaei, formerly the lead researcher on PFCs with the Minnesota Pollution Control Agency (MPCA), "persistent, bioaccumulative, and toxic (PBT) to mammals, fish and other aquatic organisms." PFCs are linked to various human health problems, including liver damage, infertility, low birth weight, birth defects, immune system disorders, and cancer.

Consider perfluorooctane sulfonate (PFOS), just one of the PFC derivatives found in the Mississippi. Since 1953, Minnesota Mining and Manufacturing Company, or 3M, a multinational conglomerate headquartered in St. Paul, used this compound in Scotchguard and other products. The discovery of this compound was serendipitous. In 1953, a 3M lab assistant accidentally dropped a bottle of fluorochemical rubber. Some of the fluid splashed on her white tennis shoes. When chemists Patsy Sherman and Sam Smith later noticed that the part of the worker's shoes covered by the solvent had resisted stains, they realized that they had discovered a fluorochemical polymer that could protect fabrics from oil and water. Since then, 3M has made $300 million annually on the sale of this product. And since 1953, 3M has disposed of the chemical wastes left over from the manufacture of Scotchguard in the ground and in the Mississippi River. Two of the several facilities in Washington County, Minnesota, where 3M burned or buried its chemical wastes have been designated as Environmental Protection Agency (EPA) Superfund sites. In 2002, the nonprofit Environmental Defense Fund ranked 3M as the United States' second-worst industry in terms of its Toxic Release Inventory (TRI). In 2005, Minnesota Public Radio reported that according to the MPCA, 3M dumped at least 50,000 pounds of eight different PFCs, including PFOS, into the river *each year*.

In 1999, the EPA began investigating the toxicity of PFOS. Shortly thereafter, 3M, which has the distinction of being the world's largest producer of PFOS-related fluorocarbons, "voluntarily" agreed to end production of the toxin. In 2003, 3M replaced the compound with perfluorobutane sulfonate (PFBS), a PFOS "cousin," with dangers of its own. 3M continues to manufacture PFCs at its Chemolite facility in Cottage Grove, just west of St. Paul.

Even though 3M had stopped manufacturing PFOS, the dangers it posed hadn't been eliminated. After all, perfluorochemicals are persistent, bioaccumulative, and toxic. Among the fish collected near Cottage Grove in 2004 for

Oliaei's study was a smallmouth bass that contained "the highest PFOS levels found in fish liver to date worldwide." Oliaei also found that blood collected from fish in the Mississippi River Pool No. 2 near Cottage Grove had the highest PFOS levels "of any animals tested worldwide."

When Oliaei called for more testing of the soil, water, fish, and deep sediments at the bottom of the river, she was ignored and denied funding. She brought a whistle-blower lawsuit against the MPCA and its commissioner and state pollution-control chief, Sheryl Corrigan. Corrigan, a Governor Tim Pawlenty appointee, was a former 3M executive who in 2005 owned $20,000 of 3M stock. In a letter to Corrigan, the Environmental Working Group, a nonprofit organization that advocates on Capitol Hill on health-related environmental issues, wrote: "Your refusal to test for PFCs in Minnesota water adds to an apparent, disturbing trend in your Agency to make decisions influenced more by politics than science, to the potential detriment of public health." Oliaei settled her whistle-blower lawsuit against MPCA out of court; in February 2006, she was forced to leave her job of sixteen years. Even though she was no longer a state employee, Oliaei, the Rachel Carson of the Upper Mississippi, completed a hefty report for the Minnesota Senate's Environment Committee entitled "Investigation of Perfluorochemical (PFC) Contamination in Minnesota, Phase One." In June of 2006, Corrigan announced her resignation from the MPCA. Some speculate that Governor Pawlenty had come to see her as a liability to his reelection campaign. Since then, the MPCA has heeded Oliaei's suggestions by issuing warnings about the consumption of tap water and fish from the Mississippi, and it continues testing.

When I was a child, I heard stories about people who swam the river from shore to shore. These were tales of heroism but they also were cautionary tales, since some strong swimmers had succumbed to the power of the river's whirlpools, eddies, currents, and undertows. Days after the contender dove in, some unsuspecting person might find the swimmer's bloated, wrinkled body floating back up, head down, or snagged on vegetation near the bank. If the swimmer survived, he or she might need a tetanus shot because of the metal junk jutting out of the mud or the debris that the water carried. While the Mississippi has been restrained so that it no longer carves meanders with bank-colliding currents, there are other, newer dangers. Now you swim in an alphabet soup, the letters spelling nothing that you can decipher.

Philosophies

During the Iowa Flood of 2008, two of the four lanes of the U.S. Highway 136 Bridge between Keokuk and Hamilton were closed. The other two were only open to local traffic. Portable caution signs stood nearby. On the Illinois shore, trucks had dumped loads of gravel in concrete barriers thirty inches tall to raise the highway leading to the bridge so that it was twenty-eight feet above the river bottom: passable, provided the river didn't top its projected crest. Still, water seeped through seams in the concrete wall and pooled on the road, miring some vehicles. I wanted to help sandbag either at Niota or in the Warsaw Bottoms on the Illinois side of the river. But I wouldn't be joining the volunteers that day, since I was afraid to cross the river in my little, low-to-the-ground Mazda Protege.

Several people were walking across the bridge, some in the lanes that were closed to vehicles, some on the pedestrian walk attached to the north side of the bridge. I parked at the Keosippi Mall on the east end of Main Street/Highway 136 in Keokuk and joined them. Illinois seemed far away and the water far below. At Keokuk's Victory Park, along what normally was the edge of the river, trees were submerged all the way up to their crowns: little green islands in a gray-brown ocean. The statue of General Samuel Curtis, who had led Union troops to victory at the Battle of Pea Ridge, now battled the river. The retired paddleboat and museum *George M. Verity*, which had pushed barges on both the Ohio and the Mississippi, looked as though it was in the process of turning around and heading downstream. Two people in a red Coast Guard motorboat moved through the turbulent water. Anyone else on the river would be arrested.

About a third of the way across the bridge, I stopped to get my bearings. The white-streaked, swirling, and debris-strewn water beneath me was twenty-eight feet deep: twelve feet above flood stage. I felt dizzy and nauseous at the sight of so much water moving beneath me. Semis rumbled past. A man with a fancy camera photographed Victory Park. Branches, logs, and a creosoted utility pole shot past in the water. Mayflies hurled their pale, winged bodies against the railing. Some fell; some flew off. Though mid to late June is mayfly hatch time in southeastern Iowa, I saw few near the river that day.

About two-thirds of the way across the bridge a green sign announced the Illinois state line. At first glance, the Illinois shore looked as it always did in the early summer. But then I noticed how high the water was compared to the trees. When I looked back toward the Iowa shore, I saw another green sign several feet behind me on the bridge marking the Iowa state line. Apparently, one or both states were ignoring the 1893 Supreme Court ruling that stipulated that a state line in a river falls in the middle of its main channel. Between the two signs lay an unclaimed strip of bridge and water. It struck me as a good place to steer one's raft—once the water dropped.

In *The Adventures of Huckleberry Finn*, Mark Twain presents this brawny river as a place apart, a sanctuary, free from the worst aspects of civilization: social class, conventionality, hypocritical religion, lynch mobs, parents who brutalize their children, and laws that protect slave owners. In his famous essay "Mr. Eliot, Mr. Trilling, and Huckleberry Finn," Leo Marx maintains, "The river is indifferent. But its sphere is relatively uncontaminated by the civilization [that Huck and Jim] flee, and so the river allows [them] some measure of freedom at once, the moment they set foot on Jackson's Island or the raft. Only on the island and the raft do they have a chance to practice that idea of brotherhood to which they are devoted." When Huck returns to the river following his misadventures with the Wilkes family in Arkansas, he says, "It did seem so good to be free again and all by ourselves on the big river, and nobody to bother us." But, as Marx points out, it's not that the river is a freer, more egalitarian place. Rather, Huck and Jim bring their code to the river, and the river is simply the place where they can practice it.

Other philosophies are also adrift in this water. One presents the river as in a constant state of renewal, rebirth, or regeneration. After you dump your sewage or industrial wastes, your evidence or treasures, you needn't give them another thought, since an unending supply of water from the north will carry your refuse south and away. Another says that the river in its powerful, sometimes terrorizing natural state must be broken and tamed. The Corps of Engineers, with its locks and levees, its dams and nine-foot navigation channel, isn't the only one bent on mastery. River dwellers create legends about monster catfish and record-setting bass and the strong, brave people who bring them in; about strong, brave people who swim from shore to shore; about strong, brave people who'd rather endure one 500-year flood after another than leave the river; about strong, brave people who fight the powers that be in order to keep the river safe for those creatures that depend on it. The corollary says that the feeble, neutered river, with its navigation channels and flood-control structures, isn't a river at all but a series of lakes that pale in comparison to that real river, the Upper Missouri. Because of the broken, enervated river's lack of integrity, it brings out the worst in those who live near it. "For what manmade entity has worked more evil upon the land than has this accident of nature?" asks former southern Illinoisan Ben Metcalf in his essay "American Heartworm." "What other waterway has been the seat of more shame, or has inspired us to greater stupidity, or has inflicted more brutal and embarrassing wounds upon our culture? Have not the basest qualities to be found in the people of the middle states been quickened by the river's example, or by its seeming impulse for self-promotion?"

At one time or another, I've held each of these views. But now, the truest thing that I can say about the Mississippi is this: it is the Great Assimilator. It takes lesser waters, the Minnesota, St. Croix, Black, Chippewa, La Crosse, Root, Wisconsin, Rock, Iowa, Skunk, Des Moines, Illinois, Missouri, Ohio, Arkansas, Yazoo, and Atchafalaya, into its greater waters, diluting or eliminating differences.

At the confluence, the Missouri flows brown into the lighter Mississippi, but it's a single, thoroughly mixed, brown, rank, and murky river that flows past St. Louis. The river drew both sides of my family: my mother's people, southerners of British descent who arrived at the Mississippi via Virginia, Kentucky, and Illinois in the mid-nineteenth century and probably crossed the river into Missouri and Iowa on a ferry; and my father's father's people, late nineteenth-century immigrants, Germans from Russia, who entered the country not at Ellis Island but at New Orleans. From there, they traveled by boat up the river, took the Burlington Route from Catfish Bend to Hastings, Nebraska, a riverless city, and a few years later, returned to the railroad town on the Mississippi. All were inexorably drawn to the river to swim, fish, work, live, and, if we're lucky, die near the river's once shifting but now regulated channels, its bald eagles, pesticides, rippling reflections, rotting carcasses, delicately veined mayfly wings, bass and carp, toxins and treasures, history and legends.

Part II

The Missouri

7

Point of Departure

When I moved to southern Illinois in 1995, I thought I was going someplace familiar, like the relatively flat, midwestern landscape of Illinois' west-central bulge. But much of what I encountered in the southern tip of the state was new to me. The rugged, forested hills reminded me more of the Missouri Ozarks than the corn and soybean fields of the part of Illinois that I knew. In the American Bottoms, that fertile strip of floodplain on the eastern bank of the Mississippi across from St. Louis, were chemical plants, oil refineries, and pipeline companies instead of the grain- and meat-processing plants of eastern Iowa and western Illinois. The culture and economy of some towns in southern Illinois were shaped by coal mining, which I knew nothing about. Near the Mississippi, I encountered a far more extensive French and Spanish history than I'd known at Catfish Bend; throughout southern Illinois and Missouri, I encountered a far more extensive involvement with both slavery and the Civil War. And I found a more southern and eastern flora and fauna: bald cypress swamps, magnolias, black tupelos, mockingbirds, a dizzying number of warbler species, wild sarsaparilla, celandine poppies, peach orchards, and tulip poplars, which quickly became one of my favorite trees.

This wasn't a geography I had chosen. I moved from Lincoln to the southernmost part of Illinois, nicknamed Little Egypt because of the similarities between its confluence of the Ohio and Mississippi rivers and the Nile River delta in Egypt, because I had divorced my daughter's father and accepted a position as an Assistant Professor of English at Southern Illinois University in Carbondale. Suddenly, I was surrounded by the new: making a home without a husband; mothering a daughter who split her time between two homes, one in Illinois and one in Nebraska; mothering a son from an earlier relationship, who was entering puberty and the teen years; settling into my new profession. Though I found the geography of southern Illinois fresh and exotic, I also found it rather familiar since my old friend the Mississippi flowed twenty miles west of Carbondale. I wasn't a river dweller in my new home, but because

Meredith flew back and forth between the St. Louis and Omaha airports, I drove to St. Louis four times a month to pick her up or put her on a plane. Each trip involved a Mississippi River crossing. Seeing my river in this unfamiliar place settled me.

For my children, the Mississippi River Valley was terra incognita. Though Ian had been born at Catfish Bend, lived there until he was two, and visited often until his grandparents moved to Ohio, he had no real attachment to the river. Because of sharp differences of opinion between my daughter's father and my parents, Meredith had rarely visited Catfish Bend. But the Mississippi that I encountered in southern Illinois and eastern Missouri was much like the river I'd known in my hometown. People fished and told stories about monster catfish. Tows pushed barges laden with grain, scrap iron, or petroleum. Steamboats docked near the shore as gambling parlors or cruised the river with dinner guests aboard. Flocks of waterfowl and songbirds migrated to Canada or the Gulf of Mexico via the Mississippi Flyway. Bald eagles wintered near the dam at Alton and the Old Chain of Rocks Bridge, and pelicans fed south of the Alton Lock and Dam. The water carried toxins from industry, agriculture, and human settlements. Some of the same floods that I remembered were part of the environmental history of this place, too.

But there was also much about this stretch of the river that was unfamiliar to me, and so Ian, Meredith, and I spent our weekends sightseeing. We explored Cahokia, a city built on the American Bottoms around 600 or 700 AD by Late Woodland people. Cahokia was strategically positioned: it was midway between the Great Lakes and the Gulf of Mexico, and it was in the vicinity of several watery highways—the Mississippi, Illinois, Missouri, and Ohio—which made a wide trade network possible. Because rivers flood, the Cahokians wisely built their city a few miles inland. Until the fourteenth century, as many as forty thousand people lived in Cahokia and its satellite communities, making it the largest pre-Columbian city north of Mexico City. From the top of Monk's Mound, which rises one hundred feet above the floodplain, we listened to the roar of traffic on Interstate 55/70. St. Louis's soaring, silvery Gateway Arch seemed near enough to touch. Two great civilizations had built cities not at but near the confluence of the Mississippi and the Missouri. One thrived for about seven hundred years; the other is about 350 years old and going strong.

We explored Cairo, Illinois' southernmost city. Illinois' extreme southern tip is a curious place where one sees midwestern cornfields on one side of the road and lakes rimmed with tupelo gum, bald cypress, and swamp cottonwoods on the other. Decades ago, people grew cotton and tobacco there. Cairo, the point of division between the Upper and Lower Mississippi, is positioned just north of the point where the blue waters of the Ohio pour into the brown waters of the Mississippi. The two rivers separate Illinois, Kentucky, and Missouri, and so it is an edgy, marginal, liminal place. During the Civil War, the Army Corps of Engineers built tall levees to protect Cairo (during floods, the city was, as one writer called it, "an island behind seawalls"), and General Ulysses S. Grant commanded Union troops from Cairo at Fort Defiance. Charles Galigher, who grew rich selling flour to the government during the Civil War, built a mansion, Magnolia Manor, with ten-inch-thick walls to keep out the humidity. Since the racial strife of the sixties drove away businesses and residents, leaving the downtown filled with empty buildings with broken or boarded-up windows, the Cairo that we encountered was a dispiriting shadow of its former, thriving self.

We also explored Kaskaskia Island near Chester, Illinois. When Kaskaskia was a French colony with over seven thousand residents, it was attached to Illinois. But during the Flood of 1881, the Mississippi cut a new channel, turning Kaskaskia into an island, the only Illinois town west of the main channel of the river. Following the Flood of 1893, Kaskaskians rebuilt Immaculate Conception Church from the bricks and beams of the original church. Even so, during the Flood of 1993, the water rose to the middle of the stained-glass windows. When we toured the island in 1996, the church reeked of mold and mildew, and only a handful of people still lived on the island's soggy ground.

We drove past the limestone bluffs near Alton, Illinois, where Marquette and Jolliet saw the original Piasa Bird, a winged panther-like creature painted on the bluff by Cahokians. We strolled through Ste. Genevieve, Missouri, a French colonial village dating back to 1735, now a quaint tourist village. We photographed Tower Rock, the eighty-foot limestone island, a big, rocky head, rising from *within* the river near Grand Tower, Illinois. Everywhere we went along this portion of the Mississippi, I had a paradoxical sense that I was both near and far from home.

Exploring my river two hundred miles south of the stretch that I knew best was like seeing my child doing well in a context that to me was unfamiliar. I was proud and a bit mystified that my progeny had a life independent of me. I loved my river even more.

Sometimes when I was in the St. Louis area, I saw that other great river, the Missouri, a river I barely knew. In my mind it was a narrow, brown, and bland river, lacking the fine music, literature, and the great cities that I associate with the Mississippi. What I did associate with the Missouri—boxy western states, fur trappers, Plains and mountain Indians, wheatfields, cattle ranching, Cold War missiles, big dams and reservoirs, grizzly bears, ponderosa pines, elk, and bitterroot—was too western to be mine. I felt about the human and natural history of the Missouri the way I do about, say, Tanzania, Nepal, or New York City: interesting but foreign.

On one of my drives back from the St. Louis airport in 1996, I decided to introduce myself to the point where my river and that other river met. I drove north of East St. Louis on Illinois Highway 3, past oil refineries, past steel and chemical plants, past bleak, run-down towns with shuttered factories, past tall, grassy, earthen levees that blocked my view of the Mississippi, until I came to the sign that directed me to the "Lewis and Clark State Historic Site and Starting Point of Lewis and Clark Expedition."

I followed the paved road past trees in standing water, past a great blue heron perched on an old, partially submerged tire. The road looped before an incongruous site: a miniature Stonehenge–like circle of yellowish stone pillars. When I drew closer, I could see that each stone bore the name of a present-day state that Meriwether Lewis and William Clark had passed through or by on their trek west: Illinois, Missouri, Kansas, Iowa, Nebraska, South Dakota, North Dakota, Montana, Idaho, Washington, and Oregon. Since the Spanish commandant had denied Lewis and Clark's group, the Corps of Discovery, entrance into Louisiana, the Corps had built its camp not on one of the banks of the Missouri, the logical place, but on the east bank of the Mississippi, in the Indiana Territory, which belonged to the United States, the sponsor of the expedition.

During the winter and spring of 1803–1804, Lewis and Clark and the recruits were headquartered at Camp River DuBois, built at the confluence of the Mississippi and Wood rivers, the official starting point of their epic Missouri River journey. In Lewis and Clark's day, the mouths of the Missouri and Wood rivers were directly across from each other. During that winter and spring of preparation, the members of the Corps of Discovery could gaze upon the object of their desire.

At the historic site, cars and camper trucks were parked near the stone pillars. People dried clothes on a line in the clearing and fished. Apparently, the fishing was good at this point of convergence of the Wood, Missouri, and Mississippi rivers. And there was the view: if you looked west from about any high point in the area, you could see where the two colors, the two temperaments of the Missouri and the Mississippi, become one.

When I returned to the land near the confluence in June 2010, I barely recognized it. In 2004, the National Park Service built the Lewis and Clark Interpretive Center, where visitors can view a full-scale, cut-away replica of the Corps' keelboat and a life-size reconstruction of the log buildings at the winter camp. Because of changes in the riverbank, the Stonehenge-like memorial is gone; in its place, a dark, plain stone no bigger than a laundry basket marks the starting point of the expedition. No one was fishing there when I visited. There was another addition, Hartford's Lewis and Clark Confluence Tower, which offers an excellent view of the three rivers. While I appreciate the efforts of federal and local entities to memorialize this site, the scruffy, out-of-the-way place where people fished and camped and dried laundry seemed closer to the spirit of the winter camp than what is there now.

As I surveyed the confluence from the 150-foot-high observation deck on the Hartford tower, I wondered about that other river, the one rolling in from the west. How was it similar to and different from the Mississippi? If I were to follow it, where would it take me? With a full-time job and only a mild interest in rugged, outdoor adventures, I couldn't undertake a Lewis and Clark–style expedition along the entire length of the river. But I could make my own voyage of discovery through maps and the tales of travelers and experts. Perhaps I'd even grow to love the Missouri as a parent does a second child—differently than the firstborn, though every bit as deeply and as irresistibly.

When I set out to trace with a black pen the course of the Missouri River, I had only a vague idea of where to find that place where three mountain streams, the Madison, Jefferson, and Gallatin, unite to form the Missouri. Once I found the point of confluence in the mountains of western Montana, I followed that single stream northward and then east. Between Helena and Great Falls, the river emerges from the mountains and forests into the openness of the Great Plains. Near the Montana-North Dakota state line, the Missouri picks up water from the Yellowstone, its largest tributary; then, in a great and sweeping downward arc, it crosses North Dakota into South Dakota. Near Pierre, it turns east and then southeast and then east again, forming part of the border between South Dakota and Nebraska; it turns south-southeastward again, forming the entire wavering state line between Nebraska and Iowa and then between northeastern Kansas and northwestern Missouri. At Kansas City, the river makes a sharp turn to the east and winds its way across Missouri until finally, it joins the Mississippi. At the confluence, the Missouri nearly doubles the volume of the Mississippi with waters once named Marias, Musselshell, Milk, Yellowstone, Little Missouri, Grand (South Dakota), Moreau, Cheyenne, Niobrara, James, Big Sioux, Boyer, Platte (Nebraska), Platte (Missouri), Kansas, Grand (Missouri), Chariton, Osage, and Gasconade.

I stepped back and looked at the line I'd drawn on the map: it was a weak and shaky attempt at drawing a backward, top-heavy, tipped-over letter *S*—so different from the Mississippi, which, after winding its way across Minnesota, flows in a more or less straight line to the Gulf of Mexico. The Mississippi is the disciplined, steadfast firstborn; the Missouri is the unruly, erratic secondborn.

Just as the Mississippi River has a more direct course, so, too, its sibilant name has a shorter lineage. The Ojibwa called it *Mici-ziibe,* meaning "great river" or "gathering of the waters." When Jacques Marquette and Louis Jolliet paddled down the Mississippi in search of the Northwest Passage to the Orient, they recorded the name as "Mitchisipi." The French translation of *sipioui* is *rivière,* or "river." Thus, to say "Mississippi River" is to say "river" twice. By 1699, Mitchisipi had become Mississipi—the preferred spelling of the name for over a century. At some point, someone added a second *p.* When my third-grade teacher taught our class how to spell the name of the river that flowed past Catfish Bend, she turned it into a chant that rocked back and forth between the "high" single letters and the "low" repeated consonants: M-I-ss-I-ss-I-pp-I.

Just as the course of the Missouri is less direct, so, too, is the history of its name. Marquette was the first Euro-American to write about his experience of the confluence of the two great rivers and so, the first to record a name for the Missouri. At the Piasa Bird painting on the Mississippi bluffs above Alton, Marquette and Jolliet were distracted by a rushing sound: the rivers at flood stage. "While conversing about these monsters sailing quietly in clear and calm water, we heard the noise of a rapid into which we were about to run," Marquette wrote. "I never saw anything more terrific, a tangle of entire trees from the mouth of the Pekitanoui with such impetuosity that one could not attempt to cross it without great danger. The commotion was such that the water [of the Mississippi] was made muddy by it and could not clear itself."

On Marquette's 1673 map, he labeled the river "Pekitanoui," an Algonquian word that means "muddy it flows." He labeled the village of American Indians living upstream on the Pekitanoui as "Oumessourita." By 1681, that name had been shortened to "Oumissouri." Gradually, "Pekitanoui" was replaced by "Missouri," the name bestowed by the Illinois, the indigenous people who lived near the mouth of the Muddy-It-Flows. In the Illinois dialect of the Algonquian language, *Missouri* means "the people or the place of the big canoes." On his 1718 map, Guillaume de L'Isle labeled the upstream portion of the river "le Missouri ou R. de Pekitanoui" and the downstream portion "le Missouri R." When Aaron Arrowsmith drew his 1795 map, he dropped the possessive and simply wrote, "River Missouri." The French tried to name the river St. Philip, but it was the local rather than the foreign name that stuck.

When one country conquers another, the winner usually imposes its name upon the loser. In many cultures, when a couple marries, the woman relinquishes her family name and assumes her husband's. But through such naming customs, one country or heritage is no longer named, so that contribution to the union is buried and knowledge of it eventually lost. So, too, with rivers. Neither name, Mississippi nor Missouri, does justice to the stream formed by the marriage of these two rivers. A new or blended name would be more fitting. Missouri writer William Least Heat-Moon offers "Missourippi," pronounced "Mizza-rippi," as fitting for the combined waters. I offer the more dignified "Mississouri." Another option is to take what is common in both names, "Missi" or more simply, "Miss," and bestow that upon the single river that flows past St. Louis.

If the river is to bear the name of only one of the two streams below the confluence, Heat-Moon argues that it should be the Missouri. "Had history taken a slightly different turn, the Missouri would be the longest river in the world," he argues in *River Horse*. "From its *true* source to the Gulf of Mexico, its length was more than five thousand miles before shortening by the Corps of Engineers, a thousand miles longer than the Nile or the Amazon. . . . In the early days of white exploration and settlement many travelers and rivermen considered the Mississippi to be the tributary of the Missouri."

Heat-Moon and others offer several reasons why people saw the combined rivers as the Mississippi. From its source at Lake Itasca to the Gulf of Mexico, the Mississippi runs a relatively straight, north-to-south course. The Missouri, west of its confluence with the Mississippi, runs a comparatively irregular course from northwest to southeast. The name of the river with the more direct route won over the name of the river that seemed to change its mind. In addition, the Mississippi was the better known, more predictable river, and it was ready for commerce. Running neatly down the center of the nation and halfway between the coasts, the dividing line between east and west, it was a mapmaker's dream. Smack dab in the middle of the Mississippi is its confluence with the Missouri. Yet the Missouri came brawling out of a territory that most people living three or four centuries ago had never seen and couldn't imagine.

Biologist Calvin R. Fremling offers yet another reason why we call the marriage of the two rivers the Mississippi. If explorers had probed the Mississippi from the Gulf of Mexico northward instead of from top to bottom, when they saw the terrific Pekitanoui roaring in from the West, they would have believed that the Missouri was the main river and that the Upper Mississippi was but a large tributary. At the confluence, they would have taken a turn to the northwest and paddled upriver and declared the confluence of the Madison, Jefferson, and Gallatin the true source of the river that flowed into the Gulf.

To know the river's essential nature, I needed to plant myself in its presence and pay attention, both to what others had experienced and what I saw and heard and felt. Fort Belle Fontaine Park, tucked away in northern St. Louis County on the Missouri River, was a place layered in history. It seemed like a good place to begin.

Finding this park required diligence. While it appears on the map in my atlas, it doesn't appear on the St. Louis Area inset on the state road map. While the address places it in Spanish Lake, an unincorporated township in northern St. Louis County, the directions I tried to follow place it north of Spanish Lake. I asked several people, including a former St. Louis cop, for help finding the park, but no one had heard of it. Finally, a construction worker that I chatted with when I stopped for gas directed me to the former fort at the north end of a lovely suburban neighborhood on Bellefontaine Road. The reason Fort Belle Fontaine Park was so unheard of was suddenly clear. Between the front gate and the bluff-top park was the Missouri Hills Home, a residential facility in the Missouri juvenile justice system, established there in 1913 in what was then a secluded part of the county far from the city. To visit the park, I had to sign in at the guard's station and drive past cottage-style dormitories where the boys and girls lived. The actual park was but a small part of the riverfront and bluff. At the bluff top, I stood between a cannon, a period piece, and one of the National Park Service interpretive signs and watched the murky river drift toward the confluence—a comforting, primal sight. According to my map of St. Louis, the heavily wooded bank across from the overlook was Cora Island. I couldn't see the shape of the island from my vantage point, but on various maps, the island looks like an elm leaf with the stem and the tip pointing west and east.

Connecting the bluff top with the riverbank and the Coldwater Creek Valley is a five-tiered staircase. Some levels consist of paired and curving flights of stairs with high, fortresslike walls between the levels. Other levels are connected by a central flight of stairs. Positioned midway between the top and bottom of the staircase is a rectangular lily pond. In the 1930s, the Works Project Administration (WPA) quarried limestone within the boundaries of the park and built an outdoor "living room," comfort stations, a patio, stone culverts, and a stone fireplace. But the crowning glory is the Grand Staircase, which once led to a swimming beach and bathhouse. Now the almost eighty-year-old staircase is overgrown with thistles, foxtails, and other weeds; the stones are powdered with orange lichen. Some stones have slipped or are broken and on the north side of one tier, the steps are so badly deteriorated that they've been fenced off with orange tape. The lily pond is dry and weedy.

I took the steps to the bottom of the bluff and walked through a clearing to the water's edge. The Muddy-It-Flows was brown and frothy and carrying logs and brush. The river earned this name from Marquette because of the great organic and sediment load that it carried. Even though the suspended sediment load of today is but a fraction of what it used to be, about 80 percent of the fine-grained particles of silt and clay borne by the river that flows past St. Louis come from the Big Muddy. Yet another reason why "Missouri" or some other designation might be a better name for the river that runs south of the confluence. At Fort Belle Fontaine Park, the water flowing past me carried ground rock from the Rockies and silt from the Great Plains.

Several famous expeditions of the Missouri either were launched from Fort Belle Fontaine or stopped there early in the trip. Zebulon Pike stayed at the fort in 1806 before setting out to find the headwaters of the Arkansas and Red rivers. Stephen H. Long of the U.S. Army Corps of Engineers, who led several river expeditions, including ones on the Platte and Missouri, stayed at the fort more than once. After Captain Clark and the Corps of Discovery set out from their campsite near Wood River on May 14, 1804, they camped on what Clark described in his journal as the first island in the Missouri "opposit a Creek on the South Side below a ledge of limestone rock called Colewater." Because of changes in the river, it's hard to say what island Clark was referring to and whether it's still there, but some experts believe it was Mobile Island, now dry land on the north side of the river. Because the Corps didn't get started until four in the afternoon, they traveled only 4½ miles of the 8,000-mile journey on their first day. They surely realized then what a hard journey against the current, snags, and shifting channels awaited them. From there, they traveled to St. Charles, Missouri's westernmost white settlement, where they waited for Captain Lewis, who was finishing up business in St. Louis.

What an excellent campsite this must have been for the Corps of Discovery. Because of rain on the morning of my June 2010 visit, the foliage was bright and the air smelled incredibly good and green. "Cotton" from cottonwood trees floated on the still air, and American spikenard and trumpet creeper were in bloom. A bluebird passed overhead; mockingbirds flashed their white wing patches; red-bellied woodpeckers rhythmically "churred." On the first night of their expedition, the Corps would have been greeted by blooming redbuds. On the last stop of their expedition, September 22, 1806, also at Fort Belle Fontaine, they would have found wild grapes, pawpaw, and walnuts ready to be gathered and eaten.

Yet, it would also have been a challenge for the crew to camp at Fort Belle Fontaine on a day like this. The campers would have had to clear a place in the thick woods; in the absence of the WPA staircase, the wooded, poison ivy–covered bluff would have been difficult to ascend. Because of the downpour a few hours before I arrived, the grass was wet and the air was oppressively heavy and humid. I batted at flying insects with my rolled-up map.

Some of what I saw on the bluff Lewis and Clark would not have seen. The brassy green Japanese beetles making lace of the wild grape leaves hadn't yet arrived in the western hemisphere when the Corps of Discovery paddled up the Missouri. Nor had the tree of heaven, Japanese honeysuckle, house and Eurasian tree sparrows, wintercreeper, Chinese bush clover, purple loosestrife, zebra mussels, and the Asian carps. These exotic interlopers crowded out the native species, some of which are now threatened, endangered, extirpated, or extinct.

Though I see and understand this small piece of the river and river bluff almost entirely through the lens of my knowledge of Lewis and Clark and their expedition, the truth is that the explorers spent only two days here. Like me, they were travelers, tourists, sightseers, and excursionists, and so their vision of the place was limited. Like me, they lacked an understanding of the ways in which people, plants, animals, river, bluff, prairie, and sky interacted with each other in this place. Like me, they could only imagine what it's like to live in this place over time.

Many others have had a longer and more intimate association with the part of the river at the foot of the Grand Staircase. Those stationed at the fort—soldiers, American Indians, and the Indian agent—could have told me more about the behavior and appearance of this stretch of the river through the seasons than Lewis and Clark. Those who came here frequently to swim, bird-watch, hike, fish, flood-watch, or forage could tell me how it felt to descend the new stone steps to the beach and swim in the swift, muddy current in a skirted swimsuit; where and when one could see wood ducklings jump from the nest in the tree to the ground and follow the mother duck to the river; the validity of local fishing lore; where to find ginseng and gooseberries; how high the water rose in greater and lesser floods; how the pallid sturgeon disappeared after the river was channelized. A native guide, one who has a long history of closely observing this place, who sees the terrain as steeped in the personal and communal stories and associations that confer value upon a place, and who sees the place as integral to those stories, is what I need if I am to understand this river.

But, too, outsiders see what insiders can't. One who has loved the Grand Staircase for many decades might not see how shabby and neglected it has become. Because of their deep familiarity with a place, inhabitants might not question whether the names they have for what flowers, flies, burrows, swims, and slithers in their home place are the correct ones. One who has never known and loved another river can't draw on such an experience when seeing this river. Looking for the similarities and differences between the subject at hand, the Missouri River, and the river of one's childhood—Georgia's Broad River for Meriwether Lewis, Virginia's Rappahannock for William Clark, the Mississippi for me—leads the viewer to single out features and characteristics, make connections, see patterns.

Even so, Lewis and Clark are valuable guides. Their story draws attention to what I can't see: how the two great rivers have revised, re-created, and redrawn this place. By comparing the area of the confluence as drawn on a Public Lands Survey map made in 1815–1817, not long after Lewis and Clark were here, and the map of the St. Louis area in my Rand-McNally atlas, I see that the channels of both the Mississippi and the Missouri are narrower and less variable than they were in the early nineteenth century. At an earlier time, the river freely migrated in response to erosion and deposition. In Lewis and Clark's day and earlier, the relatively calm place where the two rivers now meet was an enormous, dangerous body of water. The most obvious change is that two hundred years ago, the old Missouri River channel ran north of Cora Island, but now it runs south of the island. The river took land from St. Louis County and gave it to St. Charles County, the county directly north of the Missouri. What was once the main channel on the north side of Cora Island is now a chute. Mobile Island, probably the place where the Corps camped on the first night of their expedition, is now dry land north of the main channel. The Corps' winter camp, once in Madison County, Illinois, is in what is now West Alton, Missouri, proving the 1907 claim of Illinois writer George Fitch that the Missouri is a river that "goes traveling sidewise, that interferes in politics, rearranges geography and dabbles in real estate." Whatever map one drew of the river was soon inaccurate, outdated, and practically useless.

In Lewis and Clark's day, the water level in the river varied greatly. It was high in the early spring from snow melt on the plains and ice melt on the river and its tributaries. Levels dropped in May but rose again in June from snow melt in the Rockies and rainfall in the basin. Throughout the summer and fall, the flow declined until sometimes the water in the main channel was less than ten feet deep. The width of the river also varied: from 1,000 to 10,000 feet during normal flow to 25,000 to 35,000 feet during floods. Because of the frequent flooding and the shifting channel, in the spring of 1810 General Daniel Bissell moved the cantonment from the lowland near the river, slightly northwest of the clearing at the foot of the Grand Staircase, to higher ground, slightly northeast of the top of the staircase. Bissell made the right choice because when the main channel moved south, it inundated the site of the original fort. How much better to camp on the bluff top, where there are fewer insects, fewer snakes, firmer, drier ground, and a better view of the yellow, gold, apricot, fuchsia, and purple sunrises and sunsets than at the water's edge.

As I begin my explorations of the Missouri River, I need a double, double vision: one, to see the U.S. Army Corps of Engineers' fast, straight, narrow, and relatively stable river; one to see the river as it was for almost its entire existence—braided, sinuous, and wandering, characterized by logjams, snags, whirlpools, chutes, bars, cutoff channels and secondary channels around bars, with continuous bank erosion and deposition reshaping the channel and the floodplain and creating sandbars and islands. And I need to see this river that now flows past the fort with both the distance of a traveler and the intimacy of an inhabitant.

What we determine to be the beginning of something is, in many cases, constructed after the event, after we see that something is different from what came before it, after we become aware of a defining, structuring order. Rarely do we find honest accounts of conversions, new awareness, or new eras written in the moment, without the benefit of hindsight. Instead of proclaiming, "Today is a turning point in my life," we are more likely to say, "I realize now that on that Monday afternoon three Junes ago, something shifted and everything changed."

When exactly did the Lewis and Clark Expedition begin? Was it when they arrived at Fort Belle Fontaine, their first stop on the Missouri? Or was it when the Corps of Discovery set forth from the Wood River encampment on May 14, 1804? Perhaps the odyssey began when Clark and company arrived at Camp River DuBois in December of 1803. Or did it kick off on August 31, 1803, when Lewis picked up the keelboat he had ordered in Pittsburgh, bought a Newfoundland dog that he named Seaman, and pushed off down the Ohio to pick up his co-commander and the recruits? Perhaps it commenced when Congress ratified the Louisiana Purchase on October 17, 1803, thus adding to the United States the area through which the Missouri flowed. Or did the epic journey really get underway on June 20, 1803, when Jefferson instructed Lewis that the object of his mission was "to explore the Missouri river, & such principal stream of it" that "may offer the most direct and practicable water communication across this continent for the purposes of commerce"? Perhaps the expedition began with the earliest preparations—Jefferson's efforts to educate Lewis about North American geography, medicine, botany, astronomy, celestial navigation, mineralogy, and ethnology? Perhaps it more properly began the summer or fall of 1802, when Jefferson told his personal secretary, Meriwether Lewis, that he wanted him to command an expedition to the Pacific. Or was the journey set in motion when Jefferson began his first term as president in March 1801 and finally had the power to order a federally financed transcontinental expedition? Perhaps it began even earlier, when Jefferson first dreamed of a northwest passage to the Pacific.

I can point to several beginnings of my own Missouri River journey—visiting Fort Belle Fontaine Park, visiting Wood River, moving to southern Illinois. But more likely my outward journey started at some hazy point in the past when I first noticed how the Mississippi shushed and shimmered as it flowed past me, and so I fell fast in love with rivers.

As I imagined the iconic explorers setting out from Fort Belle Fontaine in their keelboats and pirogues, fresh and eager for the journey, I realized that I had chosen a fitting point of departure for my own Missouri River journey of discovery.

8

Little Dixie

I visited the Jesse James Farm and Museum near Kearney, Missouri, not because I'm related to the outlaw, as many visitors claim to be. Nor am I particularly interested in James's biography, except for the extent to which he was shaped by this place. Rather, I visited because I'm interested in the history of Little Dixie, an area along the Missouri River between Jefferson City and Kansas City. People from the Upper South—Kentucky, Virginia, and Tennessee—migrated to this region in the first half of the nineteenth century. My mother's people were part of this migration, though they settled in Knox County in northeastern Missouri and in Lee County, just north of the Iowa-Missouri border. Northern Missouri is midwestern; Little Dixie is southern.

Once in Little Dixie, the newcomers transplanted their southern traditions, lifestyle, agriculture, and politics onto the new soil. In the mid-nineteenth century, towns along the Missouri bustled with activity as farmers, planters, and traders moved the hemp grown in the fields of Little Dixie downriver to factories and warehouses in St. Louis. Where new housing developments and strip malls now stand were slave-tended hemp fields. In Little Dixie, Union and Confederate militiamen and bushwhackers, who were Confederate guerrilla forces, once gunned each other down. The latter were fed home-cooked meals in the three-room house where Jesse James was born and raised, which is now a museum. If the newcomers to this region had planted orchards and vineyards or tended wheat, corn, oats, and flax instead of hemp, cotton, and tobacco, if they'd hired hands from town to work in their fields instead of relying on chattel labor, if they hadn't exerted such an extraordinary influence on Missouri politics, we might not count Jesse James as one of the nation's bloodiest outlaws.

Jesse James's mother, Zerelda, was the quintessential Little Dixian. She was born in 1825 at Black Horse Tavern, in Woodford County, Kentucky, halfway between Lexington and Frankfort. There in Kentucky's Bluegrass Region, settlers flourished from the combination of good soil and the steep-bluffed, meandering Kentucky River that carried their hemp, corn, tobacco, and whiskey north to the Ohio River. When Zerelda was two, her father died. When her mother, Sarah ("Sallie") Lindsay Cole, married Robert Thomason, Zerelda was old enough to voice her opposition. The newlyweds moved to Clay County, Missouri, and left Zerelda behind with relatives in Kentucky.

Like many Kentuckians, Sallie and Robert Thomason wanted land and found it easier to acquire in the less-crowded and less-settled state of Missouri, which had just achieved statehood in 1821. The newcomers appreciated the woodlands and rich bottomlands near the river, the dark, fertile prairie soil beyond the river, and the watery highway that wound its way across the center of the state and formed the jagged southern boundary of Clay County. And, they appreciated that slavery was legal in Missouri.

While her mother and stepfather were far away in Missouri, Zerelda attended St. Catherine's Academy near Lexington. At a revival, she met Robert Sallee James, a student at Georgetown College. They married in 1841, and the next year, they, too, migrated to Clay County and moved in with the Thomasons.

In 1843, Zerelda delivered Alexander Franklin ("Frank"). Her second son, Robert, born in 1845, lived only five days. The next year, Robert James bought the farm and the twenty-year-old house that is now the museum, located just a few miles northeast of Kearney, then called Centerville. Whenever the Jameses had put aside two, three, or four hundred dollars, they bought another slave to work on their farm.

In 1847, Zerelda delivered Jesse Woodson. In 1849, Susan ("Susie") Lavenia arrived. Following Susie's birth, Robert James, a pro-Confederacy Baptist minister, again headed west, this time to California to preach to the forty-niners. He died there in 1850. At twenty-five, Zerelda was a widow with a farm, a house, three small children, and six slaves.

Because Reverend James had not left a will and because women had few legal rights then, one of his relatives, Tillman West, became the guardian of the James children, and an administrator was appointed to make decisions about the farm. The administrator held two auctions to pay off the family's debts. At the second auction, he sold the farm equipment, Zerelda's livelihood. With money she borrowed from West, she bought back her hoe and her husband's silver watch.

In a time when women had few opportunities, marriage was about the only legal means of improving their financial well-being. To save her family, land, and livelihood, Zerelda changed her last name two more times. In 1852, she married Benjamin Simms, a much older neighbor, whose wealth lay in land and slaves. Through this marriage, Zerelda regained possession of her children and her farm. But when Simms forbade her children to live with them, Zerelda left him. Before she could begin divorce proceedings, an audacious, stigmatizing act for a woman at that time and place, Simms died in a horse-riding accident. In 1855, Zerelda married Dr. Reuben Samuel, a fellow Kentuckian, three years her junior. Reuben was a compliant man. When Zerelda asked him to give up medicine to work on the farm, he agreed. When she asked him to sign a prenuptial contract that guaranteed her 160 acres and six slaves should he die before she did, he obliged. Together, the Samuels had four children: Sarah Louisa, John Thomas, Fannie Quantrell, and Archie Peyton. On their approximately 200-acre farm, Zerelda and her family raised hogs, sheep, corn, vegetables, and until the 1860s, hemp and tobacco for market.

The first hemp crop was grown in Missouri in 1835. By 1860 Missouri had surpassed Kentucky as the nation's leading producer of hemp, and so the leading producer of the cordage and baggage used to bale the southern cotton crop. Without the Missouri River to connect them with markets in St. Louis and beyond, Little Dixians might have grown other crops and relied on markets closer to home.

In the mid-nineteenth century, hemp, which towered far above the heads of grown men, dominated the landscape. Like the marijuana leaf, the hemp leaf is comprised of a fan of five to nine narrow, lance-shaped leaflets, alternately attached at the stem or near the base of the plant. Each leaflet is coarsely serrated; the leaflets in the middle of the fan are longer than those on either end. The green female flower forms loosely clustered spikes; the green-yellow male flower forms rather star-shaped, short, tight clusters. Hemp is a wind-pollinated plant.

The crop was planted in mid-April through May in soil that had been plowed, harrowed, and rolled. When the tall, closely set stalks were ripe, field hands cut them down with a sickle-like hemp hook. Two workers could harvest one acre per day. As with flax and jute, the bast fibers in the hemp stalk are in the phloem, just beneath the bark, and run the entire length of the stalk. Workers spread the cut stalks in the fields to "dew ret," a process in which moisture and microbial decay dissolve the softer parts of the plant surrounding the long-fiber bundles. Workers periodically turned the stalks so that all the outer parts rotted.

After Christmas, workers dragged the hemp brake, a pair of wooden jaws on a stand, to the field. One worker laid the dry hemp across the brake while the operator repeatedly moved the brake handle up and down, causing the woody outer shell to shatter and fall away. To knock out the remaining bits of stalk, workers whipped the long strands of fiber against the brake and then ran the strands through a set of hackles. Then they bundled the cleaned and combed fibers and took them to the hemp house to be weighed and baled.

Later, workers spun the fibers into a rough yarn that they twisted into rope or wove into canvas or burlap. From start to finish, the process of producing hemp rope and bagging in Little Dixie was dependent upon slave labor. During "idle" time between cultivating, harvesting, rotting, braking, and spinning, the slaves grew cotton, tobacco, or other crops.

On average, Missouri's slave population was 10 percent of the total population. But in Little Dixie, slave populations ranged from 20 to 50 percent. In 1860, Clay was one of seven Missouri counties (the other six are Callaway, Boone, Howard, Saline, Chariton, and Lafayette) where the slave population was at least 25 percent of the total. In general, the more hemp a county produced, the more slaves it had. Unlike the plantation system of the Deep South, where the average slaveholder owned twelve slaves, slaveholding in Little Dixie was small scale, with perhaps but a half dozen slaves on a few hundred acres. For instance, in 1860 in Clay County, where the James-Samuels lived, there were 651 slaveholders and 3,455 slaves—an average of about five slaves per slaveholder.

In 1850, Zerelda and her first husband owned six slaves: Charlotte, who was about thirty, and five children, Nancy, Alex, Maria, Mason, and Hannah. When Zerelda became a widow, either she or the administrator of the estate sold Alex and rented out Nancy and Maria. There is no record of the middle or last names of the James-Samuel slaves or where any of them came from. After the Civil War, Charlotte and a new slave named Ambrose stayed on as servants at the Samuel farm. In 1868, Charlotte or another slave on the Samuel farm gave birth to a biracial son, Perry. The father's name (Frank? Jesse? Reuben?) was not recorded.

When the Jameses moved to Missouri in 1841, the state was already twenty years old. The achievement of statehood had been contentious. Missouri's admission into the Union as a slave state upset the balance between "slave" and "free" states. In 1820, Kentucky senator Henry Clay, the namesake of the county where the Thomasons and Jameses settled, offered a compromise, which was approved: Missouri would enter as a slave state; Maine would enter as a free state; the remaining territories would be closed to slavery. In 1854, the Missouri Compromise was repealed with the passage of the Kansas-Nebraska Act. Thereafter, the question of slavery was to be decided by popular vote in new territories.

As more and more abolitionists settled in the Kansas Territory after 1854, fighting broke out on the Kansas-Missouri border between the "Jayhawkers," pro-Union guerrilla fighters from Kansas, and the "Border Ruffians," pro-Confederacy bushwhackers from Missouri. Consequently, during the Civil War, Missouri ranked third among the states in the number of military engagements fought within its borders. But, too, there were numerous small-scale and sometimes bloody nonmilitary clashes, since Missourians were divided between Union and Confederate positions, with differing factions within the two camps, including one that supported both the Union and slavery. One's political enemy wasn't an abstraction living in some other part of the country but a live person at the farm down the road, in the house next door, or across from one at the dinner table every evening.

The Civil War began in Missouri on April 20, 1861, ten miles from Zerelda's home, when secessionists seized the Liberty Arsenal and stole about a thousand rifles and muskets, dashing Missouri's hopes of remaining neutral in the war. A month later, Zerelda's eighteen-year-old son, Frank, joined the pro-Confederate Missouri State Guard under the control of former Missouri governor General Sterling Price. Soon Frank was battling state and federal troops across Missouri. He was at Boonville on June 17, 1861, when Union troops arrived via steamboat and quickly defeated the Guard. After this victory, the Union controlled northern Missouri and Little Dixie. Frank was at the Battle of Lexington September 13–20, 1861, when Price and his army defeated Union soldiers holed up in the Masonic College. The soldiers of the Missouri State Guard took hemp bales, each bale weighing as much as five hundred pounds, from a warehouse near the river and soaked the bales in water. Then they created hemp breastworks, with pairs of men pushing single bales up the river bluff, forming a barrier that allowed their soldiers to move close enough to Union trenches to attack. Bullets and cannonballs couldn't penetrate the damp bales, and hot shot couldn't ignite them. The militia also defeated Union troops at Wilson's Creek near Springfield and held southern Missouri until March of 1862, when Union troops defeated the State Guard at Pea Ridge, Arkansas.

One of the hardest times for the James-Samuel family was in May of 1863, when members of the local Union militia, neighbors, really, learned that Frank and other bushwhackers were camped in the woods near the James-Samuel farm and so paid the family a visit. Fifteen-year-old Jesse and a slave were working in the tobacco field when the militiamen came and whipped or beat Jesse. They dragged Jesse to the house, where he saw his stepfather with a rope around his neck and the other end slung over a tree branch. When Reuben failed to answer questions about the whereabouts of Frank and the other bushwhackers, the militiamen jerked the rope several times, each time pulling Reuben off the ground. Finally, Reuben led the militiamen to the woods, where they attacked the bushwhackers, shooting five. The militiamen took Reuben to jail in St. Joseph. Later, they returned for Zerelda, who was five months pregnant with Fannie Quantrell. Before the Samuels were released from custody, they had to sign oaths of loyalty to the Union. Though Zerelda signed, she remained loyal to the Confederacy. Some believe that the brutal attack upon the Samuel family is what violentized Jesse, violentizing being the process through which one comes to reject the religious and cultural mores of the society in which one lives and is transformed into a dangerous criminal.

The following April, Jesse joined the bushwhackers under the leadership of William T. ("Bloody Bill") Anderson, a sadist and sociopath who wore a necklace of Union scalps into battle and frothed at the mouth while fighting. On September 24, 1864, Frank and seventeen-year-old Jesse participated in the Battle of Centralia, also known as the Centralia Massacre. Bloody Bill and his bushwhackers pulled twenty-two unarmed Union soldiers returning home on leave from a train at Centralia and shot them. Then they beheaded, slashed the throats of, disemboweled, and further mutilated the bodies of the 150 federal troops who pursued them. Jesse was credited with killing a Union commander at the massacre.

Zerelda provided refuge and home-cooked meals for both Bloody Bill and the notorious guerrilla leader William Clarke Quantrill. Quantrill, whose fighters included Frank and Jesse, Cole and Jim Younger, and Bloody Bill, terrorized Union sympathizers along the Missouri-Kansas border. In 1863, Quantrill led 450 bushwhackers into Lawrence, Kansas, an abolitionist stronghold, and slaughtered 200 men and boys and burned 185 homes. When Zerelda and Reuben's daughter was born in 1863, Zerelda named her Fannie Quantrell (a popular misspelling of the leader's name)—"just to have a Quantrell in the family," she explained.

On October 23, 1864, General Price and his troops invaded Westport near Kansas City. There, Price and his pro-Confederate Missouri Army were decisively defeated by General Samuel R. Curtis, thus ending the Civil War in Missouri. In January of 1865, the Samuels and other Confederate sympathizers in Clay County were driven from the state. In his "Report Recommending the Banishment of the Samuel Family," Captain William B. Kemper, the assistant provost marshal in Liberty, wrote, "Samuel lives in Clay County. I regard his wife as being one of the worst women in this State." Kemper wrote that he heard someone ask Zerelda if she wasn't ashamed of her sons. "She rejoined that she was not—that she was proud of them—that she prayed to God to protect them in their work." Following their banishment the Samuels bought a farm in Rulo in the southeastern tip of Nebraska, near the Missouri River, and lived there until August of 1865. It was as close as they could get to Missouri without entering the state.

After a bullet lodged in Jesse's left lung during a fight with Wisconsin cavalrymen in May of 1865, he was taken to his mother and stepfather's house in Nebraska to recuperate or die. On August 25, he told his mother that he didn't want to die in a northern state. The next day, she put him on a boat and sent him downriver to his uncle's boardinghouse in Harlem, now part of

Kansas City, where Jesse's first cousin and future wife, Zerelda ("Zee") Mimms, who was named after his mother, cared for him. Because the war was over, the James-Samuels were able to return to their farm near Kearney. In October, Jesse returned home, too, and Frank joined them shortly thereafter.

After the war ended, many in Little Dixie who had supported the Confederacy were able to put aside their feelings of shame, resentment, and victimhood and work alongside the victors. But some were not. They rejected the new, postwar government and chose to live outside of the dominant society. Frank and Jesse, for instance, turned to crime as a way to retaliate for the loss of the Confederacy. For several years after the war ended, bands of pro-Union and pro-Confederate guerrilla fighters terrorized Missourians. Though slavery and the labor-intensive hemp industry had ended, for some Little Dixians, like the James-Samuel family, there was no apparent change in the way they treated the African Americans who tended their children and worked in their fields.

In late winter, farmers brought the fibers from the previous year's hemp crop to river ports in towns including Rocheport, Lisbon, Glasgow, Waverly, Lexington, Missouri City, Liberty, and Weston, where it was made into rope or stored and then shipped after the ice broke up and the river was flowing again. In St. Louis factories, the hemp from Little Dixie was turned into rope and bagging and shipped down the Mississippi to southern ports.

The most prosperous and populous town in Little Dixie was Lexington, twenty-five miles southeast of Kearney. This town was built on the bluffs and riverfront on the south bank of a curve in the Missouri. In 1860, Lexington had a population of 4,122, making it the fifth-largest town in the state. Lexington was not only the center of the frontier hemp industry, but at one time had been the headquarters for the freighting business of Russell, Majors, and Waddell, the company that operated the Pony Express. Lining the riverfront below the town were ropewalks, where hemp was corded and knotted into rope, as well as furniture factories, slaughterhouses, foundries, and warehouses. According to the January 9, 1848, *Lexington Weekly Express,* during 1847 1,000 to 1,200 tons of baled hemp had been shipped from the port in Lexington, as well as "4,500 coils of bale rope; 800 hogsheads of bacon; between 2,000 and 3,000 barrels of lard; 25,000 bushels of wheat; 8,000 barrels flour; 600 barrels whisky; and a variety of other descriptions of produce, such as dry hides, beeswax, flaxseed, hempseed, &c., the value of which was considerable." Farmers and planters raised almost everything their families and slaves needed to eat and wear, and the hemp brought ready money for taxes, more slaves, and some of the luxuries—eyeglasses, inkwells, medicines, needles, buttons, guns, glass windows, doorknobs, coffee, sugar, gold, silver, pianos, books, and fine cloth— that packet lines brought upriver to Little Dixie.

The Little Dixie hemp markets crashed because Union blockades of southern ports closed off access to southern markets. In Lexington and other river towns, people were driven out of business or went bankrupt. As the railroads replaced the steamboats and as Kansas City grew as a trade center, Little Dixie declined in both economic and political power

Frank and Jesse James were poor losers. When the war ended, they turned to crime, choosing as their targets banks and trains associated with the Union, which in their minds justified their acts as revenge. The James-Younger Gang's first bank robbery occurred when Jesse, Frank, and six others robbed the Clay County Savings Association in Liberty. The robbery occurred two weeks after a rally of the newly formed Republican Party of Clay County, to which the bank owners belonged. Jesse and his cohorts went on to rob banks in Missouri, Iowa, Kentucky, Alabama, West Virginia, and Minnesota. On September 7, 1876, in Northfield, Minnesota, they attempted to rob the First National Bank because two high-profile Republicans and former Union officers had investments there. The robbery backfired when the citizens of Northfield shot back and a posse hunted down the robbers. In the end, two gang members were killed; Cole, Jim, and Bob Younger were eventually captured; and only Jesse and Frank escaped.

When Jesse and his gang robbed the Alexander Mitchell bank on Lexington's Main Street in 1866, they received a very different treatment: the townspeople made little effort to catch the thieves. And when the gang robbed a stagecoach in August of 1874, Peter Donan, the pro-Rebel editor of the *Lexington Caucasian*, reported, "Lexington has just had the honor of one of their [the James Gang's] Robin Hood–like, rattling visits. . . . The whole proceeding was conducted in the coolest and most gentlemanly manner possible." Donan and John Newman Edwards, a former Confederate general and editor of the *Kansas City Times*, were responsible for portraying Jesse as a just and heroic man who was persecuted for his defense of the socially and economically oppressed.

Where I grew up in southeastern Iowa not far from the Iowa-Missouri state line, it seemed that every cave in every bluff was rumored to have been one of Jesse James's hideouts. I believed then that Jesse was the American Robin Hood, robbing from the rich in order to give to the poor. But I'd also heard that same claim made about Pretty Boy Floyd, Bonnie and Clyde, Billy the Kidd, John Dillinger, and quite a few other outlaws. Perhaps we justify our fascination with criminals by reading something redeeming into their misdeeds and by downplaying that which is most offensive about them. As a child, I knew nothing of Jesse's allegiance to the southern cause, that he came from a slaveholding family, and that because of his bitterness over the loss of the Confederacy, he killed many innocent people and injured many more, including a little girl.

Jesse sometimes left press releases at the scene of his crimes, providing details about the crime and telling where he wanted the missive published. But none of these communiqués contained messages about the ways in which the banks and railroads were exploiting the working class. None contained messages about Missouri's Drake Constitution, which made it illegal for ex-Confederates to hold political or church office or to vote in elections unless they swore allegiance to the Union, effectively disenfranchising most white men in Little Dixie. Some theorize that in order to right these wrongs, Jesse turned to crime; yet the killing and stealing continued after the General Assembly repealed the loyalty oath in 1871. The motive behind Jesse's crimes was personal financial gain and revenge for the loss of the Confederacy and perhaps for the loss of his family's livelihood from slave-grown hemp.

In 1874, the Adams Express Company, which delivered mail and packages via the railroads, hired Allan Pinkerton's National Detective Agency in Chicago to stop Jesse and other outlaws from robbing trains. Pinkerton, an abolitionist and former Union soldier, sent several agents to Clay County. One Pinkerton agent, Joseph Whicher, thought that if he went to the Samuel farm, he could easily capture Frank and Jesse. "The old woman will kill you if the boys don't," the president of Commercial Bank in Liberty warned. Zerelda didn't kill him, but neither did she tell him anything he could use. Shortly thereafter, Whicher was found dead near Independence, Missouri.

On January 25, 1874, Jesse, Frank, and gang member Clell Miller spent the evening at the Samuel home, leaving before the family went to bed. After midnight, Pinkerton agents threw an incendiary device into the Samuel kitchen. The intent was to force Frank and Jesse out and to burn down the house. When Reuben rolled the fireball into the hearth, the heat from the coals made it explode. One can still see the charred spot on the back wall of the fireplace. Chunks of the shrapnel hit Reuben and eighteen-year-old Ambrose, a servant and former slave, in the head; shrapnel hit eight-year-old Archie's ribs and penetrated his bowels; and a large piece smashed Zerelda's right arm just above the wrist. "The first thing that came to my recollection as I gradually grew to myself, my arm was hanging loose by my side, it being my right arm, it being broken just above my wrist," Zerelda told the *Kansas City Times* a few days later. Reuben put Zerelda to bed, sent for three doctors, and tended to Archie, the couple's youngest child, who died within the hour. "I had often thought of what might happen to Jesse and Frank, and was prepared to hear almost anything; but I never expected to see this. I never thought I should live to see my pet child stricken down at my side. I used to be a woman of fortitude and resolution; it is all gone now. I could stand anything but this," Zerelda told the *Times*. January 26, a Dr. Allen amputated Zerelda's arm just below the elbow without anesthesia. She had enough fortitude and resolution to participate in the coroner's inquest that evening. The family buried Archie in a suit of Confederate gray. In *Jesse James Was My*

Neighbor, Homer Croy wrote that after the attack, Zerelda "plowed her fields alone, with one hand."

Dan Askew, a neighbor of the Samuels and a Union sympathizer who had allowed a Pinkerton agent to work undercover on his farm, turned up dead after this incident, and the Pinkerton agent disappeared. In March, a deputy sheriff, two other Pinkerton agents, and John Younger, a member of the James gang, were found dead almost a hundred miles south of Kearney in St. Clair County. Neither Pinkerton nor his agents were charged for the injuries or Archie's death. But the raid created a national sympathy for Jesse and Frank. A bill almost passed in the Missouri legislature that would have given amnesty to the James gang members for crimes committed during the Civil War and a fair trial for crimes committed after the war.

On November 8, 1881, Jesse, his wife, Zee, and their two children moved into a little house in St. Joseph and lived under the surname Howard. There "Tom Howard" formed a new gang that included Robert and Charley Ford, with whom he was planning to rob the Platte City bank. Robert Ford was a new recruit, a small-time crook charged with killing Jesse's cousin Wood Hite. Unbeknownst to Jesse, Robert Ford was negotiating with Governor Thomas Crittenden, a former Union cavalryman who persuaded the railroads and express companies to offer a bounty of ten thousand dollars for the capture of Jesse and Frank. Crittenden promised Ford a full pardon for Hite's murder and the reward if he killed or captured the outlaws. On April 3, 1882, Jesse took off his coat and pistols and stood on a chair in his living room to dust off a picture. Ford, his housemate, shot him once in the head. Jesse died immediately.

I've never read or heard anything about Zerelda Samuel's response to Jesse's death. Jesse, who had been baptized at Mount Olivet Baptist Church in Kearney, sang in the choir, went to school until he was thirteen, grew up with and was probably cared for by slaves, and knew hard farm labor. Jesse, who at twenty-seven married a first cousin named after his mother. "There is always a smile on his lips, and a graceful word or compliment for all with whom he comes in contact," wrote John Newman Edwards of the *Kansas City Times*. "Jesse laughs at everything. . . . Jesse is light-hearted, reckless, devil-may-care." Jesse, with the shockingly clear blue eyes. Was it a numbing, paralyzing grief? Was it grief mixed with relief, since the inevitable had finally happened? Because she feared grave robbers, Zerelda buried his body extra deep beneath the coffee-bean tree in her front yard, where she could keep vigil. On his gravestone, she had inscribed: "In Loving Memory of my Beloved Son, Murdered by a Traitor and Coward Whose Name is not Worthy to Appear Here." In 1902, twenty years after Jesse's death, his widow exhumed his remains and buried them in a new casket at Mount Olivet Cemetery in Kearney. Now one sees two markers at Jesse's grave. The white vertical one says "Jesse W. James / Taylor's 50 / Todd's Co / QUANTRELL'S / Regt / CSA / Sep 5 1847 / Apr 3 1882," as if his only claim to fame were his service in the Missouri militia. A horizontal stone with "James" across the top marks the resting place of Jesse and Zee. His inscription reads: Jesse W. / Born Sept. 5, 1847 / Assassinated / April 3, 1882." The verb is provocative.

A promoter who wanted to take Jesse's remains on a national tour offered Zerelda ten thousand dollars for the body, but she decided that she alone would profit from her son's death. When the curious turned up at her door, Zerelda collected an admission fee and took them on a tour during which she dramatically recounted the Pinkerton raid in which she'd lost her arm and showed them the burn marks on the fireplace. The tour ended at Jesse's grave, where, for twenty-five cents, visitors were allowed to take a pebble. Before the next day's tours, Zerelda would gather pebbles from the creek to replenish the supply of souvenirs on Jesse's grave. Neighbor Homer Croy noted in his book about Jesse that Zerelda also sold shoes from the horses that Jesse and Frank had ridden—"enough to fill a wagon bed." And she allowed tourists to take pictures of her if they agreed to send her prints, which she turned around and sold to other tourists.

Zerelda dropped dead on a train near Oklahoma City on February 10, 1911. At the time of her death, she was returning to Missouri from a visit with Frank, who was then farming near Fletcher, Oklahoma. "Mrs. Samuels [*sic*] was 86 years old and considering the thrilling vicissitudes of her life, she was exceptionally well preserved and was in fairly good possession of all her faculties," reported the *Holden Enterprise*. "Heart disease is supposed to have caused her death." Zerelda was buried alongside Reuben, her sons Archie and Jesse, and Jesse's wife in Mount Olivet Cemetery in Kearney.

Kearney is now a bedroom community of Kansas City, with commuters rushing past it on Interstate 35, which runs along Kearney's west side. Highway 92, which I followed from Interstate 29 through Kearney and to the James farm, is a two-lane, winding road. Now that there are more housing developments than farms, the traffic on Highway 92 is heavy, even at eleven o'clock on a Monday morning. Now, like most of Missouri, Clay County's chief agricultural products are corn and soybeans. Now, the county is aligned with the Republican rather than the Democratic party.

Each year during the third weekend of September, the Jesse James Festival is celebrated at the James farm with a carnival, parade, rodeo, dog show, demolition derby, historic reenactments, craft exhibits, a barbecue cook-off sanctioned by the Kansas City Barbecue Society, the Jesse James Showdown Mud Run, and the Little Mr. and Miss Contest. At the festival, which has been held yearly since 1970, James is celebrated not as a bushwhacker, Rebel, or

Confederate, but as a rather glamorous, likeable outlaw. The festival website defends its romanticized version of the robber and murderer:

> One might ask why there is so much going on related to an outlaw whose reputation preceded him to many cities during his career as a bank robber, train robber, and even appearing as the local Robin Hood. Rumor has it that Jesse was noted for taking from the rich carpetbaggers and Yankees who had all the money. He is alleged to have given much to more deserving Missouri farmers. The reality is that Kearney hosts a festival that brings a large collection of people from all walks of life together. They gather, not to pay tribute to an outlaw, but to be reminded of an historical era which had a great impact on our country.

Yet, there's nothing that I saw at the festival that revealed what is most essential: how efforts to turn the valley of the Missouri into the valley of the Kentucky produced a distinct region, a Jesse James, and a Zerelda Cole James Simms Samuel.

9

The Overlook

I'd had a good, though hot, hike on the Meadow Trail at the Missouri River Basin Lewis and Clark Interpretive Center near Nebraska City, Nebraska. I'd seen some of the same flora and fauna that Lewis and Clark had seen when they camped in the area in 1804. Monarch butterflies drifted above the switchgrass, goldenrod, and milkweed. Turkey vultures floated high overhead on an updraft. On the trail was a wild turkey that had been torn into pieces. The tracks of white-tailed deer were pressed into the trails.

But there is much that the Corps of Discovery couldn't have seen. On a bare patch on the prairie trail, I found a beautiful spiral, the shell of a brown snail, an agricultural pest from the Mediterranean. Rock County Road was lined with tree of heaven, an invasive species from China, whose shrubby growth and compound leaves resemble the native sumac that also grows near the Meadow Trail. A ring-necked pheasant, another native to China, crowed. On the trails and in the interpretive center were people whose ancestors came from Europe and Africa, the likes of which Lewis and Clark wouldn't have encountered on this stretch of the river, sixty-four days into their journey.

After my meadow stroll, I followed the River Overlook Trail through the woods to the edge of the cliff. I long had admired this bluff above the Missouri whenever I passed it on Highway 2. To commemorate the bicentennial of the expedition of Lewis and Clark and the Corps of Discovery, the National Park Service in 2004 built an interpretive center devoted to the Corps' scientific discoveries atop the bluff. A brilliant placement. Through an opening in the trees 190 feet above the river, I could see the chain of dark, wrinkled loess hills in the far distance; between the hills and the fast, glinting river, a wide floodplain. On the Iowa shore, three people fished. At the bottom of the wooded bluff on which I stood was a railroad track.

As I sat at the overlook and watched the river, I imagined what a drastically different landscape I would have seen from this vantage point at earlier times. During the Pleistocene, about 2.6 million to 12 thousand years ago, I would have seen the advance and retreat of the great continental ice sheets. Later, the river cut a valley through the gravels, sands, and other debris that the glaciers left behind. In the spring months of many years, enormous volumes of sediment-laden meltwater from the glaciers filled the valley. In the late summers and falls, the river grew lean, exposing loess on the sandbars and valley floor. Winds from the west swept up clouds of the fine-grained, yellow-brown particles and deposited them in depths of up to two hundred feet or more on the east side of the river valley. When the glaciers finished melting, the deposition process ended. Then rainwater, snowmelt, creeks, and rivers carved the heaps of "sugar dirt" into the curiously steep, corrugated peaks of the loess hills.

From the overlook, I would have observed how the landscape evolved as the climate changed from humid subtropical forests to savannas and open grasslands. Mammoths, mastodons, ground sloth, musk ox, camels, and other exotic animals roamed the area; nomadic, spear-hurling hunters followed. When the megafauna died out, the hunters shifted to smaller game. Eventually people settled into villages near the rivers. In the eighteenth century, the Otoe, a Siouan people from the Great Lakes, arrived in skin boats. They lived in earth lodges, grew corn near the river, and hunted bison on the prairie.

From the overlook, I could have watched the Corps of Discovery pass by in their keelboat and pirogues. On July 18, they camped south of Nebraska City; on July 19, they camped a few miles upstream in Fremont County, Iowa. "This is the most open country I ever beheld," Clark declared in his journal on the eighteenth. For breakfast the next day, he had coffee and the "rosted Ribs of a Deer." Afterward, he walked along the shore, apace with the boat, until he saw "some fresh elk Sign," which he followed into the hills. When he emerged from the other side of the woods he had entered, he "Came Suddenly into an open and bound less Prarie." Clark found the sight so pleasurable that he forgot the elk and turned his attention "to the Variety which presented themselves to my view." Today Clark would find old cottonwoods instead of groves of saplings on the floodplain, fields of corn and beans, "bound less" highways, a couple of truck stops, and, on the west bank of the Missouri, a town of about 7,200 people.

From this overlook a few years after the Corps passed by, I could have watched northbound keelboats loaded with beads, rifles, knives, sugar, alcohol, cloth, tools, and other supplies and trade goods. On the return trip, the barges would have borne bales of beaver pelts, which hatters fashioned into soft, durable top hats, then the rage. After Europeans nearly trapped to extinction the beavers on their continent, they turned to Canada and the United States for the resilient, shape-holding underfur, or wool, of the beaver. When the fashion trends shifted from beaver to silk hats a decade later, the fur traders shifted to different prey: bison, whose hides were cut into lap or bed covers, as well as foxes, otters, and minks.

From the overlook in the 1830s, I could have watched Nebraska Citians, some frightened, some curious, gather to watch boats with water-churning paddlewheels and tall, smoke-belching, steam-spouting smokestacks. Soon, steamboats were common, welcome sites on the Muddy-It-Flows. In the early 1860s, as many as three hundred docked at the Nebraska City wharf each day during the shipping season. Some carried as many as five hundred passengers and several hundred tons of cargo.

From the overlook, I could have watched John Boulware ferrying troops and supplies between the first Fort Kearny, established near the overlook in 1848 to protect travelers on the Overland Trail, and the Iowa shore. Boulware built his keelboat from local cottonwood trees and strung cables to tow the boat over the river. In 1850, he built a larger, steam-powered ferry. A ride on Boulware's ferry was costly: one dollar for a loaded wagon or carriage and two horses or oxen; ten cents per horse, ox, mule, or person; five cents per sheep or swine. (One dollar in 1855 is the equivalent of about twenty-three dollars in 2010.) In the 1860s and 1870s, two steamboats, the *Capitola Butt* and the *Lizzy Campbell*, shuttled people, cattle, and wagons between East Port, Iowa, and Nebraska City. Many of those who paid the toll—Colorado gold rushers in the 1850s, Montana gold rushers and Mormons in the 1860s—crossed the Missouri at Nebraska City in order to follow one of two trail spurs that originated there: the Nebraska City–Fort Kearny Cutoff, which joined the Overland Trail on the Platte near Columbus; and the Oxbow Trail, which joined the Overland Trail on the Platte near Kearney. Other travelers arrived in Nebraska City by steamboat.

From the overlook, I could have watched U.S. and territorial officials and the chiefs of the four affiliated bands of the Pawnee come to Nebraska City in 1857 to put their signatures or X's on the Treaty of Table Rock. Once the Pawnee had ceded all but a few acres of their vast holdings to the United States, the territory opened to a rush of new settlement. One of the officials at the Treaty of Table Rock was J. Sterling Morton. In 1855, he and his wife, Caroline, bought land just west of Nebraska City that had recently belonged to the Otoe-Missouria Indians. Morton edited the *Nebraska City News*, farmed, tended his orchards, and held various public offices. What most people remember him for is that in 1872, he founded Arbor Day, a holiday that encourages people to plant trees, whether they are appropriate for their ecosystems or not. In a speech entitled "Fruit Address" to the Nebraska State Historical Society that year, Morton declared his goal as nothing short of making Nebraska our nation's "best-timbered state." While that goal was never achieved, certainly Nebraska City is one of the state's "best-timbered" towns. When I meet people who have moved to Nebraska from wetter, more forested parts of the country, I tell them about the arboretum at Arbor Lodge, the Morton estate. Spending some time at the arboretum, with its heavy shade, high bluffs, and trees native to other parts of the continent (magnolia, sassafras, tulip poplar, golden rain tree, bald cypress, a stand of American chestnut, groves of white and yellow pines) can ease their homesickness and sense of dislocation—just as seeing the Mississippi River when I moved to southern Illinois did for me.

From the overlook, I could have watched packets bound for Nebraska City. Once they docked, workers unloaded the crates and barrels of food, whiskey, tools, guns, and ammunition and loaded them onto wagons. The wagons headed west on the Overland Trail or south on the Santa Fe Trail, carrying supplies to military forts and those on the trails. Because the Nebraska City–Fort Kearny Cutoff provided a shorter, drier route to the Overland Trail than did the spurs one could pick up in other Missouri River towns and because Nebraska City had a good, gently sloping river landing, sixty-four freighting companies, including Pony Express operator Russell, Majors, and Waddell, located there. Nebraska City grew to support the freighters with boarding houses, saloons, boot shops, warehouses, wagon shops, whip makers, blacksmiths, and foundries. By 1860, the population of this wild, western town had grown to 1,922. By 1870, it had more than tripled to 6,050. A Nebraska State Historical Society photograph from 1860 shows a muddy street crowded with covered wagons and a couple dozen long-horned oxen. About a dozen men and boys stand before or lean against the brick storefronts as they watch the commotion in the street.

From the overlook, I could have watched slaves, slave owners, and abolitionists crossing the Missouri. Abolitionists guided slaves from Missouri through Kansas and to the Mayhew Cabin, a station on the Underground Railroad, in Nebraska City. One of the abolitionists who sometimes stayed in this little cabin was John Kagi, the secretary of war in John Brown's provisional government. Like Brown, Kagi was executed for his part in the raid on Harper's Ferry, where he was second in command. Abolitionists hid fugitives in the Mayhew Cabin and, as legend has it, in underground tunnels and a cave near Table Creek until they could be concealed in cargo and ferried across the river after dark. In Civil Bend, now Percival, Iowa, Dr. Ira Blanchard, a conductor on the Underground Railroad, started refugees on their journey across Iowa.

From the overlook, I could have watched billowing smoke rise above the trees. On May 12, 1860, a fire started in Coleman's butcher shop. Since it was a windy day during a dry spring, the fire spread quickly along Sixth Street and Main (now Central Avenue) to houses and thirty-eight businesses, including the post office, the U.S. Land Office, all Otoe County offices, a bank, two drugstores, a hotel, a dentist's office, three saloons, a bowling alley, a stable, a barber shop, and two boot shops. The following year, Nebraska City organized its first volunteer fire fighters. In the 1870s and 1880s, the fire-damaged buildings on Main and Sixth streets were replaced with the two-story brick buildings that now line those streets.

From the overlook, I could have watched the train stop in East Port, where the *J. S. Joy*, a railroad transfer boat, waited. The passengers boarded the *Joy*'s upper deck; the train cars were moved onto the boiler deck, which held as many as eight cars at once. Did the travelers see this stop as an aggravating interruption in their journey or as a welcome source of entertainment? After crossing the Missouri, the train was reassembled in Nebraska City, and the passengers reboarded and continued their journey. The Chicago, Burlington and Quincy Railroad put the *Joy* out of business when it built a steel trestle bridge over the Missouri in 1888.

From the overlook, I could have watched workers piece together over one hundred flatboats, upon which they built a plank road and a pedestrian path across the river, also in 1888. This floating bridge was 24½ feet wide; with the approach on either side, it was over 2,000 feet long. The cable-operated, V-shaped midsection, the apex of which pointed downstream, could be opened to provide passage for boats and barges. The toll was fifty cents per double team; forty cents per single team; five cents per pedestrian; twenty-five cents per horse and rider; two to ten cents per horse, cow, sheep, or hog—cheaper than the rates charged by the railroad to cross its bridge. A Nebraska State Historical Society photo of the newly opened bridge shows the roadway and pedestrian paths with short, evenly spaced posts on either side but no railings. The grand opening was a festive occasion, as one can see from looking at the photo. Women in long white dresses stand near the tollbooth on the Nebraska side; three men raise a flag; a parade of pedestrians and horse-drawn buggies cross the bridge from East Port. I suppose that people stood on the overlook where I now sit and watched the festivities from afar. Since the bridge was easily damaged by ice or high or low water and sometimes was closed for weeks, it was a fair-weather friend and was used only for a short time. In 1891, the CB&Q laid planks beside the tracks on its railroad bridge so people could drive over it in wagons and buggies when it was not being used by a train. This bridge served until 1930, when the Waubonsie Bridge, a truss bridge built by the Kansas City Bridge Company, opened to nonrailroad traffic. Each "invention"—ferry, pontoon bridge, transfer bridge, railroad bridge, truck and auto bridge—brought the two shores closer together and made the river more passable.

From the overlook, I could have watched people break the prairie, cut the riverine forests, and drain the wetlands. With each passing decade, I could have watched the number of bison, wolves, bald eagles, pallid sturgeons, river otters, false map turtles, bobcats, terns, plovers, regal fritillaries, western fringed prairie orchids, and other native species decline and the number of house sparrows, pheasants, Asian carp, purple loosestrifes, Eurasian mussels, rusty crayfish, Russian olives, Bradford pears, buckthorns, gypsy moths, bluegrasses, brown snails, trees of heaven, and other nonnative species increase. And, with each passing decade, there were more and more people.

From the overlook, I could have watched as the U.S. Army Corps of Engineers turned the once-wild river, whose forces of erosion and deposition and seasonal variations in flow continuously reshaped the channel and floodplain, into a relatively controlled and predictable river. A plaque at the overlook explains that in 1927, the Corps began dredging the Lower Missouri, that stretch of river between Sioux City, Iowa, and St. Louis, to create a channel that was six feet deep and two hundred feet wide. In 1945, the Corps expanded the channel so that it was nine feet deep and three hundred feet wide, in order to control flooding and make the Missouri safe for barges. In spite of these measures, the river rose far over its banks in 1952, 1967, 1978, 1993, and during the record-breaking flood of 2011. In spite of these measures, tows never became a common sight on the Missouri as they did on the Mississippi. While on some stretches of the river, there are mitigation projects, attempts to restore the Missouri to something closer to its natural state by opening side channels and planting natives grasses, what I see from the overlook is, more or less, just as the Corps left it: a relatively straight drainage ditch.

From the overlook, I could have watched the construction of the four-lane Nebraska City Bridge that opened in 1986 and the demolition of the old Waubonsie Bridge. The Nebraska City Bridge carries tourists to the Apple Jack Festival, an annual celebration of the apple harvest in September, my favorite small-town festival; to tour Morton's grandiose Arbor Lodge and arboretum and the unassuming Mayhew Cabin; to hike and explore the exhibits at the Missouri River Basin Lewis and Clark Interpretive Center or to sit at the overlook and watch time and the river. And, the bridge carries people to jobs and shopping and home again, as well as those just passing through.

I take a last look at the murky, brown river, the hills beyond, and several millennia of river-shaping and river-shaped history. I follow the Limestone Bluff Trail through woods and emerge north of the Interpretive Center. There I see an emblematic scene: a row of burr oak saplings, a native tree; an earth lodge, like those that the Otoe once lived in; and in the distance, massive grain elevators and the tall bridge girders. Cars and trucks zing past on Highway 2. Suddenly, my attention is pulled in close: a turkey hen crosses the path about ten feet in front of me; several gangly chicks follow. They are not alarmed by my presence. They linger, foraging in the native and introduced plants near the trail, and then disappear into the woods.

10

Missouri River Music

Warble (River Mile 2,341, the Headwaters, to River Mile 700)

I am listening to a crude recording by Turkey Legs, a Northern Cheyenne. I can hear him capture a lungful of air before he blows a plaintive melody into his flute. His sound isn't clear, pointed, and constant like that I can make on my silver, side-blown flute, but reedy and wavering, with wide spaces between the notes. At the end of a held note, the pitch rises quickly like the tail-flick of an alarmed white-tailed deer. The melody resumes. At the end—or is it the beginning?—of several phrases I hear a curious sound: a loud, low note that resembles the sound of a flag fluttering in a stiff wind.

In the early years of the twentieth century, ethnomusicologist Frances Densmore paid American Indian musicians twenty-five cents for each song that they played or sang into the morning glory horn, at once speaker and microphone, on her Edison phonograph. The wax cylinder into which Turkey Legs's haunting melody was cut was one of almost 3,500 on which Densmore stored songs for the Smithsonian Institution's Bureau of American Ethnology. Eventually, Turkey Legs's song was transferred from the delicate, brittle, perishable cylinder onto a thin ribbon of tape. Even so, the scratchy sound of the rolling cylinder almost overwhelms the melody.

The curious fluttering sound that Turkey Legs makes with his flute on Densmore's recording is a "warble." The Reverend Alfred Riggs, the Congregational missionary who in 1870 founded the Santee Normal Training School in northeast Nebraska, provides one of the earliest written descriptions of the warble. He explains that the Santee Sioux called their flutes *cho-tan-ka*, which means "big pith," because the flute was made by cutting a straight piece about twenty inches long from a pithy sumac branch. To distinguish the wooden from the bone flute, the former is called a "murmuring" or "bubbling" *cho-tan-ka* because of the tremulous or warbling note it makes when the player stops all the holes and blows forcefully, causing the pitch to leap quickly and repeatedly up and down an octave.

117

What Turkey Legs was playing was a courting song. It was a widespread custom in the northern Plains tribes for a young man to play his flute to woo a woman. The warble was a highly coveted sound. If a young Lakota woman was moved by her suitor's warbling song, she left her family's tepee and went to him, where he stood waiting, wrapped in a blanket big enough to envelop both of them. Within the blanket, they could talk privately. The Lakota name for this ritual is *ina aopemni inajinpi,* or "standing wrapped in the blanket." When Lakota youth were sent away to boarding schools in the late nineteenth century, the practice of this courtship ritual declined until finally it existed only in memory or in written accounts.

Turkey Legs's flute was typical of those made by northern Plains Indians of various tribes. Within the hollowed-out tree branch, the flute maker constructed two chambers, a shorter one in the head and a longer one in the body. Between the two chambers is the whistle mechanism: two holes and a shallow channel connecting the chambers. A separate piece of wood, the "block," or "saddle," is lashed in place above the whistle mechanism, or flue, to limit the amount of air flowing between the two chambers. On some flutes, the block is just an unadorned chunk of wood. But on others, it's carved to resemble a rabbit, bird, dog, or duck.

When a flautist wanted to perfect a song that had been handed down or to bring forth a new one, I imagine that he stood on a wooded bluff above the Missouri when the trees were aflutter and listened to the slurred whistles, trills, buzzes, chitters, and warbles of the finches, robins, wrens, doves, kingfishers, warblers, and vireos. He breathed into his flute and played back what he'd heard.

Another Golden Age (River Mile 617)

Dark clouds have rolled in over Memorial Park, a large green space in the center of the city. This doesn't bode well for those of us who have come to the City of Omaha's free, annual June concert in the park. Conor Oberst, the thin, pale, twenty-six-year-old guitarist for the band Bright Eyes, wears the hood of his brown sweatshirt pulled over his head. His fingers brush the strings on his guitar. "Thanks for coming. We're going to play as long as . . . as long as you want us to play," he says into the microphone. "So if you don't care about the rain, we don't either." We cheer. Oberst turns his back to his audience. When Maria Taylor clicks her drumsticks, he bends his knees, strums his guitar with gusto, and turns to face the crowd. He has pushed back the hood and a long shock of dark hair hangs over his forehead. To his right is guitar player Mike Mogis. To his left is Anton Patzner, who plays a rollicking melody on his violin. After a long intro, Oberst finally sings:

Your class, your caste, your country, sect, your name or your tribe
There are people always dying trying to keep them alive
There are bodies decomposing in containers tonight in an abandoned
  building
Where the squatters made a mural of a Mexican girl
With fifteen cans of spray paint in a chemical swirl
She is standing in the ashes at the end of the world
Four winds blowing through her hair

Oberst seems pensive and vulnerable; his voice is distinctive, clear, and quavering, as if he's on the verge of tears. Rain falls on the band, the crowd, the war memorials at the top of the hill, the pedestrian walk over five-lane Dodge Street, and the University of Nebraska–Omaha, where Oberst was a student for a few semesters.

"Four Winds," the second song on the album *Cassadaga*, is a spirited tune, reminiscent of the Waterboys, an Irish folk-rock band that I listened to in the late eighties, or the Band's accompaniment of Bob Dylan on *The Basement Tapes*. What's particularly satisfying is how easily Bright Eyes blends genres— rock, country, emo, and folk. The lyrics of "Four Winds" are typical of those that Oberst writes: more cerebral than almost anything you'll hear on radio stations owned by Clear Channel Communications, the media conglomerate whose business practices Oberst opposes; more words crammed into one line than will comfortably fit; lyrics that are either mildly confessional or starkly political; lyrics that almost add up to something. Or, to quote William Butler Yeats, whose poem "The Second Coming" Oberst alludes to twice in "Four Winds," often "the centre" in Oberst's ambitious lyrics "cannot hold."

The story of Conor Oberst, Bright Eyes, and the record company that produced the band's albums fits the pattern of an old and cherished American story: that of homegrown inventiveness and determination; that of a local product gone national. Oberst was born in Omaha in 1980 to an inner-city elementary-school principal and an information manager at Mutual of Omaha. When he was ten, his father and brother taught him to play the guitar. Within a few years, Oberst, a quick study, was writing songs and playing at gigs. At thirteen, he made his first collection of songs, *Water*, recording the cuts in the basement of the family home on his father's portable four-track tape machine with his friend Mike Mogis. In the midnineties, Oberst attended Creighton Preparatory School, a Jesuit, boys' high school by day; by night, he played in a number of bands, whose members later formed Cursive, the Faint, and Tilly and the Wall.

Oberst's brother Justin and friend Mike Mogis sold one hundred cassette copies of *Water* under the name Lumberjack Records as a project in a class on entrepreneurship at the University of Nebraska–Lincoln. When they learned that the name was already taken, they renamed the label Saddle Creek Records after a street that runs diagonally through midtown Omaha. As a result of this project, the company became an incorporated entity. Now, Robb Nansel, who assumed Justin Oberst's role, is the owner of Saddle Creek Records; his friend Jason Kulbel is the label manager; Mike Mogis has produced, engineered, and performed in many Saddle Creek releases. Though Bright Eyes is its most well known act, Saddle Creek also produced albums for such independent ("indie") groups as Cursive, the Faint, Azure Ray, Rilo Kiley, and Spoon.

Conor Oberst was only twenty-one when his success as the lead singer, songwriter, and creative force behind Bright Eyes and the success of Saddle Creek Records began drawing national attention. In 2001, displaying a questionable sense of geography, the title of a *Rolling Stone* article proclaimed, "King of Indie Rock: From the Badlands of Omaha Comes Conor Oberst of Bright Eyes— The Best Young Songwriter in America." In July 2003, *Spin* dubbed Omaha, which it described as "a beige city of 390,000 perched on the Missouri River bluffs," "America's new indie-rock capital." In 2005, Saddle Creek Records simultaneously released two Bright Eyes albums, the acoustic-based *I'm Wide Awake, It's Morning* and the electronic *Digital Ash in a Digital Urn,* cementing Oberst's reputation as the United States' King of Indie Rock. Two singles from those albums, "Lua" and "Take It Easy (Love Nothing)," were numbers 1 and 2, respectively, on Billboard's Hot 100 Singles Sales Chart in November 2004. This rating was based not on commercial radio playtime but on sales, which is remarkable for indie rock releases. Two years after the Memorial Park concert, *Rolling Stone* would name Oberst the best songwriter of 2008.

Omaha, the name of which is variously translated as "against the current" or "upstream" in the Omaha Indian language, is one in a long line of American cities where a musical innovation burst forth: the Motown sound in Detroit in the sixties; psychedelic rock in San Francisco in the late sixties; hip-hop in the Bronx in the midseventies; the B-52s, Pylon, and R.E.M. in Athens, Georgia, in the eighties; grunge rock in Seattle in the midnineties. To compare the phenomenon to an earlier period, Omaha in the early years of the new millennium is to indie music what Kansas City was to jazz in the twenties and thirties. A golden age. Perhaps the greatest factor in the flowering of Kansas City jazz was a corrupt political boss who kept the nightclubs open during Prohibition. Though Count Basie, Mary Lou Williams, Lester Young, Big Joe Turner, Charlie Parker, and others eventually left Kansas City for New York, Kansas City still claims them as its own. The Omaha sound and the city's golden age are the result of a fortunate confluence of creative talent, entrepreneurism, a small, tight-knit music community, and a city that was eager to be seen as something other than a beige river town and to not be confused with the badlands of western South Dakota. Though Conor Oberst now lives in New

York City, works on albums in Mexico, and records on Merge Records of Durham, North Carolina, he is still Omaha's own.

Oberst tilts his head toward his right shoulder and stomps his right foot, as he belts out the final chorus of "Four Winds":

> But when great Satan's gone . . . the whore of Babylon . . .
> She just can't remain with all that outer space
> She breaks. She breaks. She caves. She caves.

Before the last note has finished ringing, Oberst takes a step back, turns his back to his audience, and slips off his guitar. The exuberant hometown crowd goes wild.

Osage Orange (River Mile 465)

The growling roar of the classic tractor pull has finally stopped; the smell of engine coolant hangs in the air. Faint strains of music draw a small crowd to a parking lot behind the grandstand, where an old man in worn overalls, a plaid shirt, and a seed-corn cap is playing tunes on his fiddle that his audience recognizes—"Grey Eagle," "St. Anne's Reel," "Soldier's Joy"—and ones that it doesn't. Cyril Stinnett, the small, unassuming performer, shows little expression as he plays, in part because his mouth folds in on itself. Compared to the fiddling one hears at bluegrass festivals, his tunes are relatively free of vibrato and double-stops (playing two different notes simultaneously). Where most fiddlers would hold a note, Stinnett continues playing melody, moving the tunes relentlessly forward so one finds little rest there. His sound is overly bright; his G string is surprisingly resonant. Since he pays slight attention to the shaping of a phrase and the effects produced by varying the levels of loudness and softness, his playing lacks musicality. Instead of shifting his hand position on the fingerboard to play the higher notes, most of the time he simply reaches. Because he holds his violin in his right instead of his left hand, he tips the instrument toward him to ease the angle when he plays the E and A strings. Nonetheless, Stinnett is extraordinarily dexterous. His contorted pose reminds me of an Osage orange tree in a hedgerow. The tree in the living fence has grown around the barbed wire in the newer fence, embedding the thorny wire in the gnarled, twisted, yellow-orange wood. In spite of the irritation, the tree flowers, makes shade, and bears fruit. Stinnett rips through one tune after another. "Frisky Jim." "Swallow Tail." "Wake Up Susie." "Whiskey before Breakfast."

Before Stinnett died in 1986, he recorded three hundred songs; rumor has it that he knew at least that many again. "The Fiddling Computer," some call him. While Stinnett was adept at imitating southeastern, French Canadian, and bluegrass styles, his gift was his ability to make the tunes associated with those styles sound midwestern. An often-repeated story about Stinnett's versatility and his utter devotion to the midwestern style tells about a time when he was playing, probably in a parking lot like this one, with a small crowd gathered around. "Can you play 'The Orange Blossom Special' like X does?" someone shouted. Stinnett could and he did. When he finished, someone else asked, "Can you play it the way Y does?" He could and he did. Finally, someone asked him how *he* played "The Special." Stinnett answered, "I really don't play that tune myself."

One hundred and six years after Pierre Cruzatte fiddled his way up and down the Missouri with the Lewis and Clark Expedition, Stinnett was born, near Savannah, in Andrew County, a county in northwestern Missouri watered by two rivers: the Missouri and the Nodaway. When he was eight, Stinnett started practicing in the basement so he could surprise his fiddle-playing father. Because of a childhood accident that injured his right hand, Stinnett played a conventionally strung violin left-handed, or "over the bass." A few years later, he was moving feet and hearts at dances. At eighteen, he won the first of many fiddling contests. Stinnett lived what appears to have been a simple, uncluttered life. He never married; lived in Holt County, just a short distance from his birthplace; worked on the family farm until his death; cared for his aged parents; and practiced his fiddle. He is buried in the Fillmore, Missouri, cemetery among other Stinnetts. On his gravestone are carved two fiddles and bows and "Uncle / Cyril W. Stinnett / Jan. 27, 1912 / July 27, 1986."

Stinnett was one of the chief practitioners of the Missouri River Valley style of fiddle playing, also called the North Missouri hornpipe style, which developed in northwestern Missouri, western Iowa, and eastern Nebraska. Because this style of fiddling is sparing in its use of the drones, double-stops, and embellishments that characterize the southeastern style, the notes sound clean, separate, and energetic, appropriate for a style of fiddling born and raised in such an open, spacious land, a land once lush with tall asters, lead plant, milkweeds, wild roses, orchids, and tall grasses, a land drained by a great river and lined on the east side by steep, rugged loess hills. Though the hills and river are still there, the river has been squeezed into a deep, narrow channel; its impounded upstream waters are released according to a schedule drawn up in conference rooms by the U.S. Army Corps of Engineers. The tallgrass prairie is now covered with houses, lawns, asphalt, and chemically treated fields of genetically modified corn and soybeans, parted by wire fences.

Because Stinnett died several years before the explosion of easily accessed information on the Internet, there are few facts about him there. No interviews in publications devoted to old-time music; no newspaper obituaries for him and his family; no reports about him winning first prize at the fiddling contests at Weiser, Idaho; Avoca, Iowa; or Montreal, Quebec. A reference librarian at the Rolling Hills Consolidated Library, which serves Stinnett's hometown and several others in Andrew and Buchanan counties, tells me that she has never heard of him and finds no information about him in her library. Yet Stinnett's stature is large among other fiddlers and old-time music aficionados. When Kenny Baker, who fiddled for Bill Monroe and the Bluegrass Boys for a quarter of a century, was asked, "Who's the best fiddler?" he answered, "I don't know anybody can beat that old man up in northwest Missouri." One of Stinnett's disciples preserved the performance of his teacher on a camcorder. Thirty years later, someone posted these blurry, black-and-white videos on the YouTube website. As I watch and listen, I imagine myself into a parking lot behind the grandstand in a county fairground in northwest Missouri, where an old man plays one gnarled, knotty, and golden tune after another.

Jamming (River Mile 365)

After a long, full night playing jazz and blues and sweet, popular songs for the white people who came from their enclaves to the clubs and cabarets in downtown Kansas City; for the underworld characters who profited from the bootleg whiskey and the three hundred or so nightclubs that urban boss Tom Pendergast kept open during Prohibition; for the black people who scraped out a living as cooks, maids, porters, doormen, barbers, hairdressers, and gravediggers, who clerked in the shops in the black district, who killed and cleaned in the stockyards; and for all those who came from other cities and towns to dance to that joyous, light, loose, spontaneous music, heavy on head arrangements and improvised solos, simple riffs delivered and answered, and that crisp, buoyant, lilting swing from the rhythm section that was the Kansas City sound, after that performance, the musicians played for themselves and each other.

Those who showed up to play at the after-hours sessions at the Hi-Hat, the Chocolate Bar, Dante's Inferno, and the many other clubs and dance halls, had to be technically proficient; they had to know the repertoire of the Bennie Moten and the Count Basie orchestras; and they had to have endurance. But what separated the wheat from the chaff was the ability to play it, play it again in a new way, play it again in a newer way, play it again in an even newer way, and so on, always flowing: a river of spirit and innovation. You couldn't hear anything like this at home on your Victrola or in any other American city during the twenties and thirties.

The jam session was a chance for the musicians to be unfettered, no longer bound by what the dancers or the club managers or the marketplace demanded. The spontaneous solos and the riffing behind them unfolded generously, extravagantly, daringly, in defiance of time and convention. One evening at about ten o'clock, Sam Price, a blues pianist from Dallas who had migrated in the early thirties to the place where the Missouri and Kansas rivers meet, stopped in at the Sunset Club at Twelfth and Highland, where a jam session was going full throttle. Price had a drink, went home, rested a bit, bathed, and changed clothes. When he returned to the club around one o'clock, the band was playing the same song that it had been playing three hours earlier when he left. Yet, every musician on the bandstand, with the exception of the pianist, had been replaced. Price listened as the melody, an undammed, unchannelized river, meandered, looped, braided, ran straight through tall limestone bluffs, and meandered again. He relieved the exhausted pianist and stepped into the current.

Occasionally, the jam sessions ushered in a new order. Mary Lou Williams, the eclectic pianist and prolific arranger for Andy Kirk and his Twelve Clouds of Joy, tells about a December 1933 jam session in which Coleman Hawkins, the reigning king of the tenor sax and member of Fletcher Henderson's New York City band, competed against the Kansas City tenor sax players—Dick Wilson, Herschel Evans, Herman Walder, Ben Webster, and twenty-four-year-old Lester Young. At four in the morning, Webster awakened Williams because the pianists were spent. When Williams arrived at the Cherry Blossom at Twelfth and Vine, she saw that Hawkins, who had stripped off his jacket and shirt, was taking turns with the Kansas City saxophonists. Just as the Missouri, which flows southeasterly through most of its course across the northern plains, takes a left turn at Kansas City and flows northeasterly before resuming its southeasterly course, the Kansas City sax men had thrown Hawkins something he hadn't expected. Hawkins had a gig with the Henderson band in St. Louis that evening and knew he ought to get started on the 250-mile drive across Missouri. Yet, he also knew that there was something at the Cherry Blossom that he had to beat or at least hold back. A decade earlier, Hawkins, under the influence of Louis Armstrong, had transformed the saxophone from a novelty, comic, or vaudevillian instrument into one to be reckoned with, appropriate for the most swinging or heartrending jazz solos. He had developed a sound that was dark, somber, hard-toned, and so aggressive that it sometimes growled. Lester Young's sound was more lyrical and streamlined, played in the upper range of his saxophone with slower vibrato and a lighter sound that, in my mind, floats gracefully above the bar lines, above time itself. "I don't like a whole lot of noise," Young said in an interview just months before he died in 1959. "I'm looking for something soft. It's got to be sweetness, man, you dig?" When Hawkins finally gave up the fight that night in 1933, he got into his new Cadillac and drove straight to St. Louis, blowing out his engine on the way.

The following year, he left Henderson's band and moved to Europe, where he remained until the war started. When he returned to the States, he continued performing and recording, though he was no longer the dominant force among saxophone players. Three years after the famous session at the Cherry Blossom, Young went to New York with the Count Basie band and became the most emulated jazz performer for a new generation of musicians.

The jam session was also a proving ground where the young or inexperienced tested their mettle. At the Reno Club, young Charlie Parker sat in the balcony over the band shell, fingering his pawn-shop saxophone as he watched Young improvising with Basie's orchestra. One night at the jam session that followed the show, Parker stepped up to play his solo. When he faltered, Basie's drummer, Jo Jones, threw his cymbal, which landed at the novice's feet. Parker stepped down. Four years later, in 1939, when Parker went to New York City, a virtuoso and innovator that no one could spell or replace, he took with him the practice of the spirited, all-night, time- and convention-defying Kansas City jam session.

Shimmer (Almost Any River Mile)

The old cottonwoods, with their wide, open, towering crowns and deeply furrowed, ash-gray bark, have survived floods, droughts, lightning storms, and channelization projects. A dense band of cottonwood seedlings germinate in the wet earth near the river.

The scientific name for the eastern cottonwood is *Populus deltoides*, a member of the poplar family with delta-shaped leaves. A more accurate name would be *Populus cardarninaefolia*, the poplar with the heart-shaped leaves, since the glossy leaves are broad at the base and taper to a point like Valentine's Day hearts. But the most evocative name would be *Populus ripa*, the river poplar, since in each leaf, I see an entire watershed: the straight, midrib vein is the channelized Missouri; the smaller, branching side veins are the river's tributaries—Marias, Milk, Yellowstone, Cannonball, Little Missouri, Cheyenne, White, Niobrara, Platte, Nodaway, Kansas, Chariton, Osage, Gasconade, and Mississippi. The headwaters are at the tip of the leaf; the mouth is near the stem.

Because their petioles, or leaf stalks, are flat instead of round, cottonwood leaves ripple and flutter in the slightest breeze. The shiny tops of the leaves reflect the sunlight, just as sunlight flashes and glitters on the surface of the river. Muffling the sounds of the vehicles whizzing past on the highway, fishing lines unspooling, raindrops tinkling, flutes warbling, vireos whistling, and car stereos thumping are the whispering, shushing, sighing, glossy leaves. This is the sound of many millions of shimmers.

Harmony (River Mile 97)

Pairs of dancers circle the floor of the Bavarian-style Festhalle at the Hermannhof winery in Hermann, Missouri. Some do a simple two-step. But those who know how to polka, mostly older couples, including pairs of women, travel around the room in a series of quick, tiny steps. Making this music is the Loehnig German Band. Their repertoire includes polkas, marches, schottisches, and waltzes. You can't hear this energetic, joyous music and sit still.

Unless you're Marilyn Loehnig, a blonde, bespectacled woman in her mid-sixties. She sits on a chair, holding a black-and-white Monarch accordion on her left knee. She is extraordinarily well coordinated: her right hand plays the keyboard; her left hand pushes the buttons and expands and contracts the bellows. She smiles broadly as she taps her right foot and rocks from side to side.

Hermann is a pretty town of 2,800 snugged against the hills near the confluence of the Missouri and Gasconade rivers in the "Missouri Rhineland," about seventy highway miles west of St. Louis. If you visit this town of old brick houses and wineries and streets named Mozart, Goethe, Gutenberg, and Schiller, chances are good that you will see and hear the Loehnig German Band. The band plays at Wurstfest, the sausage-making festival in March; at Maifest, the annual celebration of spring; at the month-long Oktoberfest; and at just about every other event in or near Hermann. The Loehnig German Band has been making this happy music for almost forty years.

Loehnig has been playing the accordion even longer. In 1950, when she was five, she received a red, plastic, Sears and Roebuck accordion for Christmas. She picked out the songs she heard at Sunday school like "Jesus Loves Me" or on the radio like "How Much Is That Doggy in the Window?" She would leave her accordion out of the case near the radio so that when she heard a song she liked, she could dash into the kitchen and try to play along.

When Loehnig was twelve, her parents bought her a real accordion and one year of music lessons at a studio twenty-five miles away in Washington, Missouri—her only formal training. By the time she was thirteen, she and her future husband, Terry, were playing their accordions with a local group, Sonny Bottermuller's Peace Valley Orchestra. As a young woman, Loehnig worked at the Florsheim Shoe Company in Hermann and gave lessons. She and some of her students formed an accordion band and strolled the streets of Hermann during Maifest, at church picnics, and at the Gasconade County Fair.

In 1968, Marilyn and Terry married and moved to a U.S. Army base in Bavaria. The setting was auspicious, since the accordion, an important part of German folk music, was probably invented in Bavaria in the early nineteenth century. It was there that the Loehnigs conceived of the idea of forming a German folk band.

Accordions have long been an important part of the Hermann music scene. In 1837, members of the German Settlement Society of Philadelphia founded the village of Hermann, Missouri, a haven where German immigrants could preserve their language and customs. They chose the site because the hills and valleys, the winding Gasconade and the temperamental Missouri reminded them of their homeland near the Rhine and Weser rivers. While the soil on the ridges, hills, and bluffs near the Missouri wasn't good for farming, it proved to be fertile ground for the cuttings that the German transplants brought from their old-country vineyards and their knowledge of wine-making. In their immigrant trunks, these settlers also brought button-box accordions and concertinas.

In 1973, after the Loehnigs returned to Hermann, they started their band. When the three Loehnig children played in it, they called themselves the Loehnig Family Band. After the children grew up and left, Marilyn and Terry changed the name of the group to the Loehnig German Band. Now it consists of Terry playing the guitar, Marilyn the button-box and piano accordions, and their cousins on their various instruments: Jim Oncken, trombone, Bonnie Oncken, drums, and Ehren Oncken, button-box accordion and bass guitar. All but the drummer sing; Marilyn and Ehren yodel.

The band is bouncing through the familiar strains of "Beer Barrel Polka," though the words aren't familiar to many of us since Terry is singing "Rosamunde Polka" in German. The music is lively, full bodied, and unpretentious, content with its simple chord progressions. Pairs of dancers are whirling about the room in a joyous, dizzying circle. Marilyn is seated at the center of the group, her handiwork in full view. Between the verses and the choruses, the accordion, at once melody and accompaniment, at once humble and aggressive, swells, floods, and dazzles with the fullness of an entire ensemble.

The Bowman (River Mile 1, the Mouth)

"An EXCELLENT Bowman" is how Captain William Clark referred to Pierre Cruzatte, the oarsman in the bow of the keelboat on the Lewis and Clark Expedition. It's an appellation that points in two directions. Before Cruzatte enlisted as a private in the Corps of Discovery on May 16, 1804, he had been an employee of the St. Louis fur-trading Chouteau family. Since the search for beaver pelts had taken him as far up the Missouri as the Platte River in what is now Nebraska, he had direct knowledge of the Lower Missouri. From his mother, an Omaha Indian, he may have heard stories about a more northerly stretch of the river he hadn't yet seen. Lewis and Clark valued Cruzatte because he could find the best channel for a vessel in a river swollen with snowmelt or in low water during a late-summer drought.

In his personal baggage, Cruzatte carried a fiddle. In his head, he carried his repertoire: singable, danceable popular songs, waltzes, jigs, and quadrilles. Like most fiddlers of the time, he had learned these tunes by ear rather than eye—which is a good thing, in Cruzatte's case, since his eyesight was not the best. On August 12, 1806, he accidentally shot Captain Lewis in the butt. "This Crusat is near Sighted and has the use of but one eye," Clark wrote.

Apparently, the expedition's journal keepers weren't musicians, for not one of their many entries noting that Cruzatte provided the evening's entertainment mention the name of a tune that he played, the quality of his sound, or his bowing technique. Lewis's entry from June 9, 1805, when the Corps camped near the confluence of the Missouri and Marias rivers in present-day Montana, is typical: "In the evening Cruzatte gave us some music on the violin and the men passed the evening in dancing singing &c and were extreemly cheerfull."

No one knows what kind of violin Cruzatte played. He may have saved enough money from his fur-trading days to buy a well-crafted European instrument with the latest alterations. Or he may have played a homemade instrument with a bow cut from a barrel stave, the pearl on his bow slides punched from mussel shells that he found near the river, the strings sliced from sheep guts, the bow hairs plucked from horse tails, and the belly, back plate, and ribs carved from local wood.

Like other fiddlers of his time, Cruzatte held the instrument in front and vertically instead of horizontally and to the left. Because shoulder and chin rests hadn't yet been invented, he supported his violin with his left hand, which made shifting to higher positions awkward. Because of the difficulties in shifting and the shorter strings, Cruzatte, like other early nineteenth-century fiddlers, favored tunes such as "Yankee Doodle," "Pop Goes the Weasel," and "Marlborough" (the melody is that of "The Bear Went Over the Mountain") because they have a narrow range of notes. My daughter demonstrated for me with her fine, Italian-made violin the manner in which Cruzatte probably played "Soldier's Joy." She sawed away with an endless stream of simple, up-and-down bow strokes, slurring the notes since her bow seldom left the strings. Because the near continuous vibrato that one hears from a contemporary violinist wasn't the fashion then, her notes were steady. I found her re-creation of Cruzatte's version to be flat, choppy, and entirely danceable.

As Cruzatte traveled upriver, he played songs the way he'd heard them performed in St. Louis. But the longer he was away from "civilization" and the influence of other fiddlers and with each dip of his paddle in the river, the more the tunes changed. The "Soldier's Joy" that he played when he returned to St. Louis on September 23, 1806, wasn't the steady, straight-down-the-middle tune he'd left home with, but a meandering, eddying, rippling, lapping, flooding, dwindling, turning-over-and-under-upon-itself improvisation.

11

The Taking

The village was named after Maga Ska ("White Swan"), the chief of the Ihanktonwans ("Dwellers at the End Village"), the Friendly People, the Yankton Sioux. White Swan brought his *tiospaye*, his friends and extended family, to the bottomlands on the north bank of the Missouri in the early nineteenth century. He chose this site northwest of present-day Yankton, South Dakota because it provided everything the people needed. The Yankton called the bottomlands along the Missouri *Pte ta-tiyopa*, or "Gate of the Buffalo," because migrating bison passed through the narrow corridor between the river and the bluffs.

The people of White Swan cut timber in the bottomlands and gathered the driftwood that the Missouri River left on the shore for their stoves. In the summer, their livestock found cool shelter beneath the trees near the river. They put river water in barrels and hauled it to their houses. Because the water was swift and cleaned by the rocks and sand on the bottom, no one ever got sick from drinking it.

The people of White Swan grew corn, oats, alfalfa, and vegetables in the bottomlands. They hunted deer, rabbits, pheasants, ducks, geese, prairie chickens, and grouse. They pulled catfish, pike, sturgeon, paddlefish, bass, and turtles from the river. They trapped muskrats, minks, otters, skunks, and beavers. They gathered and ate wild onions, wild plums, buffalo berries, lamb's quarter, hog peanuts, groundnuts, spring cress, gooseberries, crab apples, wild roses, cow parsnip, morel mushrooms, and wild turnips. June was the strawberry moon; July was the chokecherry moon. Beebe Island was the best place to pick wild grapes. They smoked red-willow bark. They could cure about anything with May apple.

White people chose this site, too. Across from White Swan on the south bank, they built Fort Randall Military Post. The soldiers that fought many Plains tribes, especially the Teton Sioux or Lakota, were stationed there, including the buffalo soldiers, the "negro" cavalry. The U.S. Army held Sitting Bull, the

Hunkpapa Lakota chief who defeated Crook and Custer, there as prisoner. In 1858, about the same time that Fort Randall was built, a treaty took most of the land of the Yankton Sioux and gave the people a reservation that's been shrinking ever since. In 1952, the government closed the floodgates of the newly built Fort Randall Dam and the water spread behind it. Ever since, the town of White Swan has been at the bottom of the lake, Lake Francis Case. Tourists can visit the shell of the old chalkstone church, the parade grounds, and the cemetery at Fort Randall. But nothing remains of White Swan.

The village of White Swan had a post office, a ferry, two cemeteries, two churches, two schools, and a cannery where residents could put up fruits and vegetables and show movies with a portable generator. The barracks and stables that the Army had built were also there. The residents of White Swan moved a dance hall from Yankton, seventy-five miles away, to their town so they'd have a place to hold ceremonies and meetings. In the 1940s, the people of White Swan lived in log cabins or frame houses with dirt floors; some lived in tents year-round. Only three or four families had cars or trucks; none had electricity or heating oil. Whenever the river flooded, no one had to tell the townspeople to evacuate: they were used to moving to higher ground and living in tents until the river receded and the land dried out. The river jumped its banks almost every spring. Once every decade or so, there was a big flood. Then the people stayed longer in the camp on the bluff.

In 1943, an unusually warm spring caused rapid snow melt in the Dakotas, swelling the Missouri and its tributaries and causing disastrous flooding downstream. This was followed by several consecutive days of rain. In March, the Missouri breached the levees between Sioux City and Kansas City. At peak flooding, the river between Onawa, Iowa, and Decatur, Nebraska, spread for fifteen miles. At Omaha, the river broke the levee, killing one, destroying about one hundred houses, and causing the evacuation of one thousand people. Eight feet of water covered the runways at the Omaha airport. One could travel through the streets of Kansas City by boat. In May, the Missouri breached or overtopped most levees between Jefferson City, Missouri, and St. Louis, closing war-munitions factories and flooding freight yards.

In what *Life* magazine called the worst flood in sixty years, the Missouri inundated 1.24 million acres, many of which were planted fields. The estimated damages exceeded $32 million (which would be about $400 billion in 2010). There had been other major Missouri River floods: 1844, 1881, 1903, 1927, 1937. What was different about the flood that occurred in 1943 was that Congress and the U.S. Army Corps of Engineers vowed that it would be the last.

~

Perhaps the people of White Swan were butchering hogs during the rutting moon of 1941, when workers with the Corps of Engineers arrived at the village and at Fort Randall to drill the earth. Perhaps after the Corps left, the villagers looked at the burrows the government men had made and wondered what they wanted with the soil and the rock they'd taken. Next came the surveyors, who looked through theodolites, laid down steel tapes, and drew a map of the land.

Government officials told the people of White Swan that they wanted to build a dam there to stop and store water so there wouldn't be another flood like that of '43, and so there'd always be enough water for crops and electricity for homes. But the people of White Swan had plenty of water and didn't need electricity. They knew what to do when the water rose. The Flood of 1943 was just an excuse to take their tribal land.

On May 13, 1943, Colonel Lewis A. Pick, the Corps' Missouri River Division engineer, appeared before the House Committee on Flood Control to testify about flood-control needs in the Missouri River Basin. Though Pick had been senior engineer of the division for just one year, Congress asked him to draft the plan to harness the river. Pick called for 1,500 miles of levees on both sides of the Missouri between Sioux City, Iowa, and St. Louis; eighteen dams on the river's tributaries; and five massive, multi-purpose dams and reservoirs on the river above Sioux City and below Fort Peck Dam in Montana. The chief objectives of his plan were to control floods and to maintain deep, reliable channels for commercial barge traffic. Secondary goals were to produce hydroelectric power and to provide jobs for returning veterans.

The Office of the Department of the Interior's Bureau of Reclamation had been studying the water and irrigation needs of the Missouri River Basin and developing its own plan of action for several years when it learned of the Pick Plan. The Bureau of Reclamation rushed its proposal to completion in hopes of receiving congressional approval before Congress had time to review what Pick had put together. The Bureau's plan, developed by William Glenn Sloan, an engineer and the assistant director of the Bureau's regional office in Billings, Montana, proposed to deliver subsidized water and cheap electricity to farms, ranches, cities, and towns. The Sloan Plan, which was largely a response to the severe and prolonged water shortages of the 1930s, featured smaller dams near the headwaters, three main-stem dams, and massive diversion systems for irrigation, while reducing water in the channel below Sioux City.

How best to tame the Missouri was a contentious, divisive issue. Residents and politicians in the lower Missouri River Basin states, whose economies depended on navigation (Missouri, Kansas, Iowa, Nebraska), tended to favor the Pick Plan, as did South Dakotans. Residents and politicians of the upper river basin states, who would benefit from the proposed irrigation developments (Montana, Wyoming, and North Dakota), tended to support the Sloan Plan.

Congress received the two competing plans at the same time that it was considering establishing a Missouri Valley authority (MVA), which would put a regional entity similar to the Tennessee Valley Authority (TVA) of 1933 in charge of developing the river basin. The TVA, with its holistic concept of basin improvement, built dams for flood control, deepened the rivers for shipping, generated electric power, developed fertilizers and mineral resources, and managed forests. Those who opposed the fragmentation that can result when different federal entities (i.e., the Bureau and the Corps) determine policy tended to support the MVA. Those who objected to the centralized management of a regional authority tended to support either the Pick or the Sloan plan.

In spite of the wide differences in their plans, Sloan from the Bureau and Brigadier General Roscoe C. Crawford, who represented the Corps after Colonel Pick was sent to Burma in October 1943 to build roads for the Army, were in agreement that a TVA-style system should not be put in place on the Missouri River. They met at the Stevens Hotel in Omaha and hammered out a compromise. "A shameless, loveless shotgun wedding" was what James Patton of the National Farmers Union called the compromise between the Corps and the Bureau. With its five large dams and reservoirs on the Missouri in North and South Dakota and its 107 tributary dams, the Pick-Sloan Plan was patched together and redundant, "in no sense an integrated plan," the Hoover Commission would conclude in 1949. But it protected the interests of the Corps and the Bureau and their backers. Congress passed the plan, called the Missouri River Basin Development Program, as part of the Flood Control Act of 1944. This program established that the Corps would design the main-stem reservoirs and set storage requirements for flood control and navigation on the Upper Missouri, and that the Bureau would determine irrigation capacities for reservoirs on both the main stem and the tributaries. The two agencies were to work together to develop hydroelectric power and other beneficial uses of the river. Through Pick-Sloan, technology and engineering prowess were to triumph over nature and in the process end floods, create electricity, provide water for drinking and irrigation, and create jobs for a nation recovering from a depression and a war.

But before the Corps could tame the Missouri, it had to gain title to riverfront properties.

It was during the planting moon of 1946 that Corps contractors and laborers began preparing the way for the Fort Randall Dam. First, they scared away the nesting birds and the does that were ready to give birth. Then they cut down the trees. Some of the cottonwoods were older than anyone alive. The wild plums were in full bloom—giving off the sweetest smell on earth. Then the workers built a railroad line and a road that connected Highway 18 at Lake Andes, South Dakota, to White Swan.

The next year, the Corps took the land. By the time the people of White Swan heard that the federal government wanted their land and houses for the dam, the debate was over. The Corps appraised the land and houses and told homeowners that they could accept or reject what it was offering for their properties. The people of White Swan didn't know if the Corps was offering them fair prices or not, and if not, what recourse they had. The Bureau of Indian Affairs (BIA) hadn't even advised the Yankton to seek legal counsel. In 1948, the government started charging those who were still living in their own homes rent on what had been reservation land near the river. But the people of White Swan had lived rent-free before. If they had earned money selling firewood, milk, eggs, and vegetables in town, they had formerly used it to buy sugar, salt, and coffee. Because the Corps put the money that it paid for their properties into BIA trust accounts temporarily, the people not only couldn't pay rent, but also didn't have the money to secure other housing. Altogether, twenty families from White Swan lost their homes.

In 1950, three years after the U.S. government took the land and knocked down houses, churches, and schools and moved the remains of the dead, the people of White Swan received money for their land and homes. Some bought other property on the reservation or had other allotments. Some rented rooms in a Lake Andes motel that had gone bankrupt. Others bought or rented one- or two-room shacks, each one just like the others. A family of fourteen lived in one of those shacks. Some remained there the rest of their lives. Some stayed until they were driven out by the two tornadoes that hit Lake Andes in May 1962. Everywhere the people of White Swan went, living was more expensive, since they had to buy heating oil, electricity, food, and water. People who had always been neighbors and had helped each other were scattered. They had to walk far to see the river.

The Yankton lost 2,851 acres to the dam, and it wasn't just any land. Since it was bottomland, it was the best land for growing crops. At the time of the taking, the government paid the Yankton $39.45 per acre. It would have been less if the BIA hadn't finally intervened. Eventually each of the White Swan families that had been forced to move received an average of $5,605 for their homes and land (about $50,000 in 2010).

The treatment the Yankton received from the U.S. government was nothing new. Under the Treaty of Washington in 1858, the United States took over eleven million acres of tribal land between the Missouri and Big Sioux rivers, land that stretched all the way from Vermillion in the southeast corner of the state almost to North Dakota, land that was good for farming and hunting. In exchange, the Yankton received $1.6 million paid out over fifty years, a shrinking reservation, and use of the sacred Pipestone Quarry. In 1892, the U.S. government bought 170,000 acres of unallotted land from the Yankton for $600,000 and then turned around and sold it for quite a bit more. In the 1890s, it built an American Indian boarding school at Pipestone for the children of many midwestern tribes and laid railroad tracks on the sacred ledge. The Yankton didn't get paid for their quarry until 1929.

The Yankton were the first to have their land taken from them for the dam. Other tribal losses followed. The Corps took part of Rosebud Reservation for Lake Francis Case from the Brule. It took part of the Crow Creek and the Lower Brule Sioux reservations for Big Bend Dam and Lake Sharpe. It took part of the Santee Sioux reservation for the Gavins Point Dam and Lewis and Clark Lake. It took part of the Cheyenne River and Standing Rock Sioux reservations for the Oahe Dam and Lake Oahe. It took 150,000 acres of Fort Berthold Reservation from the Three Affiliated Tribes for the Garrison Dam and Lake Sakakawea. It took more land from the Mandan, Hidatsa, and Arikara than from any other tribe or tribal group and paid them the least amount of money per acre. The Rosebud, Santee, and Yankton Sioux didn't receive rehabilitation funds to build and fix houses on their reservations and to help tribal members become farmers and ranchers, as did the other Sioux tribes. The Yankton only received payments for their houses and land. What made White Swan different than other places taken for the dams and reservoirs is that it was the only town that wasn't relocated. Of all the towns on the Yankton reservation, White Swan was the most traditional and the least dependent on government support.

If the Sioux had known what the government surveyors had planned in 1941, if they had known that the Corps would take two hundred thousand acres of tribal land in the Dakotas and evacuate twenty thousand people, mostly Sioux, they might have banded together and fought—just as they did at the Battle of the Greasy Grass near the Little Bighorn River. If they had had an attorney, if the BIA had done more to protect them, the Corps might have had to put the dams somewhere else. But they didn't know and the Corps didn't tell them.

When Major General Eugene Reybold, the Corps' chief of engineers, submitted a letter to the House Committee on Flood Control on December 31, 1943, recommending the implementation of the Pick-Sloan Plan, he flatly stated that "the proposed reservoirs will inundate Indian lands at several points." The estimated costs of the plan included funds to cover the cost of taking lands and buildings and relocating burial grounds. The plan called for forcing tribes to turn their property over to the federal government, which in turn was to pay the dispossessed fair values for their properties and relocation.

What Reybold didn't mention but surely must have known is that the Corps' method of acquiring titles to tribal lands was unlawful. The "Takings Clause" of the Fifth Amendment of the U.S. Constitution provides that private property can be taken for public purposes if the government provides "just compensation." But according to the 1920 U.S. Supreme Court case *United States v. North American Transportation and Trading Co.,* no federal agency could repeal American Indian treaties through eminent domain without Congress's authorization. Though the Corps didn't have the authority to condemn and purchase any land held in trust by an American Indian tribe, it proceeded, certain that the defendants in the condemnation proceedings didn't know their legal rights. Moreover, the Corps didn't abide by the policies of fair payment for property. Nor, in the case of White Swan, did it relocate those whose homes it had taken.

Though the Yankton had accepted the Indian Reorganization Act of 1934, they hadn't organized according to its requirements, so their tribally elected officials weren't recognized by the U.S. government. This hindered them in their dealings with the federal government. Within the tribe, there were at least five factions competing for power at the time of the taking, so there wasn't strong, united leadership. Moreover, because the various Sioux reservations were isolated and geographically scattered, those most affected by Pick-Sloan weren't unified and so lacked the political power to influence the placement of dams and reservoirs. The Corps acted under the assumption that treaty obligations, reservations, and tribal sovereignty would soon end. In 1943, a Senate commission ordered a survey of conditions on the reservations in order to prepare the way for the Eisenhower administration's Indian Termination Policy. The ultimate goal of this policy was for American Indians to be assimilated into the dominant culture and for tribal lands to be converted to private ownership. By 1948, the Corps of Engineers had illegally acquired all of the Yankton land that it needed for the dam and reservation.

Overnight, one town disappeared and another sprang up.

East of White Swan, the government built Pickstown, where the dam workers and their families lived. It was a remarkable place. Over three hundred new houses, one family per house. Spaces for over six hundred trailers. Dormitories and three cafeterias for the workers. A two-story school. A hotel. The largest movie theater in five counties. A hospital. A shopping center. A bowling alley. The Corps cut down all the trees near the river. Because there was no shade after the trees were gone, they planted shelterbelts around the new town.

Nobody stayed long in Pickstown. One wave of workers would finish their jobs at the dam and move on so the next wave could come in. In other towns, Yankton, Platte, Gregory, and Sioux Falls, the new is mixed in with the old. But

Pickstown was only new—new buildings, new streets, and new people, who knew little or nothing about what had once been there.

The Corps brought in heavy equipment and reshaped the earth where the Yankton had hunted and grown corn, where babies had been born and old people had died and been buried. Draglines took bites of earth and dropped them into Mack trucks, two scoops per truck. The trucks took the earth to the embankment and dumped it there. Then the workers leveled it, sprinkled it with water brought by trucks, and rolled it with heavy, spiked rollers until it was hard packed. When workers uncovered the graves of Rebecca Highrock's aunt and Jesse O'Connor's brother, they dumped those bones into the embankment, as well.

A train arrived on the new track carrying pieces of a dredge, the *Western Chief*, which the workers assembled on site. The *Chief* loosened the river bottom with a rotary cutter; then it sucked the mud and soft rock through a pipe until instead of a river, there was a very, very deep lake. Bright lights shone all night so the dam builders could work twenty hours a day, six days a week. People from Pickstown and other towns came to watch the machines move earth and cut through the ancient chalk and limestone. The workers built a row of towers that look like silos, a slidelike spillway with big gates at the top, and a powerhouse in the water, which was connected to the dam by a bridge.

The water was churned up and full of raw sewage from Pickstown, the earth was torn up and moved around, machines growled, blasted, and roared, men worked day and night, and the sky was never dark. There was nothing left to show that this had been the Yankton homeland, that their ancestors had walked here, that Maga Ska had chosen the bottomland near the river because it had everything that they would need.

Like other hydropower plants, the one at Fort Randall Dam converts the energy in flowing water into electricity. Like most hydropower plants, the one at Fort Randall consists of a dam to stop the flow of water, a reservoir to store the water, pipes, a powerhouse, and an electrical-power substation.

The amount of electricity generated at a hydro plant is determined by two factors: the amount of water going through the system ("flow") and the gravitational energy or the distance the water falls from the highest level of the dammed water to the point where it goes through the power-producing turbines ("head"). The dam raises the water surface in the reservoir, which permits the water to be diverted by the natural pull of gravity. At Fort Randall Dam, four tunnels, or conduits, each 1,013 feet long and 22 feet in diameter, carry water from the lake through the embankment. The water falls 140 feet before hitting the turbine blades. The spinning turbines drive the rotors in the eight generators, each of which produces as much as forty thousand kilowatts of electricity. Nearby are eight surge towers, one for each generator, to regulate fluctuations in the water flow. The electricity produced by the generators is transmitted to a substation near the powerhouse, where transformers convert the electricity to usable voltage levels. Then the electricity is sent through transmission lines to distribution stations and finally, to homes, schools, hospitals, businesses, and factories.

The dam rises 165 feet above the riverbed and is formed from twenty-eight million cubic yards of rolled earth. It is just over two miles wide, and the two-lane U.S. Highway 18/281 runs over the top of it. The thousand-foot-long spillway, fashioned from five hundred thousand cubic yards of concrete, has twenty-one tainter gates, each forty by twenty-nine feet. During floods, the gates close to hold back and gradually release over the spillway from the reservoir the flow of excess water, which then flows into the deep stilling basin.

Northwest of the embankment is Lake Francis Case, a reservoir of stored energy, which runs for 107 miles northwest of the dam. With a maximum depth of 140 feet, its storage capacity at maximum operating pool is 5.7 million acre-feet. The reservoir is named after South Dakotan Francis H. Case, a great promoter of dams and waterways and the only U.S. senator who questioned the Corps' plans for taking tribal lands.

The Corps closed the floodgates on July 21, 1952, and the reservoir began to fill. This wasn't the first time that the river flooded White Swan. But unlike past floods, this one never ends.

If you stand on a high hill and look downstream, you'll see that directly south of the dam, the river flows in three branches. The left branch is topped by the grate-like spillway. The long middle branch is topped by the intake structure. The right branch is just a stub. This is an ugly, unnatural place of boxes, cylinders, grates, wires, and switches. Now, a different spirit inhabits this part of the river. Farther to the southeast, the Missouri again becomes a single stream with a wavy course and islands within. There, it looks like a river again—until you reach Lewis and Clark Lake and Gavins Point Dam near Yankton. If you look northwest of the dam, you'll see the impounded waters: a huge, artificial lake of dead, slack water—so dead that it has to be stocked with fish.

If you look at a map, you will see that the Corps raised a dam north of Bismarck to protect it from flooding. But that flooded the reservation of the Three Tribes, which is north of the dam. The Corps built a dam north of Pierre, which flooded the Standing Rock and Cheyenne River reservations. It built a dam north of Chamberlain, which flooded the Crow Creek Reservation. It built a dam north of Yankton, which flooded the Yankton Reservation and

White Swan. What the Corps did to protect white towns and farms, it could have done to protect the towns and farms of native people. But it didn't.

From the White House on March 15, 1954, President Eisenhower spoke over the radio to six hundred state and federal officials gathered at the Fort Randall Dam. After greeting those participating in the ceremony, he remarked that the occasion was significant not only for those who would benefit directly from "the flood control features, the navigation, the power, the irrigation," but that this dam was a symbol of what Americans "must do about our most precious natural resource." Eisenhower said that one of his "most earnest ambitions," an ambition shared by all political leaders of both parties and his cabinet members, was to find "the best and most intelligent ways of participating through a combination of Federal, State, and local assets in developing the water resources of our country so as to be of lasting benefit for the whole Nation, now and always." With that, the president pushed the remote-control button that started operating the first of the eight power-generating units at Fort Randall Dam.

After Eisenhower spoke, a former governor of South Dakota reminded the audience that South Dakota was sacrificing five hundred thousand acres of land for the construction of the Pick-Sloan dams and reservoirs—dams and reservoirs from which South Dakotans would reap great benefits. He didn't mention that a disproportionate percentage of those five hundred thousand acres were tribal lands.

A half century later, the successes and failures of Pick-Sloan are evident. The cost of the Fort Randall Dam and Lake Francis Case Reservoir alone were $200 million; the annual benefits are $242 million. The reservoir can store 5.7 million acre-feet of water—water that would otherwise flood cities, towns, and farms. The maximum hydroelectric output of Fort Randall Dam is 320,000 kilowatts, and the dam produces enough electricity to power about 250,000 homes. Together, the six main-stem dams provide about 9 percent of the total energy used within the Mid-Continent Area Power Pool, which serves Manitoba, Montana, North Dakota, South Dakota, Nebraska, Minnesota, Iowa, and Wisconsin—hydroelectric energy that reduces the United States' reliance on coal, oil, gas, and nuclear power.

The Corps estimates that each year, two million visitors camp, fish, hunt, water-ski, swim, hike, and watch bald and golden eagles along Lake Francis Case's 540-mile shoreline. When Congress passed Pick-Sloan as part of the Flood Control Act in 1944, no one anticipated that the lake would be in such demand for recreation and would generate so much revenue through the sale of park permits, hunting and fishing licenses, and camping fees.

Pick-Sloan was to have irrigated 5.3 million acres in the Missouri River Basin. But by 1989, the Bureau had watered only 1 percent of that total. Much of the grassland slated for large-scale diversion projects was found to be nonirrigable because of the quality of the soil. However, farmers and ranchers continue to develop private, small-scale diversion projects in the region.

The nine-foot-deep channel between Sioux City and St. Louis was created for commercial traffic, but since the 1970s, towboat traffic has fallen steadily. In 2008, tows hauled only 175 tons, the fewest since 1949. Because the nine-foot channel disconnected the river from the floodplain, the taking of floodplain forests and wetlands has significantly impacted the well-being of those who depend on such places—beavers, minks, king rails, cottonwood groves, migrating waterfowl, yellow marsh cress, tufted loosestrife, star duckweed, and people.

Crops still burn up. The Missouri still floods, and sometimes quite severely, as it did in 2011. Because trees that once held the shore in place were removed, waves from the powerboats on Lake Francis Case have taken over four hundred more acres of reservation land, so the Yankton have lost even more land since the dam was built. In 2002, Congress put $23 million in a trust fund for the Yankton to compensate for some of what they lost because of the dam project. Most of those who lost their homes didn't live to see this reparation.

The Yankton are still finding broken promises. According to the Corps, it relocated 509 graves of Yankton tribe members, including those from St. Philip's Episcopal Church, where the graves date back to 1869, and from the cemetery at St. Francis Catholic Church. Some of the isolated, unmarked graves the Corps claims to have moved were even older than those at St. Philip's. During the spring and summer, the St. Philip's cemetery is under water.

Many Decembers, or what the people of White Swan used to call "the moon when deer shed their horns," the water in Lake Francis Case is low. Then, fishermen, hunters, and park rangers find skulls, skeletons, coffins, and parts of coffins exposed on the shore. Sometimes, they find graves that have been dug into and the bones scattered. In December 1999, skulls, an entire skeleton, and a baby's coffin turned up. The Corps' plan to remedy the situation was to raise the level of the lake within a week, which would have washed the remains downstream. In 2000, the Yankton went to district court and got an injunction to stop the Corps from opening the dam, so they could search for and remove remains that had been exposed that winter.

In May of 2002, at North Point Recreation Area, which some know as East White Swan, workers who were building a waste dump for RVs and campers and a place to clean fish unearthed human remains. Again, the Yankton went to court, this time to ask to have the dump site moved. In 2003, a judge ruled that the state had to return some of the dirt it had taken from the site of the exposed remains. But the judge also ruled that some of the dirt brought there from another location could remain as a foundation for the waste dump.

The Yankton believe that the living are responsible for the dead and the dead, in turn, look after the living. When the remains of the ancestors are disturbed, their spirits become restless. To restore harmony, the living must perform the proper ceremonies and rebury the dead. But the living can't take care of their ancestors if the ancestors are beneath a dump or reservoir.

Those who come to Lake Francis Case to picnic, camp, fish, hunt, water-ski, swim, bird-watch, bike, hike, and drive off-road vehicles probably don't know that this used to be a river, a homeland, and a burial ground where the living and the dead were once at peace.

12

Restorations

Ian and I are spending the day at Boyer Chute National Wildlife Refuge ten miles north of Omaha. I want to hike along the riverbank, through the prairie grasses on the island, through the stands of cottonwood trees across the road, and see rarer birds than those that gather at my bird feeder. Then I want to sit and watch the water rushing through the chute. Ian wants to fish.

Ian, my grown son, loves Boyer Chute because he rarely gets a chance to fish in a river. Most evenings, he fishes in a lake–Pawnee, Bluestem, Wagon Train, or Holmes—near his riverless home in Lincoln. Often, he catches a whole stringer of channel catfish in one of these lakes. But the Missouri River is alluring: it offers blue and flathead, as well as channel, catfish; its water moves at different speeds at different depths; its current makes one's fishing pole hum with an irregular, pulsing energy; its forward movement calls to mind other origins, passages, and destinations.

I love Boyer Chute because it looks like a mistake. When I think of rivers, I think of water flowing in a relatively straight, single channel. But here, part of the Missouri River bulges eastward, taking a good bite out of what should be Iowa and giving it to Nebraska. The 2½-mile long Boyer Chute draws a squiggly line down the back side of this half circle of captured land. Together, the river and the chute form a sloppy capital *D*. On the map, the slim line of water that is the chute looks like it should be the main channel, since it is the shorter, more direct route, while the wider, main channel, which appears to veer off course, looks like it should be the side channel.

We drive to the main parking lot near the middle of the stem on the *D*. Planted along the banks are signs that say "Caution! Current can be Swift and Dangerous." The last time we were here, I strolled the Meadowlark and Oriole Trail loops on the island while Ian fished near the bridge. But on this June afternoon, we hear the roar of machinery. A man operating a small crane on the bridge dislodges logs and branches caught between the bridge piles. A man standing near the crane hollers that the last storm deposited all of this (he waves his hand toward a tall heap of brush on the opposite shore) beneath the bridge in just two hours. If you want to fish, he says, go to the north end of the chute.

We drive north, past old cottonwoods, some as big around as four or five of me. The trunks of some are smooth and pale, the bark long gone. I stop to photograph a leafless, Y-shaped branch snapped at the point of intersection with the trunk and held precariously in the branches of a nearby living cottonwood. Between the road and the cornfields to the west is a field of cottonwood saplings all about the same height, all skinny and strappy. Their heart-shaped leaves flutter in the hot breeze and flash their silvery undersides. I snap a picture of the cottonwood grove, too. The cottonwood is my favorite tree, and I know where to find several in the center of the city where I live. But these wide and unbroken stands seem about as natural to me as a Christmas-tree farm.

From the north parking lot, we follow a path through the woods. A snake slithers into the grass at our approach. We step out of the darkness of the woods and stand in the bright light and the yellow sweet clover on the west bank of the side channel. To the north, the Missouri sends some of its water into the chute, less than 5 percent, I read, though it seems like more. Bank swallows swoop low over the choppy water, hawk insects, and rise again.

When Lewis and Clark paddled their keelboats up this stretch of river over two hundred years ago, they encountered a very different river than the dammed, channelized, and tightly regulated one that I know. In 1804 the Missouri wasn't just flowing water but logjams, snags, whirlpools, meanders, chutes, cutoff channels, sandbars, and lesser channels around the bars. "The river here is very crooked and winding," Clark wrote on August 5, 1804. "To arrive at a point only 370 yards from this place, the passage by water is twelve miles." At that time, the river was deeper in the spring and early summer, shallower in the fall and winter. The river meandered over the floodplain, bluff to bluff, with the width of the main river channel varying from 1,000 to 10,000 feet during normal flow periods and swelling to as much as 35,000 feet during spring rises. Shallower streams flowed on one or both sides of the main channel.

Two centuries ago, the land near the river was different, too. On July 30, 1804, Clark wrote that he saw "a Prarie . . . of High Grass & Plumb bush Grapes &c" and, near the meandering river, "open and butifull Plains, interspursed with Groves of timber, and each point Covered with Tall timber, Such as Willow, Cotton, sum Mulberry, Elm, Sucamore Lynn [linden] & ash (The Groves contain Hickory, Walnut, coffee nut & Oake in addition.)" During most of the twentieth century, Clark would not have recognized the place since the chute and the surrounding area had been converted to corn and soybean fields.

The 1814 "Map of Lewis and Clark's Track Across the Western Portion of North America" shows nothing remarkable about the point where the

"Bowyers" River, which flows through west-central Iowa, enters the Missouri. No eastward bulge into Iowa; no chute. But between 1820 and 1937, the river gradually moved three miles east of where Lewis and Clark had found it and cut a channel through the mass of sand and sediment that the Boyer River dumped into it: the chute and the island. An 1879 map shows Boyer Chute attached directly to the island- and sandbar-filled river. Connected to the west side of Boyer Chute was Horseshoe Chute. A 1926 map shows that though Boyer Chute was still joined to the river, it had moved far enough to the east that Horseshoe Chute, a meander scar, a channel cut off from the river, was no longer connected to it.

These were the natural movements of a wild river. In the mid-twentieth century, the river continued to change, but these alterations were the result of human engineering and hubris. In response to unemployment during the Depression, Congress passed the National Industrial Recovery Act in 1933. This provided money and workers to build Fort Peck Dam in northeastern Montana, which provided a steady and sufficient flow in the river for barge traffic and the development of hydropower. The Recovery Act also paid workers to channelize the stretch of river between Sioux City, Iowa, and Kansas City. In 1937, the U.S. Army Corps of Engineers closed off the north end of the chute and installed culverts in the cutoff wall so that some river water could still enter the former side channel. A 1944 photograph shows that the river had been channelized up to Boyer Bend. Under the Missouri River Bank Stabilization and Navigation Project of 1945, the Corps closed off side channels, including Boyer Chute, and concentrated the water flow in the center of a single channel. To create a self-scouring, nine-foot-deep navigation channel, the Corps straightened the channel, which increased the water speed. By 1981, the Corps had "stabilized" 735 miles of the river between Sioux City and St. Louis and had shortened it along this stretch by 240 miles. At Sioux City, the Missouri is 600 feet from bank to bank; it gradually widens to 1,100 feet at St. Louis. The once-wild river was, more or less, the same size and in the same place, with little variation from season to season. "But a slip of its former brawly self," Conger Beasley wrote of the engineered river.

But deep, straight channels and high levees cause the river to run high and fast. In the presence of heavy rains and quickly melting snow, the river rises above its banks and levees. After the Flood of 1993, those who managed the river began to consider that allowing floodwater to spread rather than rise caused less damage to homes, businesses, and farms. Thus, a river with meanders, chutes, and floodplain wetlands might be a better option when the snow melts and the rains come than a river running in a straight, deep, and narrow trough.

Ian chooses a fishing spot about fifty feet south of the only other fisher we'll see at the refuge that day. The other fisher sits on a low lawn chair, minding two poles, his stereo softly thumping. Nothing but bites, he says, when we ask him about the fishing. Ian works a lump of pink chicken liver onto his hook and casts out. I watch. I don't fish or hunt, nor do I eat animal flesh. Yet, I'm proud that my son kills, cleans, and butchers the meat that he eats. Unlike the birds, fish, and mammals that one buys cut up and plastic wrapped at the grocery store, the creatures that Ian kills and eats have lived a wild, free life and had a decent chance of escaping his hook, bullet, or arrow. If one must eat meat, this is the way it should be done: honestly and ethically.

Ian has always been interested in wild things and places. His first fishing trip was probably with my dad in the Mississippi or Lake Geode in southeastern Iowa when Ian was two or three. When he was seven or eight, he made a scrapbook about raccoons, his totem animal. In it, he glued articles about and his drawings of raccoons, and his plan for converting his bedroom into a raccoon den, complete with a hole in the floor and a tunnel beneath, so that he and his raccoon friends could come and go without using the front or back doors. He was a Tiger, Cub, and Boy Scout more for the campouts than the meetings and badges. His favorite book in elementary and middle school was Jean Craighead George's *My Side of the Mountain,* about a boy who runs away from his family's apartment in New York City and lives in a hollow tree in the Catskill Mountains for several months, surviving on his wits and luck. And always, Ian wanted to hunt.

While Ian was in high school, he bought a bow for deer hunting. There's a lot of significance to that bow, he says. He had called his father in Kansas and told him that he needed equipment for Boy Scout camp. Ian's father, who rarely called and visited even less, had a nostalgic admiration for the Boy Scouts, so he sent Ian three hundred dollars. But Ian didn't go to camp that summer. Instead, he took the money that his father sent him and one hundred dollars that he earned at his part-time restaurant job, and bought a good bow on sale at the sporting goods store. When Ian's father found out that Ian hadn't gone to camp, he was so angry that he refused to speak to him. At the time of his death in March of 2009, he still hadn't spoken to his son about the bow incident—or anything else.

When Ian bought the bow, it was too big for him, and he didn't know anyone who could show him how to use it. At first, that mattered to him, and then it didn't anymore, because at seventeen, Ian lost his grounding in nature. Within just a few months, he stopped caring about hunting, fishing, and camping. For the next three years, the bow hung on the wall in his bedroom; his fishing poles, tackle, and camping equipment gathered dust and cobwebs in the garage.

The story of Ian's crises differs little from those I've heard other people tell about their children. While I feel compassion for the tellers of those tales, I rarely find their stories of rebellion, estrangement, and predictable consequences compelling or unique. So instead of a slow, anecdotal account with lavish details, I offer a list of the main points: Wayward friends. Drugs. Alcohol. Legal offenses. Truancies. Juvenile court. Adult court. Months of institutionalization. A tangled knot of sadness, fear, and anger that made it hard, sometimes impossible, for me to carry on. Most devastating for me was when Ian stopped going to school—he didn't "drop out," with all the conviction and finality that phrase carries; rather, he fizzled out," going to fewer and fewer classes until one day, he wasn't going to school at all. Most mornings before I was fully awake, I was flooded with dread and sorrow over the fact that my son would not be going to school that day—or the next one or the next one. Part of what made this so painful and perplexing was that I had never for a single moment considered that a child of mine would stop going to school. Nothing I or anyone else said or did changed Ian's mind about school or anything else. Like the Prodigal Son, my son had journeyed to a Far Country to escape the bonds of all that had once held him. But would my son, like the one in the biblical parable, also "come back to himself" and return home?

During the time that Ian was in the Far Country, several people suggested to me that he would find healing in nature. Two friends recommended that Ian seek employment on an Alaska fishing boat. "The work is hard, you make lots of money, and you have to cooperate with people if you want to stay alive," said one of those friends who had worked on a crab boat during his own stormy youth. I imagined driving Ian across Canada and dropping him off with his backpack and lunch money in Sitka or Anchorage or some other port city. As I drove away, I'd glimpse him in my rear-view mirror, walking the docks, looking for work on a trawler, the cold, pewter-colored waves of the North Pacific in the background.

Others suggested that I send Ian to a wilderness camp for "outdoor therapy." These camps claim to cure everything from addictions to juvenile delinquency to low self-esteem. Some are boot camps where teams of troubled youth go on long, grueling hikes in Utah canyon country. Some have a gentler approach, offering vision quests in the Adirondack Mountains. Whatever the approach, whatever the setting, the camp mission statement refers to "the transformational power of nature," or some such phrase, and bolsters the claim with a quote by an American Transcendentalist. A camp in Aspen Park, Colorado, quotes Henry David Thoreau: "I believe that there is a subtle magnetism in Nature, which, if we unconsciously yield to it, will direct us aright." Many camps quote Walt Whitman: "Now I see the secret of making the best persons. It is to grow in the open air and to eat and sleep in the earth." While I was willing to leave my son at a camp in the Rockies or the Sonora Desert so he could experience "the transformational power of nature," I certainly couldn't have paid for it. Most wilderness camps charge several hundred dollars per day; sessions run four to eight weeks. Instead, I sent Ian to a good counselor in Lincoln, and I prayed fervently.

My son's return from the Far Country wasn't the sudden, dramatic appearance of the recalcitrant son at the end of the road, as in the parable. Ian's return was more gradual. While he no longer had encounters with the police, he struggled to stay employed and in school, moved out of my house and back again several times, had friends with little ambition. During the times that he lived elsewhere, he and I frequently talked on the telephone, but I rarely saw him. If I invited him for dinner or fishing and hiking, he'd refuse, or accept and later cancel. I feared that this is what we'd always live with: no grave problems but a failure to thrive on Ian's part and a widening distance between us.

When Ian was twenty, he took his bow off the wall and practiced shooting with it. It was a perfect fit. He read books and magazines about deer and deer hunting, built a tree stand, took a couple of hunter's safety courses. Now during deer-hunting season, Ian spends more of his weekends at Lake Pawnee than in town. Some afternoons, he goes directly from work to his deer stand. When he's not hunting deer, he's processing deer meat, reading about deer or deer hunting, or tromping around in the woods looking for signs of deer. "In my dreams," Ian told me, "I'm always following deer." To tide him over from the end of one deer-hunting season to the beginning of the next, he ice fishes, hunts turkey in the spring, fishes all summer, and shoots squirrels or rabbits for stew.

I don't know if a return to nature healed Ian and brought him back from the Far Country or if his return to nature was evidence that healing had begun. Nor does he. But I know how wildness heals my own wounds both great and small and calls me back to myself. When I watch the land heal after human or natural disasters, when I consider that tidy, poisoned lawns and fields of genetically modified corn can be restored to prairie, I am solaced. People I love have died or moved away; places that were the setting of significant events in my life have been flooded, blown down, torn down, bulldozed, remade. But the plants and insects that I knew as a child—climbing jenny, cabbage moths, sweet peas, fireflies, white clover, chicory, bees, violets, corn, daddy longlegs, and apple trees—look and act as they always did. So, too, the moon continues to wax and wane over a twenty-eight-day period, chittering flocks of swirling blackbirds still roil the late summer sky, cicadas still buzz on summer nights, their songs trailing off like the last notes of a bagpipe, and Orion is forever shooting his bow in the night sky. What I see in nature—a deep story that remains the same though the surface details are ever changing—consoles and restores me.

~

To restore is to give or bring back something that was lost or taken. *Re* means "again"; *staurare* means "to make strong." To restore, then, is to return to a former condition for the purpose of making strong and whole again. The restoration of antiques, old buildings, governments, religions, or ecosystems involves more than merely repairing what's broken. The restorer seeks to bring back the original state or appearance and the functionality of the diminished thing.

Ecological restoration involves taking a degraded, damaged, or destroyed ecosystem and returning it to something close to its condition prior to the disturbance. The National Research Council's *Restoration of Aquatic Ecosystems* emphasizes the holistic nature of this process: "Merely recreating a form without the functions, or the functions in an artificial configuration bearing little resemblance to a natural form, does not constitute restoration. The objective is to emulate a natural, self-regulating system that is integrated ecologically with the landscape in which it occurs." In other words, simply digging a chute and diverting water into it isn't a restoration. The process of ecological restoration involves digging the chute, diverting water, removing invasive, nonnative species, reintroducing absent native flora and fauna, and if necessary, chemically adjusting the soil and water.

Efforts to bring back Boyer Chute began in 1989 by the Papio–Missouri River Natural Resources District in Omaha and the U.S. Army Corps of Engineers. On August 11, 1992, Boyer Chute National Wildlife Refuge was established by the authority of the U.S. Fish and Wildlife Service and the Emergency Wetland Resource Act. It was the first restoration of its kind on the Missouri and part of a larger effort to restore the Missouri to a wilder, healthier state. In 1993, the District and the Corps excavated the original channel of the chute. In a photograph on the U.S. Fish and Wildlife Service website, the area that was being made into a chute looks like a dirt road plowed through dry brush and solid ground. Next, workers installed rock girdles to hold the new channel in place. The restoration of the actual chute was completed in 1996. Once again, part of the river flowed into a slower-moving channel. Since most land near the chute, including what is now the island, had been farmed, restoration included converting corn and soybean fields into native prairies and wetlands and expanding the floodplain forest. Once again, when the river rises, the wetlands near the chute soak up water like a big sponge, hold it, and slowly release it.

The restoration continues. Nearby Nathan's Lake, a shallow lake connected to the Missouri by Deer Creek, was sediment filled and usually dry. The Corps excavated part of the lake and diverted Missouri River water into the lakebed and wetlands near it. Now, one can fish for bass, carp, and channel catfish in Nathan's Lake. With sufficient spring rises in the Missouri, larger river-fish species will also spawn in the lake. To keep the weeds from crowding out the native species at the refuge, workers and volunteers remove purple loosestrife, musk thistle, eastern red cedar, leafy spurge, and other nonnatives. Recent acquisitions have doubled the size of the refuge from almost two thousand acres in 1992 to over four thousand acres of prairie, woodlands, and wetlands in 2007. Eventually, the refuge will include land in Pottawattamie County, Iowa, where DeSoto National Wildlife Refuge is located, as well as in Washington County, Nebraska. The stands of cottonwood saplings near the chute are a sign of a successful restoration. Cottonwoods are what ecologists call a "disturbance-dependent species," which means that they can't reproduce in a well-established woodland. But if floodwaters clear out the overstory, cottonwoods find the space and sunlight they need. Before the Missouri was dammed and channelized, cottonwood seeds germinated rapidly on the mudflats and bare sandbars created by the flooding river and its eroding banks. After the Corps dammed and channelized the river, deposition rates fell sharply. One consequence of this was that conditions weren't right for new groves. Eventually, the cottonwood forests were replaced by those dominated by green ash. This resulted in less bird diversity, primarily, explains Stephen Gross in *The Missouri River Ecosystem: Exploring the Prospects for Recovery*, "because of the loss of pioneer plant species, loss of vertical structural complexity, and the loss of nesting cavities found mostly in old cottonwood trees." Fields of cottonwoods near the Missouri are good and right. So, too, are the meadowlarks, Baltimore orioles, red-bellied woodpeckers, red-tailed hawks, thrashers, kingfishers, and dickcissels that I've seen and heard at the refuge.

Boyer Chute isn't the only project that seeks to restore the river and provide habitat for endangered species. The Corps is undoing its own work by cutting notches in the thousands of wing dikes it once built to restrict the river to one main channel. The notches allow the banks to erode, thus creating new aquatic habitats. After the wing dikes were notched and detached from the banks at the Jameson Island Unit of the Big Muddy Wildlife Preserve near Arrow Rock, Missouri, the bank eroded and the river itself created a narrow chute between the bank and a sandbar. Downstream of the notched dikes, deep holes developed, thus creating habitat for a wide range of native species. The Corps and other wildlife agencies are reopening historic side channels, digging new ones, and restoring floodplain wetlands. The Corps is installing chevrons, which divert water, which in turn allows sandbars to form. Sandbars are critical nesting habitat for endangered piping plovers, interior least terns, and other shore birds. And some years, the Corps manages the release of water from the dams to imitate the natural fluctuations in the river—higher in the spring, lower in the late summer. With each restoration project, the river is becoming healthier, more dynamic, and better self-regulating.

〜

On September 1, 1804, Captain Clark wrote that his traveling companions caught a number of catfish, "those fish so plenty that we catch them at any time and place in the river." The last time Ian and I came to the chute, he would have agreed with Clark. But this time, he gets nothing but bites.

At a picnic table not far from where the crane pulls debris from under the bridge, we eat our lunch: I packed rice and vegetables; Ian packed fried catfish and morel mushrooms. Unfortunately, neither of us remembered to bring dessert. Everything, the table, the grass, and the parking lot, is furry and white with the cottony hairs that carry the ripe cottonwood seeds through the air. A clump of the fluff lands in my rice.

Our conversation turns to deer. Ian complains about people who kill bucks just for the antlers. "I'd love to catch those people," he says.

"There are jobs where you could do that," I remind him. More than once, Ian has told me that someday, he'll go to school to become a natural resource manager or a conservation officer. "But I'm not ready yet," he says. I hold on to the possibilities of *yet*. Last fall, I had talked him into enrolling in classes at the community college. But then he realized that the end of the quarter and the beginning of deer season overlapped. He confessed that when faced with the choice of going to class or to Lake Pawnee, hunting would win, and he probably wouldn't finish the quarter. "When deer season ends," Ian said, "maybe then I'll start school."

Like Boyer Chute, Ian is a work in progress. While water again flows in the historic chute, while prairie grasses and forbs again flourish on the island and near the banks, while young cottonwoods again crowd the floodplain, while rare and common birds again flash in the trees and on the water, invasive species still outcompete the natives, and irrigators, the commercial barge industry, and some politicians still fight the Corps' efforts to release water in a way that mimics the river's natural ebbs and flows for the sake of wildlife. It will be many years before there are middle-aged cottonwoods at the refuge. I hope that the U.S. Fish and Wildlife Service and the Corps will continue restoring the refuge and the river. I hope that time and nature's "subtle magnetism" will continue directing my son "aright."

Talk about jobs leads to talk about the recession, which leads to talk about the next election. Suddenly, Ian looks distracted. He climbs onto the picnic table. "Mip," he says softly, his blue eyes gazing off into the distance. "Mip." He uses this "animal-ish, fawnlike sound," as he calls it, when he wants to call deer or before he shoots a deer so that it won't be surprised by the sound his bow makes when he releases the string. I look across the road and see deer—or rather, the suggestion of deer—in the young cottonwoods and tall grasses.

"She's listening to me. I'll be back in a minute." Ian climbs down from the table and heads for the road.

I am accustomed to such behavior. I cover his food to protect it from the blizzard of fluffy cottonwood seeds and finish my lunch.

Part III

The Platte

13

The Middle Ground

I know the qualities of a real river. A real river is spanned by tall, graceful bridges and flanked, at least on one side, by lofty, majestic bluffs. A real river has dangerous currents that can yank you into the depths or whisk you downstream. A real river carries interesting things: slow, rust-colored barges the length of a couple of city blocks; paddlefish with their long, shoehorn-shaped snouts; legends about monster catfish that do wicked things to those who come near; and boats—houseboats, tugboats, rafts, speedboats, johnboats, keelboats, pontoon boats, steamboats, trawlers, and an occasional sailboat. A real river is the subject of travel narratives and novels by a funny, profound author, a giant, really, whose works are studied in high school and college classrooms across the land. A real river was explored by a colorful duo—Marquette and Jolliet, Lewis and Clark. A real river is one that you can't help singing about— "Old Man River," "Big River," "Miss the Mississippi." When a real river floods, it makes the national news.

For a long time, when I saw the Platte River, I saw a bland, flat, shallow, unstoried, unsung, boatless, shape-shifting swampy ground that sometimes ran completely dry. As a river, it failed on every count. "More of a creek than a river," I used to say with condescension.

I don't remember when I first saw the Platte. Perhaps it was when I was four, when my father was transferred from the CB&Q railroad shops in Burlington, Iowa, to the CB&Q shop in Lincoln, Nebraska. For a little over a year, my family lived in Nebraska. My mother says she and Dad were always too broke for restaurant meals, movies, shows, and anything that required a babysitter. But gas was cheap, and so they drove. Perhaps on one of those Sunday afternoon car rides, we ventured far enough from the city to see the Platte and wade in its shallow waters.

Or perhaps I saw the Platte for the first time in the early 1980s. Shortly after I graduated from Iowa Wesleyan College in 1981, I took a job teaching high school English in Omaha. One of my colleagues was fascinated by the history of the Overland Trail, which for most of its span across what is now Nebraska runs parallel to the Platte and North Platte rivers. My friend and I went to museums and festivals that celebrated the history of Nebraska's portion of the trail. Surely on one of those occasions I noticed the Platte even if I didn't find the experience worth remembering. Another one of my Omaha friends wanted to buy a little cabin, a weekend getaway, so he, his realtor, and I looked at property near the Platte. After considering a few cabins, none of which were set on stilts like the river cabins I knew, my friend and I walked to the water's edge. From this perspective, the river was even less awe inspiring than it was from afar. Yet my friend beamed with pride and delight when he repeated the old adage that the Platte is "a mile wide, an inch deep, too thick to drink, too thin to plow." How could anyone love such a flat and dreary little river? When I left Nebraska for graduate school in Illinois in 1984, I regretted leaving my friends and the big city but felt nothing about leaving the Platte and the prairie through which it meandered.

In 1988, I again returned to the Land of the Platte, this time for a doctoral program at the University of Nebraska–Lincoln. It wasn't the land or the river that had brought me back, but a better financial package than any of the other PhD programs I'd applied to. It was during my third stint in Nebraska that I became acquainted with the Platte and the land that it watered and drained. One Sunday not long after my son, Ian, then three, and I had settled into our new home in Lincoln's North Bottoms, I found myself yearning for a less-managed landscape than the city parks that he and I haunted. A couple at church gave me directions to Platte River State Park, then a rather new park, cobbled together from two camps and one privately owned woodland. Ian and I went home, changed clothes, ate lunch, and headed out for the park in our ancient, unreliable 1965 Plymouth Valiant, which made any trip beyond the city limits a risky endeavor. Once at the park, we paddleboated on the tiny lake, sat inside a tepee, played on the park toys, gathered native grasses whose names I didn't yet know, and climbed to the top of the eighty-five-foot-high Lincoln Journal Tower. Looking north from the tower, we saw the low, squat Interstate 80 bridge and a glinting stream of sandbar-filled water that curved into the northwest and disappeared. Rather beautiful, I mused. The Platte and its bluffs provided a pleasant backdrop for a perfect afternoon.

At the same time that I was learning about my new home, I was also discovering what kind of writer I wanted to be. I went to graduate school thinking that I would continue developing as a poet. But as I read essays by Annie Dillard, Loren Eiseley, Joan Didion, Gretel Ehrlich, Aldo Leopold, Barry Lopez, Maxine Hong Kingston, and others, I saw more possibilities for me in the essay than in poetry. After all, the essay could, as Annie Dillard proclaimed, "do everything a poem can do, and everything that a short story can do—everything but fake it." Instead of limiting my exploration of an idea to a trickle of words running down the left side of a sheet or two of paper, I could write a work that was deep, long, wide, and single-channeled like the engineered Mississippi or Missouri. Or, I could braid two or three streams of meandering ideas together like the Platte. I fell fast in love with this spacious, imaginative, factual, and truth-telling genre, and vowed to devote myself to reading and writing essays. I'd earn my keep by teaching others to do the same. What I was most drawn to write about was the land and what dwells there; how it shapes us and we shape it; our responsibilities to and our dependencies on it. Because my subject matter demanded that I seek a deeper relationship with the place where I was living, I began exploring the natural and human history of the river and the prairies in earnest. When I saw the Platte from the highway or interstate, I paid attention. Sometimes, I got out of my car for a closer look. The Platte still wasn't a *real* river by my standards. Nonetheless, I was growing to appreciate this sloppy, shallow, loosely knit, prairie river. I had one toe in the water, so to speak.

After I received my PhD, I left the Land of the Platte for a position at a university in the rugged, forested southern tip of Illinois. While I was there, a curious thing happened. Though I lived only about twenty miles east of the Mississippi, I saw this new landscape, with its abandoned coal mines, its cypress and tupelo swamps, its rocky, unglaciated terrain, and its comparatively short, mild winters as foreign. I found myself yearning for home. But since my parents, brothers, and grandmother had all left Catfish Bend for Ohio and the other relatives that I had been close to were dead and buried, Catfish Bend was no longer the home that I dreamed of returning to. Rather, it was the Land of the Platte that beckoned me. During my time in southern Illinois, I realized that there was something about the wild grasses, the open sky, and the flat, braided river that had won my heart. After three years in southern Illinois, I resigned from my position at the university and moved back to Lincoln.

Humanist geographer Yi-Fu Tuan says that there are two ways in which a landscape can acquire deep meaning. One way is through "the steady accretion of sentiment over the years." In other words, remaining in a place and coming to care about that place because the great and small events of your life happened there. Another way is for "an intense feeling [to] illuminate a place for life." In other words, space can become charged with meaning through some great loss, such as a trauma or separation, or some great gain, such as falling in love or having a mystical experience in the new place. I can't look back and point to a particular day or event that caused me to see the Platte as mine. But I can point to several times when I felt a strengthening of my connections to it, when I saw the place not just as the setting for the story of my life, but as a main character in that story.

One time was a Saturday in March when my daughter, Meredith, and I drove to the Big Bend between Grand Island and Kearney to see the half million or so sandhill cranes that feast and dance on the central Platte, a trip that has since become an annual spring rite for me. On one of those trips, I stopped watching cranes long enough to see what else was near the river: a red-tailed hawk dropping into the grass; a blazing gold meadowlark whistling and gurgling from a fence post; four wild turkeys watching me from the end of a driveway, the male puffed and fanned and sporting a long, red beard; many hundreds of migrating waterfowl, a black rash in the sky; many hundreds of restless, clamorous snow geese at Mormon Island. Year after year, millennium after millennium, the cranes and waterfowl migrating on the Central Flyway return to this narrow stretch of the river and the Rainwater Basin Wetlands of south-central Nebraska.

I also felt a strengthening while hiking at Schramm Park State Recreational Area, Nebraska's oldest state park. The first time I went to Schramm for solace was on a Saturday morning in November when both of my children were gone for the day, Meredith at a debate tournament, Ian at a reunion of his girlfriend's family. It was rare for both of my children to be gone all day and on the same day. First, I felt light and free; then, a heavy sadness settled in. This is what it will be like, I thought, when my children leave home. Plenty of "free" time.

I drove to Schramm on the east bank, across the river from Platte River State Park. I wanted to stand atop a bluff and survey the river; I wanted to stand at the water's edge and listen to the river: fast, slow, smooth, rippled, plashing, murmuring, gurgling, lapping, eddying. But when I arrived at Schramm, a long line of hunters were waiting to register their kills at the Ak-Sar-Ben Aquarium and Outdoor Education Center. I pictured bullets zinging through the air and the wildlife scared and hidden. I quickly decided that the first day of deer-hunting season wasn't a good time to be hiking the oak-clad hills above the river. Instead, I attended the bird-banding demonstration in the aquarium. The ornithologist and her assistants captured one bird after another—American tree sparrow, American goldfinch, tufted titmouse, black-capped chickadee, slate-colored junko, red-headed woodpecker—in nets as the audience watched through big windows. Then they brought the fluttering, frightened birds into the building in mesh bags, banded them, and gave them to members of the audience to take outside and release: a therapeutic and symbolic act for me at a time when my relationship with my soon-to-be-adult children was changing in ways that baffled and unsettled me.

The second time I went to Schramm for consolation was in January, the day after Meredith received some devastating news. Meredith didn't want to talk; nor did she want to listen to my insights and consolations. So we silently climbed the hill above the Platte, walking through old, dirty snow, porous like pumice and studded with the broken and empty bowls of the nut of the bitternut hickory. At the top of the bluff, we surveyed the scene: two cars, ours and someone else's, sitting in the parking lot near the aquarium; cabins lining the far shore of the Platte; no people anywhere. Sparrows fluttered and cheeped in the trees. Branches creaked in the wind. We descended the bluff and strolled along the river's edge. Ducks and geese clacked and preened on a sandbar. We stood silent vigil as Meredith's grief and the broken pieces of ice drifted past.

Another experience that strengthened the bonds was time I spent making weekly commutes to a western town where Ian was institutionalized for four months. Every Saturday morning, I'd drive west, bringing him home-cooked food, newspapers, clothes, and toiletries. Near Grand Island, the Platte is remarkably flat and more land than water. The bottom is sandy and unstable; the braided channels are choked with vegetation. Surely this part of the river inspired those names that stuck: *Platte,* which means "plate," bestowed by French explorers; and *Nebrathka,* which means "flat water," bestowed by the Otoe, eighteenth-century immigrants to what is now southeastern Nebraska. How could water run in such a flat place, I wondered. I was always grateful, relieved, even, when I got my first glimpse of the flat, stringy little river that would keep me company on the rest of my western journey. On the sad drive home in the late afternoon, I watched other commuters—sandhill and whooping cranes, white-fronted geese, scaups, shovelers, mergansers, and snow geese—migrating to their winter homes. But they didn't stay long that fall. Because of the long, severe drought in the early years of the new millennium, the Platte was starved and bony. Some channels were dry enough to walk across. Consequently, the "river" that I saw there looked like a scruffy field where the vegetation had been parched or worn away. This made my commutes even sadder. Is a river still a river if it has no water? Was I still my son's mother if someone else was caring for him and making decisions about him?

For the past several years, I've driven Interstate 80 between Lincoln, where I live, and Omaha, where I have a job, two or three times a week during the fall and spring semesters. Instead of being mindful of where I am and what I'm doing during my morning commutes, I listen to the news on National Public Radio; I generate discussion questions for my next round of classes; I think through thin or bloated or tangled spots in my writing, sometimes scribbling notes to myself, my reading glasses low on my nose so I can see both my notes and the road. On the return commute I'm often too tired to think, so I talk on my cell phone or sing to songs on the radio. Yet for a few minutes during each commute, I do pay attention. No matter how busy or tired I am, when I reach the Interstate 80 bridge south of Ashland and glimpse the shallow channels of the Platte, the wooded islands and bluffs, the shrinking or expanding sandbars, the high water in the spring, the low water at summer's end, the snow- and ice-covered water, or the breaking up of the ice in winter or spring, I am mindful of where I am and what I am doing.

My relationship with the Platte is informed, at least in part, by my understanding of what this river means and has meant to others. For most of those who traveled on the Great Platte River Road, the super highway over which almost a half million people passed on foot, on horse, or in wagons to what is now Utah, Oregon, Colorado, and California, the land through which the Platte flowed was transitional or even dead space between two poles of meaning: the old home in the east, the new home in the west. Theirs is the story of those who merely passed through, who didn't stay long enough to learn the deep story or to see the beauty, meanness, subtleties, and complexities of the place. Theirs is a story that runs counter to my own. But there's also a Platte River story about people who migrated here from the South and stayed for centuries. For them, the Land of the Platte was a good and beautiful place, a character as well as the setting in their stories. When the Pawnee were driven from their adopted home place on the Platte in the nineteenth century, they grieved the loss. Their Platte River story, about staying on and falling in love with a place, is more similar to mine than that other one, about the Land of the Platte as empty space to get through as quickly as possible, and so a deficient place. Unfortunately, the latter is the grand narrative that provides the collective identity for those who live on the Great Plains. It's to our own detriment that we keep emphasizing this story, through museum displays, festivals, and school curricula, as if it were the only thing that happened here, since the negative value that this story confers shapes not only how we see our home place but how we see ourselves: as flyover people.

I studied the wildlife that depends on the river, including Nebraska's threatened and endangered species—whooping cranes, interior least terns, piping plovers, pallid sturgeons, and western prairie fringed orchid—as well as less vulnerable species. The water in the Platte rises through roots and stems into leaves and flowers and seeds; seeps into the soil, rises into the atmosphere, and falls as rain or snow; is carried in the bodies of mammals, birds, amphibians, reptiles, and insects away from the banks and channels; and flows from my kitchen tap. The shallow, little Platte is the great life-giver along its course in Nebraska.

I studied and wrote about center-pivot irrigators, a machine invented by Frank Zybach of Duncan, Nebraska, that transformed the land and economy of Nebraska by allowing people to grow corn and other crops in a place that doesn't receive enough rain to support humid, eastern agriculture. The center-pivot sprinkler is comprised of a long aluminum or plastic pipe mounted on wheels and attached by a swivel connection to a well in the middle of a field.

The 1,200-foot pipe moves in a giant circle like a clock hand, spraying water and pesticides to 130 of 160 acres, all but the corners of a large square, so that from the air, Nebraska farmland looks like a full checkerboard. The abundance of center-pivot irrigators in the fields and sprinklers in front yards remind us that what we come by naturally in this part of the country isn't enough for the type of life that we want to live here.

I've also studied the complexities of Nebraska water law. Legislative Bill 962 requires the state's twenty-three Natural Resources Districts (NRDs) and the Nebraska Department of Natural Resources to work together to manage hydrologically connected surface water and groundwater—a contentious marriage in which the two partners are often at odds with each other. I learned the various ways in which Nebraska's human and nonhuman residents competed for the waters of the Platte, and I learned under what circumstances the state Department of Natural Resources would declare a river basin fully appropriated, overappropriated, or open to new development, and why the NRDs would fight these declarations.

On December 19, 2007, I put my newly acquired knowledge to work. Instead of finally starting my Christmas shopping or finishing my semester grades, I sat in a hearing room at the Nebraska State Capitol in Lincoln listening to the two sides in the water war. What was at stake was the Lower Platte, the 110-mile stretch from the river's confluence with the Loup River near Columbus to its confluence with the Missouri River near Plattsmouth, those surface waters that drain into the Lower Platte, including the Loup and the Elkhorn rivers, and all the aquifers that affect surface-water flows in the basin. What was at stake was the health and well-being of a river that I'd grown to love. One side, scientists from the Nebraska Game and Parks Commission and the U.S. Fish and Wildlife Service and environmentalists from various groups, including American Rivers and the Nebraska Wildlife Federation, wanted the river declared fully appropriated so that it would be closed to new consumptive uses and its in-stream flow would be protected for wildlife and recreation. The other side wanted the Lower Platte River Basin kept open for new development, namely, the drilling of more irrigation wells. Most of the twelve men who testified at the hearing on behalf of keeping the river open were members of boards from the NRDs in the basin—boards that were packed with water-guzzling irrigators.

As I left the hearing room, I felt uneasy—not so much about what had been said, but about what had not. Irrigators, who comprise less than 1 percent of Nebraska's population but, according to the *Water Encyclopedia*, are responsible for 94 percent of the groundwater withdrawals and use a hefty percentage of the surface water, had defended their interests. The only two people in the room who had spoken on behalf of the birds and fish that depend on the Platte were a state and a federal official. With the exception of John Knapp, a farmer from Springfield and a member of the Schramm Association for a Viable Environment (SAVE), a group committed to saving that part of Sarpy County near the Platte, not a single environmentalist or representative of an environmental organization, not a single fisher or canoeist, local history buff, cabin dweller, bird-watcher, nature writer, or Interstate 80 commuter had risen to speak on behalf of the river. And not one of the people who testified was female. What troubled me the most was that I, a woman who had grown to love this river and knew something about how it worked, had remained silent. In January 2008, Ann Bleed, then director of the Department of Natural Resources, delivered her decision: she chose to keep the Lower Platte River Basin open to new development. Groundwater and surface water could be used to expand the number of irrigated acres in eastern Nebraska. Those of us who cared about the ecological well-being of the Lower Platte would garner no protection from the state.

The deep story that I have to tell about the Platte is how I moved from being an outsider to being an insider in relation to it. It's not a story that is peculiar to the Platte. Had I situated myself in an abode house in Albuquerque with yucca and pinyon pine growing in my front yard or in a cottage perched on the rocky Nova Scotian coast, I would have had to make this change in perspective if I was to be "in place." In short, this is a story that I might have told about any landscape or river other than the one where I was born and raised. But because I chose to settle in the Land of the Platte, the details of my story are particular to that place.

In any landscape, one is either an outsider or an insider, a resident or one just passing through. The outsider's knowledge about an unfamiliar place and those who dwell there is simple, one-dimensional, and acquired through collected rather than innate knowledge. The tourist, traveler, sojourner, or visitor notices objects and surfaces, and according to Yi-Fu Tuan, composes a picture of the place with his or her eyes and judges that place "by appearance, by some formal canon of beauty." It requires a special effort, Tuan says, for the outsider "to empathize with the lives and values of the inhabitants." An outsider might comment that many Nebraskans show a low tolerance for lifestyle differences among people. But what the outsider might not see is that at least some Nebraskans take a greater pride in their wild, nonconforming, homegrown writers, musicians, and artists than you'll see almost anyplace else.

Insiders have a different vision. Inhabitants, dwellers, or natives, and those who have what Barry Lopez calls a "long-lived intimacy with a place," perceive relationships and depths. After paying attention to the ways in which prairie grasses and forbs cooperate and compete with each other, they can tell you how right and natural it is for a prairie state to have but one legislative chamber.

After paying attention to the way the sound of the train horn carries up the hill or the behavior of squirrels and swallows, they might have a good feel for the immediate and long-range weather. Insiders possess a double vision: they can see what is no longer here as well as what is. The insider sees both the new streets and buildings of the university's Innovation Campus and the Nebraska State Fairgrounds that used to occupy that site. The insider knows special places not listed in the travel guide—the little mom-and-pop restaurant tucked away in an old neighborhood that features excellent homemade soups or the colonies of Virginia bluebells at Pioneer's Park (not natives, but beautiful nonetheless)—and can tell you the story behind that unlikely restaurant and how those lovely bluebells bloom earlier and earlier each spring.

Because the native has, as Tuan puts it, "a complex attitude derived from his immersion in the totality of his environment," he or she perceives the place "with more than just the eyes." Though the insider may not be able to articulate the texture of life lived in this place, he or she understands it. The insider knows or senses the ways in which personal and communal stories and associations confer value upon a place, and the ways in which that place is essential to those stories. The insider knows his or her place in those stories, even though he or she may not understand the ways in which that role and placement limits movements and choices.

Between the two poles of perception and knowing, there is a middle ground, that of the newcomer who consciously or unconsciously decides to stay on and become an inhabitant. As the newcomer explores the place, people, and land, he or she comes to occupy a challenging and rewarding position: poised or balanced between the two visions, the two ways of knowing and being. Consequently, one who is both insider and outsider, what Gretel Ehrlich calls a "culture straddler," sees more than those at either pole. Neither yin nor yang, but the wholeness and rightness that results when the two principles are balanced. Knowing a place in such a way takes time and great commitment.

My knowledge of the Platte and the land through which it flows came through formal study as well as through experience, memory, and feeling. I know this place as an outsider who once saw it as foreign, strange, and "not mine." Then, I saw too easily the various ways in which the history, landscape, and way of life in this place fell short of my expectations. But, too, through what Tuan calls "the steady accretion of sentiment," I now perceive dense and tangled webs of connection and causality. Now I can see what is beautiful and ugly, sustaining and degrading in this place.

Because of my dual status, I see what many miss: namely, the astonishing diversity in the Land of the Platte. I read in the preface to a field guide that there's a greater difference in the flora of eastern and western Nebraska than there is between eastern Nebraska and New England. From what I've seen, that's true. All three prairie types, tallgrass, mixed-grass, and short-grass, are found in the Land of the Platte. So, too, are ponderosa pine forests, cacti, and mule deer in the west; shagbark hickory, Ohio buckeye, pawpaws, bobcats, and flying squirrels in the extreme southeast. Every year, at least a couple of Nebraska counties turn up on the list of the hundred poorest counties in the country; yet, Warren Buffet, the third-richest man in the world, lives and works in Omaha. Though Nebraska ranks fourth among the states in total agricultural receipts (topped only by California, Texas, and Iowa), more Nebraskans are employed in the service industry than in agriculture and live not on or near farms and ranches but in Omaha or Lincoln.

When compared with states of similar populations, Nebraska is fifth in the nation in refugee resettlement. Though Nebraska's Euro-American pioneer past is prominent in festivals celebrating our Czech, German, Italian, Greek, Danish, Norwegian, Swedish, and Welsh heritage, in several Platte River towns, the majority of the population is Hispanic. One can choose between several restaurants serving authentic Mexican or Guatemalan food, shop in a bodega, and learn about laws passed by city councils aimed at punishing brown people who work for low wages at the meatpacking plants on the edge of town.

Nebraska also has a growing international community. My ex-husband, a black man from the Caribbean rim of South America, immigrated to the Land of the Platte after being recruited for a position as an assistant professor at the University of Nebraska–Lincoln in 1986. Six years later, he was sworn in as a U.S. citizen. To celebrate, my children and I baked him what we have since referred to as a "citizen cake": a chocolate and yellow marble cake with chocolate frosting.

While I will never know the Platte River landscape with the depth and thoroughness of one who has spent an entire lifetime paying attention to it, I have, over the past twenty years, accumulated the historical, ecological, legendary, and personal meanings that transform space into place. While I still dream of living near my beloved, prototypal river and plan to buy a cabin someday on the Iowa or Illinois side of the Mississippi or a little house on a high bluff where I can watch barges, eagles, floods, fishers, and mayflies, it is the Platte that has taught me about the kind of love that embraces both the beautiful and the objectionable, that sees past one's own expectations to the essence of the other, and that fights for the beloved. This love is mutually sustaining: good for the beloved and the lover.

14

No Other River

It's an annual rite. Sometime between late February and early April, I drive west on Interstate 80. In south-central Nebraska, both the Platte River and the interstate swing low toward the Nebraska-Kansas state line. Somewhere along the bottom of this catenary curve, I pull off the interstate and drive gravel roads south of the river. What I'm looking for is the world's largest gathering of migrating sandhill cranes. They're easy to find. The half million cranes are concentrated, more or less, within the forty-mile stretch of the river between Grand Island and Kearney, the narrow waist on the hourglass-shaped Central Flyway and the narrowest part of the cranes' migratory route. Because this part of Nebraska is relatively flat and open, one doesn't have to look hard or far to see the elegant, leggy, four-foot-tall, red-capped, gray birds.

I come to watch them feast and dance and drop out of and rise into the sky. Most of the cranes congregating on the Platte are lesser sandhills, the crane with the longest migration. The remaining cranes are greater sandhills and the endangered whooping cranes. After the roughly 600-mile trip from their winter homes in eastern New Mexico, northwestern Texas, and northern Mexico, the sandhill cranes are lean and hungry. Once in Nebraska, they glean corn left from the harvest and slurp up snails, worms, grubs, insects, snakes, and crayfish in the wet meadows near the Platte. Each crane stays in Nebraska about four weeks and adds a pound or so of fat during this time. At night, they return to the shallow river, where they sleep standing in water, usually on one leg, in roosts of as many as ten to fifteen thousand cranes per half mile of river. From the air, these sleeping masses, some of which are a mile long, look sandbar-shaped, and the individual cranes are evenly spaced, as if, describes Steve Grooms in *The Cry of the Sandhill Crane*, "positioned on a grid of four-foot squares, each bird staying just beyond the reach of its neighbors' sharp bills." At dawn, the cranes head for the fields near the river.

And there, they dance, bowing, strutting, pumping their heads, raising their bills, flapping their wings, tossing corncobs into the air, and gracefully hopping

163

as high as twenty feet. "Great bouncing balls" is how one observer described them. "Great theater" is how I describe the dance. Scientists once considered the dance to be a mating ritual. Yet the behavior isn't limited to mated pairs. Juveniles, chicks, and unpaired cranes dance as well. Now scientists believe that the dance serves several functions: it is a courtship ritual performed mostly by unpaired cranes; it is a bonding ritual among life mates; it is a way, according to Nebraska ornithologist Paul Johnsgard, to "thwart aggression, relieve tension, and strengthen the pair bond" and so is enacted year-round.

I drive back roads with other crane-watchers ("craniacs," we're called) who creep along at ten to twenty miles per hour, radios off, windows down. We stop frequently to peer through binoculars. But if I see cranes spiraling on motionless wings on rising columns of air ("kettling," it's called), I stop, get out of my car, and watch. Johnsgard, who has been watching cranes since 1962, speculates that cranes might use these "high-altitude maneuvers as reconnaissance flights" before they leave the Platte in the spring in order "to scan the river and commit its topographic features to the collective memories of the flock members." Johnsgard believes this activity may be especially important for the younger and more inexperienced birds, since they must learn all of the species' most reliable migratory stopping points along their several-thousand-mile migration. Kettling also prepares the cranes for that time when they leave this part of the Central Flyway in a dramatic mass departure, winging north over the Nebraska sandhills and on to their breeding grounds in northeastern Siberia, Alaska, and northern Canada. When they go, they take tons of Nebraska with them: grain, insects, and invertebrates converted into flight fuel. When they leave, we craniacs go home, carrying images of these great, gray-clad "preacher birds," as travelers and settlers once called them, delivering their wild sermons near the Platte.

Though I'd lived in Nebraska many springs and many times had planned or promised myself to make the trek west to their staging grounds, I didn't see my first cranes until 2000. Then, on Alda Road south of Wood River, Nebraska, I pulled onto the edge of a gravel road and watched. At first, I didn't know what I was seeing and hearing. Movement in the cornfields. A chorus of trills, trumpets, rattles, calls, and croaks. A sky speckled with black dots. Dropping out of the sky were big birds, with broad, cupped wings, over six feet from tip to tip, fully extended necks, and dangling legs, an almost cartoonish sight that reminded me of people dangling from parachutes. I had never seen or heard anything like this great congregation. I wept with joy. Now, I return to the central Platte each spring just as the cranes do. The cranes know of no other springs than these along the Platte. How good and homey this stretch of the river must be to them after so many spring returns.

~

The sandhill crane has had many Nebraska landscapes "to scan . . . and commit its topographic features to the collective memories of the flock." Nearly ten-million-year-old crane fossils, similar to those of the Crowned Cranes, one of the two crane subfamilies, were found buried in beds of volcanic ash at Ash Falls Fossil Beds State Historical Park near Royal, Nebraska. Typical Cranes, the other subfamily, which includes the sandhills (*Grus canadensis*), first appear in the fossil record in the Miocene epoch, twenty-three million to five million years ago. In the 1920s, Dr. Alexander Wetmore, an avian paleontologist with the Smithsonian Institution, found an eight- to ten-million-year-old fossilized humerus, or "arm bone," of one of the Typical Cranes in Nebraska. Wetmore said that he couldn't distinguish this bone from that of a contemporary sandhill crane.

Grus canadensis were here when the Rockies were being uplifted and the climate changed enough that the forests contracted and the grasslands evolved. Did the Miocene cranes migrate, too, or were they permanent residents of what is now Nebraska, sharing the landscape year-round with exotic grazing mammals (rhinoceroses, elephants, camels, and the curious ancestors of the pig, sheep, deer, and horse) and equally exotic predators (lions, short-faced bears, dire wolves, and saber-toothed cats)?

The sandhill cranes were here during the Pliocene, when the world became colder and ice sheets formed and descended upon the center of North America. During this time, the cranes fed, danced, and roosted in a landscape covered by ice and bordered by arctic tundra or coniferous forests. The cranes were here as the landscape, flora, and fauna were reshaped by the repeated waxing and waning of the great glaciers. The cranes persisted as much of the megafauna, for whatever reason or cluster of reasons—volcanoes, meteorites, climate change, or the arrival of new species, namely, spear-hurling, flesh-eating humans— became extinct.

During the early Pleistocene, the cranes were here when wind-blown loess, a yellowish, "rock flour" sediment, covered glacial deposits in parts of Nebraska, Iowa, and Missouri. In this period they shared the sky with giant condors and teratorns, as well as birds that we recognize. Ten thousand years ago, at the beginning of the Holocene, the current epoch, the cranes were here when meltwater from the Rockies moved east across the Great Plains to the Missouri River in a sprawling, braided course. For ten thousand springs, the sandhill cranes have danced and loafed near the Platte.

The cranes were there as almost a half million people passed over the Great Platte River Road on foot or horse or in wagons to what is now Utah, Oregon, Colorado, and California in the mid-nineteenth century. Nebraska historians James C. Olson and Ronald C. Naugle called this road, with its "broad, flat valley" and its easy climb to the foothills of the Rockies, one of the world's "great natural highways." The cranes were there when some of those emigrants settled down, planting corn and wheat and trees, building cities, towns, roads, and railroads. The rapid decimation of sandhill crane populations in Nebraska, due to the loss of habitat and overhunting, began with gusto in the 1870s. The 1925 account of sandhill cranes in Arthur Cleveland Bent's *Life Histories of Familiar North American Birds* includes a quotation by Professor Wells W. Cooke, an expert on bird migrations, that suggests how precarious the crane's existence once was: "Its numbers have decreased decidedly in the past thirty years, and it is now rare as a breeder in the southern half of the above-defined breeding range. . . . It is interesting to note that it still breeds commonly in Florida where it can still find large tracts of uninhabited, open plains; *here it will perhaps make its last stand*" (italics are mine).

The cranes survived several waves of extinctions, including those of the nineteenth and twentieth centuries, and were here when the last passenger pigeon, Carolina parakeet, heath hen, great auk, Bachman's warbler, slender-billed grackle, Labrador duck, and numerous species of hummingbirds drew their final breaths. Because of the passage and enforcement of the United States' Migratory Bird Act of 1913 and the Migratory Bird Treaty of 1916 between the United States and Canada, sandhill crane populations increased, though in 2005 the National Audubon Society reported that when compared to their historic numbers, all sandhill crane populations are low. Perhaps they will not survive the present, human-made "extinction spasm." Currently, every Central Flyway state and Alaska permit regulated hunting of the sandhill crane except Nebraska, where it is against the law every day of the year.

The cranes were here as people diverted the waters of the Platte for irrigation, electricity, and municipal water supplies, constricting the crane's staging area from two hundred to eighty then to forty tight miles. Cranes are here in the twenty-first century as people fight each other for every last drop of water in the narrower, shallower Platte.

Because of the severe drought in the early years of the new century, as well as continuing depletions from dams and water-diversion projects in Colorado, Wyoming, and western Nebraska, the channels of the Platte in south-central Nebraska ran dry. What would you call this dry, cracked, weedy earth if you didn't know that it was a river? During those drought years, the Platte didn't flow again until it picked up water from the Loup River near Columbus.

A century ago, the Platte was a different river. Then, the channel was one to three miles wide in the spring and with far more sandbars than it has now: a river of water and sand. Because it flooded most springs and because of the scouring action of ice, the Platte was relatively free of trees and vegetation: a wide, open, shape-shifting river. Now the river carries less than one-third of its historic flow, so the channels are thick with cottonwoods, willows, goldenrod, false indigo, purple loosestrife, phragmites, salt cedar, reed canary grass, and Russian olives: a narrow, enclosed, predictable river.

I know the older river through the written accounts of those who traveled there long ago. Many traveling on the Great Platte River Road, also called the Mormon, Oregon, or Overland Trail, were struck by the flatness of the river. In 1859, emigrant Martha Missouri Moore wrote, "The river is a perfect curiosity, it is so very different from any of our streams that it is hard to realize that a river should be running so near the top of the ground without any timber, and no bank at all."

As Erwin Hinckley Barbour, a professor of geology at the University of Nebraska, was studying the homemade windmills of the Platte River Valley in the 1890s, he observed that this "singular and highly interesting river" was so "overloaded and taxed beyond its power" that it couldn't "carry its burden of sand out of the State." Barbour notes that "its energy is spent in shifting its sand bars from side to side and in forming a lace work of channels through its broad bed." Because the river was constantly receiving deposits of sand, its bed was built up fifty to two hundred feet or more—which is why it ran "so near the top of the ground."

Loren Eiseley, one of Barbour's students, was struck by the Platte's changeability. In *The Immense Journey*, he describes the river: "In the spring floods, on occasion, [the river] can be a mile-wide roaring torrent of destruction, gulping farms and bridges. Normally, however, it is a rambling, dispersed series of streamlets flowing erratically over great sand and gravel fans that are, in part, the remnants of a mightier Ice Age stream bed. Quick sands and shifting islands haunt its waters." For Eiseley, the Platte was a "treacherous place ... where neither water nor land prevails," the latter a sentiment captured in the often-repeated saw "The Platte is a mile wide, an inch deep, too thick to drink, and too thin to plow."

While I will never know the wild and free river that long-ago residents, explorers, emigrants, and cranes saw, I can imagine a Platte that has been restored to some of its former glory: rushing, scouring, braiding, flooding, emptying, gulping, frothing, sprawling, ravaging, winding, roaring, withering, nurturing, murmuring, shifting, haunting. I can imagine a Platte where sandhill and whooping cranes are comfortably spread out over the entire, 200-mile-wide bend in the river, all the way from Chapman to North Platte.

For most of its existence, the Platte, with its braided land and water, has been a place of extravagant abundance for cranes. After their long, energy-consuming flight to the Platte, they need to pack on 20 to 25 percent of their weight in fat to sustain them as they complete the journey to their still-frozen breeding grounds, where food isn't yet available. For many millennia, the cranes found enough calcium, protein, and minerals in the wet meadows near the Platte to trigger the breeding process and to make eggshells and embryos. In the past century, they met most of their caloric needs not in the prairie near the river but in the cornfields that have replaced the prairies.

And for many millennia, the Platte was a secure place for the cranes. Because cranes find safety not in concealment but in exposure, they sleep standing in water or on slightly submerged sandbars in the wide shallowness of the Platte. Dogs and coyotes or, in wilder times, wolves and bobcats were reluctant or unwilling to cross the water. But if one did, the cranes could easily spot it from the middle of a river flushed clean of vegetation by spring floods, and flee or fight the intruder with their sharp-clawed feet.

Now the Platte is a different river. While the cranes prefer channels that are five hundred feet wide, they've settled for fifty feet. While they prefer a wide open space around their roosting areas, they've settled for a place where vegetation obscures their view. With so many of these beautiful creatures concentrated in such a small space, one cluster of tornadoes, one outbreak of avian cholera or other virulent disease, one prolonged drought, or one violent winter storm could be catastrophic. Since 80 percent of the world's sandhill crane population gathers on the Platte in the late spring and early winter, and since cranes have a low reproductive rate (one or two eggs per breeding cycle, with only one of the young surviving), one catastrophe could cause the crane population to crash.

It's not only the roosting conditions that have changed. Many of the wet meadows have been drained for agriculture or houses, businesses, streets, and highways, and more-efficient combines leave less grain in the fields. Gary L. Krapu, a biologist with the North Prairie Wildlife Research Center, notes that in the late 1970s, cranes could meet their energy needs within two or three miles of the river; but by the late 1990s, they had to range several miles beyond the valley to feed. More work for the same amount of food.

Still, they keep returning. The Missouri River is too deep and hasn't the wet meadows of the Platte. Neither the Loup in central Nebraska nor the Niobrara in the northern part of the state has shallow sandbars and wet meadows. The Republican has been so tapped for irrigation along its course in Colorado, Nebraska, and Kansas that it's little more than a trickle. Quite simply, there is no other river near the middle of the sandhill crane's migratory route that meets its requirements for a staging ground with calories from grain, calcium from invertebrates, and relatively safe roosts.

When we watch a river flow past, we are seeing both groundwater and surface water. James Goeke, a hydrologist at the University of Nebraska–Lincoln's School of Natural Resources, says that groundwater makes up 50 to

90 percent of the flow of the Platte. When one pumps out groundwater that is connected to a river, one has intercepted water that would have flowed into that river. *Hydrologically connected* is the term that describes this intimate link. According to the U.S. Geological Survey, since 1950, just prior to the boom in the extensive development of groundwater irrigation, the water level in the High Plains Aquifer, an Ice Age ocean underlying most of the Great Plains, has fallen in some places by several feet per year. Currently, 94 percent of the groundwater withdrawals in Nebraska are for irrigation. As of August 2007, over 90,000 active irrigation wells were pumping water in Nebraska, with the highest density of wells (sixteen wells per square mile) in the Central Platte Valley, where the cranes stage. Even when the river shriveled and disappeared during the drought of the early years of the new century, the center-pivot sprinklers continued to rain on the corn and soybeans. It's no wonder the Platte carries less water than it once did.

Until recently, the State of Nebraska split the duties of regulating water use between the twenty-three Natural Resources Districts (NRDs), which managed groundwater, and the Nebraska Department of Natural Resources, which managed surface water. But in 2004, Legislative Bill 962 passed, requiring the two entities to manage hydrologically connected surface water and groundwater as a single, integrated unit. Moreover, LB 962 requires that NRDs in basins with water shortages lessen water use through a plan that the individual NRD and the Department of Natural Resources develop together. In April 2006, the Department added a provision to LB 962 that established a regulating formula called 10–50. According to this formula, surface water and groundwater are connected if the pumping of groundwater depletes a stream by 10 percent over a 50-year period. A 10–50 area must be treated as a single, integrated system.

Because of LB 962, the 130-mile stretch of the Platte River Basin between Columbus and Lexington has been declared "fully appropriated," meaning that no water remains for new development. The Platte River between Kearney and the city of North Platte, and the North and South Platte rivers have all been declared overappropriated, meaning that cuts must be imposed since existing water use has exceeded the supply. In other words, the wet meadows are drier and so less productive than they used to be, and the cranes are packed into even fewer roosts along an even narrower stretch of the river, in water that is already claimed, with none to spare.

Various groups are fighting to save the Platte for the cranes and for those of us who can't live without them. The Lillian Annette Rowe Sanctuary, owned and managed by the National Audubon Society, was founded in 1974, when Rowe, a New Jersey teacher, donated 7,832 acres and 2.5 miles of river channel and wetlands. Today, the sanctuary includes 1,448 acres and several miles of river channel. To preserve the river and meadows for sandhill and whooping cranes and other migrating birds, sanctuary employees and volunteers clear woody growth from the sandbars and the river channels, fight the invasive species that drink up so much water, and maintain the nearby prairies through grazing, haying, and prescribed burnsThe nonprofit Platte River Whooping Crane Maintenance Trust conserves habitat along the Platte River in central Nebraska for whooping and sandhill cranes and other migratory birds. The trust was formed in 1978 as part of a settlement stemming from the construction of the Grayrocks Dam and Reservoir and the Laramie River Power Station on a tributary of the North Platte River near Wheatland, Wyoming. The State of Nebraska filed suit claiming that the Rural Electrification Association, which was funding the project, and the U.S. Army Corps of Engineers, which had issued permits for the project, were compromising the habitat of endangered species and so were in violation of the Endangered Species Act (ESA) of 1973 and the National Environmental Policy Act of 1969. The chief species at risk was the whooping crane, though other listed species, including the bald eagle, Eskimo curlew, American burying beetle, and western prairie fringed orchid, were also affected. In order to be allowed to complete the dam, reservoir, and power station, the Missouri Basin Power Project agreed to provide $7.5 million to fund a trust. In turn, Congress granted the project an exemption from the ESA. With income from this endowment, the trust has acquired and managed ten thousand acres of habitat and conducted research about migratory birds and their habitat needs. It is one of the reasons why the whooping crane population rose from 22 in 1941 to 535 (both wild and captive) in 2010. Of the 383 wild whooping cranes, most pass through Nebraska on their path between the Gulf Coast and Alberta.

The Platte River Recovery Implementation Program (PRRIP), a major restoration program backed by the federal government, had its origins in 1994, when the U.S. Fish and Wildlife Service issued a biological opinion stating that restrictions had to be imposed on Platte River water use in order for users in the Platte River Basin to comply with the ESA. The federally threatened or endangered species listed in the opinion were the whooping crane, interior least tern, piping plover, and pallid sturgeon, the last a fish found in the Lower Platte. Like the sandhill cranes, each of the listed birds requires open river channels, bare sandbars, and an adequate stream flow.

The PRRIP, which was developed in response to the U.S. Fish and Wildlife Service opinion, is a joint, Platte River Basin–wide effort between the Department of the Interior and the states of Colorado, Wyoming, and Nebraska to provide habitat for the three listed bird species that use the central Platte. The agencies involved in the PRRIP are working to meet three goals during the first thirteen years of the plan. First, they will increase the stream flow in the central Platte to normal levels by releasing water stored in upriver reservoirs such as Lake McConaughy. Second, they will acquire, restore, and maintain 10,000 acres of new habitat in the Central Platte Valley by 2019, eventually increasing that to a total of 29,000 acres. To expose the sandbars, unclog the channels, and lessen the water loss to thirsty invasive plants, the program also funds the removal of trees and vegetation growing in the riverbed. Third, they will return the river to its July 1, 1997, level of development, in terms of water use and associated river depletion. Since irrigation takes the lion's share of the Platte, farmers and ranchers must reduce the amount of water they pump onto their fields. Any new or expanded water uses that diminish the stream flow must be offset by such methods as water rights transfer, groundwater recharge projects, relocating or retiming groundwater withdrawals, crop mixing, and changes in tillage practices.

Needless to say, the program has critics. Nebraskans First, an organization of Nebraska irrigators "dedicated to protecting Nebraska's groundwater for agriculture," claims that "it took over a century of hard work and investment by Nebraska farmers to develop the Central Platte River Basin from nothing into a productive agricultural powerhouse," and that "this success story" may now "be undone for an unnecessary and contrived species/habitat program." Several months after PRRIP was signed into law, on May 8, 2008, Mike Dobesh, a farmer from Wood River and a board member of the Central Platte NRD, presented his objections to the PRRIP in "The Platte River Boondoggle," a guest editorial published in the *Lincoln Journal Star*. Because "the first phase of the compact, as well as LB962, calls for farmers to get back to 1997 levels of irrigation development, which is more than 400,000 acres in the Platte River valley," Dobesh predicts that the economic impact on the state from the loss of crops on those irrigated acres will be devastating. Like many who oppose limits on water use on behalf of wildlife, Dobesh believes that "to address the issue of low river flows, one should look at the trees and invasive species of plants in the river, the salt cedar, purple loosestrife and phragmites" rather than the irrigators. On October 8, 2009, an article in the *Omaha World-Herald* reported that research conducted by the U.S. Geological Survey in 2002 and 2006 near Gothenburg and Odessa shows that trees along the central Platte require far less water than previously believed. In fact, the trees, which require 22.2 inches of water per year, use less water than the corn crop, which requires 26 inches per year. Annual rainfall in the central Platte during 2002 and 2006 averaged 24.3 inches per year. While there are many benefits for wildlife in removing the strip of invasive plant species along the Platte, a far greater way to increase water levels in the Platte would be to limit the number of irrigated acres.

October 2008 was the wettest on record in Kearney and the second wettest in Grand Island, but if there's another severe, extended drought here or in one of the world's other food-producing regions, if fuel prices soar and grain becomes an even more desirable way to fuel engines, will there be greater incentive to raise irrigated crops with land and water that the cranes need? If the staging grounds become more crowded, if calcium and calories become harder to find, if no other river will suffice, what will become of the cranes?

On a sunny Saturday in late October, I hike through the Lillian Annette Rowe Sanctuary to the river, hoping for cranes. The prairies and woods are tan, yellow, and seedy (curly locust pods, tiny hackberries, empty milkweed pods, hairy seed heads of little bluestem), and the grasshoppers are on their last legs. I have never gone to the central Platte during the fall to look for migrating cranes, and for good reason. They merely pass through on their way south, stopping for no more than a night, if they stop at all. In the fall, the cranes stage farther north, in the prairie provinces of Canada, in the Dakotas, and in northwestern Minnesota. Though I don't see a single crane on the ground, the sky is full of migrating birds—Canada and white-fronted geese, mallards, pintails, blue-winged teals, and sandhill cranes. I know the last because of the slow, heavy movements of their massive wings. As I watch the sky, I imagine that this is how a late-winter, early-spring morning on the central Platte might look if the cranes found another river: no cranes roosting in the river, no cranes dancing in the fields; cranes merely passing overhead. But for now, I count on a half million cranes returning next spring as surely as I count on the new, green thrust of little bluestem and common milkweed.

When I arrive here next spring, I'll look closely and carefully, as if this is my last chance to see the cranes so close to home. I'll note the texture of the red patch that starts at the base of the bill and extends just under and beyond the eyes. From photographs I've seen, it looks stubbly, more like the bare, pink-purple head of a vulture than the red-feathered head of a woodpecker. I want to discern if this blaring red, so painfully bright on a gray day, is scarlet, crimson, cherry, ruby, or some other red. I'll see for myself if the edges of the long, strong bill really are serrated and make it easier for the crane to grasp slippery food. I'll observe the crane's "true" tail, the short, stiff, unremarkable tail that I've never noticed before, as well as the more familiar false one, formed by the long, drooping, inner-wing feathers that, when folded, create a frilly, out-of-character embellishment, what many have called a "bustle." I'll watch the dance closely enough that I can join in, bowing my head, strutting a bit, tossing sticks, and leaping high above the earth. I'll listen carefully to what Aldo Leopold described as "a pandemonium of trumpets, rattles, croaks, and cries" that issue from the crane's long and convoluted trachea, until I can translate these utterances into human words and phrases. I'll hide in a blind so that I can look a sandhill crane in its yellow eye and see this and more distant landscapes reflected back.

15

Nine-Mile Prairie

Manner of Speaking

I'm going there today. But I can't find the right preposition to capture the experience. Will I go *onto* the prairie, as if it's the upper surface of something, a plane or a platform to pass over? Will I go *into* the prairie, as if it's something that can surround or envelope me like an economic recession or a waiting room? Will I go *through* the prairie, as if it's a substance like water or an ordeal like menopause to move into and beyond? Or will I go *around* the prairie, metaphorically skirting its edges, since it's an enigma whose meaning I've yet to discover?

And what of the articles *a* or *the*? Will I go to *a* prairie, *a* being a fragment of the once-vast grassland in the center of North America, or will I go to *the* prairie, the whole from which the relict is preserved or has somehow escaped destruction, a whole that still exists, even if only in the imagination? What I can say: I'm going there today.

Fervor

Nine-Mile Prairie is so named because it is five miles west and four miles north of the City Campus of the University of Nebraska at Lincoln (UNL). Not so long ago, these nine miles were more open and rural. Now, to get to Nine-Mile, you cross Interstate 80, pass new housing developments and apartment complexes, turn west on Highway 34, pass the Kawasaki factory that employs over a thousand people, pass the north side of the Lincoln Municipal Airport, pass fields planted with corn or soybeans, pass a Casey's convenience store, an RV storage site, and a pallet manufacturer, and then turn west onto West Fletcher Street. South of where West Fletcher dead-ends is Nine-Mile Prairie. At first glance, the prairie is nothing but weeds, brush, sparrows, and fences—

what you'd find at home if you let the yard go. But if you become acquainted with this prairie, you will find it remarkable. All but 20 of the 230 acres that comprise Nine-Mile have never been broken, none have been grazed since 1968, and each have been burned about every three years since 1979. This small prairie relict supports astonishing diversity: over 80 species of birds, 392 vascular plants, including the threatened western prairie fringed orchid, and the rare regal fritillary butterfly. In the early years of the new millennium, almost 300,000 of us live in Lancaster County. But if you keep your eyes to the ground at Nine-Mile, you can imagine what most of this county in southeastern Nebraska looked like a century and a half ago, when there were but 153 white residents.

My first encounter with prairie occurred at Nine-Mile in the fall of 1989 through Ecology of the Great Plains, a course I was taking at UNL. On a Saturday morning in September, I rode the bus the nine miles between the City Campus and the prairie with the other students in the class and, since I hadn't been able to find a babysitter, with my five-year-old son, Ian. We walked the rutted lane between two pieces of fenced-off land owned by the airport and entered a whole new world. When the professor showed us big bluestem, the premiere grass of tallgrass prairie, I fell in love with it. For me it was its second common name, turkey foot, a reference to the shape of the seed head (three long racemes, or flower clusters, three long turkey toes), that made this grass easy to remember at the time. Now it's the scientific name, *Andropogon gerardii*, that intrigues me because of the link it suggests between this grass and humans. The Greek *andros* means "man," *pogon* means "bearded" (the seeds of big bluestem are very hairy), and *gerardii* contains the name of the botanist who first described the species in scientific terms, Louis Gerard. Big bluestem is a tall, bearded man. The other common name, big bluestem, has always puzzled me. While the stem *is* big, there's nothing blue about it that I can see. During its growing season, it's green. Big greenstem. In a damp year, it greets my September birthday with bronze-purple stems and seed heads that I look up to. Big winestem.

I don't remember what else the professor showed us that morning, but I do remember the pond, which then had water in it, and the cottonwoods near it. I remember that the late morning was prickly hot and that my attentions were divided between the lecture I was supposed to be hearing and Ian, who had grown bored and restless. Nonetheless, something happened at Nine-Mile on that September morning that led me there again and again and led me to seek other swatches of prairie, both native ones and restorations. After my daughter, Meredith, was born in 1991, it was seven full months before I had the time, energy, and attention to finish a piece of writing. That piece was an essay about wildflowers that I'd seen that summer at Nine-Mile.

When the Cistercian monk Thomas Merton was selecting poems to be included in a new collection, he realized that those that he'd written during his early years in the monastery, when the communion, intimacy, and asceticism were so new and so intense, were his best. "The fervor of those days was special and young," Merton wrote. "It can inspire one to seek a new and different kind of fervor which is older and deeper." I, too, have sought an older and deeper kind of fervor. Seventeen years ago, I was eager to match names in the field guide to the plants that I saw and to learn the characteristic grasses and forbs and thus the boundary lines between the different types of prairies—tallgrass, mixed-grass, and short-grass; upland and lowland. Now I'm less interested in names and divisions than in learning how the prairie works, both as individual plants and as a whole, and how a prairie landscape works on my body, mind, and soul. What, in another decade or two, will an even older and deeper fervor lead me to see and love about this place?

Horizontal

On a mild December day, Meredith photographs me standing atop a knoll at Nine-Mile. I imagine that the picture will show the grassy hilltop, a little sky, and me, the only perpendicular. My presence is intended to give scale to my surroundings, yet I imagine that it will appear as an assertion, an effrontery, an impertinence. "Raise your arms," Meredith shouts before she snaps the photo. I do but then drop them. It seems that there is already enough of me in the picture. But when I look at the photo, I'm unsettled by what I see. The hilltop is not a hilltop but an ever so slightly curved horizon, the line of which extends beyond the frame of the photo. I'm just a dark dot on the horizon, smaller than the dark seed heads in the foreground, with one and a half inches of grass beneath me, two and a half inches of sky above me. I'm about to be squashed or canceled out by sky.

In *Prairie Plants and Their Environment*, grassland ecologist John Ernest Weaver defines prairie as a landscape that "appears almost monotonous in the general uniformity of its plant cover. Its main features are the absence of trees, the scarcity of shrubs, the dominance of grasses, and a characteristic xeric flora." In other words, a horizontal landscape. In the photo Meredith took, there are no trees or shrubs. The only plant that I can identify is switchgrass. What I see in the photo are flat, gold islands of that grass against a dun background. But what I remember are clumps or crowns of switchgrass the size of hula hoops, the many-branched seed heads reaching farther into the sky than me. Weaver says nothing in his definition about the sky; yet, its presence in the photo of me on the hill is overpowering. A wide open sky with its ability to divest me of any notions of my own power and importance is as essential as grass to my definition of prairie.

We're easy with horizontal landscapes. There's nothing there that can fall down, or if there was, it's already done so. No threat. Horizontal lines follow the earth and extend into places that we can visit or imagine. At Nine-Mile, that means Iowa and Colorado or South Dakota and Kansas, places I either know well or at least am acquainted with. Consequently, horizontal lines suggest repose, peacefulness, and spaciousness to me. Vertical lines, however, are dramatic and dynamic. One end touches the earth but the other extends into the blue, beyond our ability to follow or imagine. Because the tree, person, steeple, tower, tornado, or lightning bolt has defied gravity in its vertical reach, we feel tense, uneasy. What goes up must come down.

I seek prairie, but not because I find it to be an easy, tranquil setting. On the contrary, the more I learn about prairie, the more I see it as a place of keen competition between the various plants for water, light, and nutrients. Rather, I seek prairie because of the revision that this landscape demands of me. In the city, I walk or drive through a world that is crowded with perpendiculars—houses, utility poles, trees, billboards, and lots of people. The interior of my house and office are just as upright, since there I am, enclosed by walls lined with tall bookcases, looking out through vertical windows, entering and exiting by vertical doors. My days are ordered and enclosed by routine, a vertical list of priorities. When I'm in or on or around prairie, it's tempting to visually latch onto the rare perpendicular, the clump of eastern red cedars near the fence or the cellular phone tower a half mile away, because that's what I've been taught to see and value. I'm like those famous kittens who were reared in the dark except for a brief period each day when they were exposed to one kind of line, vertical for some kittens, horizontal for others. When researchers tested the kittens' visual behavior at the end of five months, they found that each group showed clear visual deficits. For instance, those exposed only to vertical lines gave no response when a researcher held a rod horizontally before them. But when the researcher turned the rod so that it was vertical, the kittens played with it. Likewise, those kittens who were only exposed to horizontal lines were comfortable only in the presence of such. Live and move in a world that is primarily vertical and that's what you come to see and expect.

Seeing and accepting the openness and the open-endedness of prairie counters what I've been taught—that open space, like silence, is an uncomfortable emptiness to be filled, even if all that one has to put there is clutter or chatter. When I'm on or in prairie, I try to keep my attention from contracting and moving in the usual up-and-down pattern. I soften my vision, loosen my grip, and allow my awareness to expand: forward, backward, and sideways. Then I feel as though I've just thrown off my corset, broken the habit, paid off the debt, been cleared of the charges. In the presence of such freedom, I'm giddy and wary. Reason enough to preserve prairie landscapes.

As a study site now owned by the University of Nebraska Foundation, Nine-Mile is relatively safe, though global climate disruption may cause, may have already caused some grasses to retreat and be replaced by others that can thrive in droughtier conditions. At the moment, the main threat to Nine-Mile is vertical and aerial. In 2005, Lincoln Electric Service (LES) planned to meet the electrical demands in Lincoln's growing northwest quadrant, where I now live, by erecting steel towers over one hundred feet tall along the western edge of the prairie to support wires carrying 115 and 345 kilovolts. Environmentalists were successful in persuading LES's administrative board not to install the towers on the prairie's western edge, but they couldn't stop the board from erecting them along the southern edge. Yet one more obstruction in the sky. An open sky above the prairie creates a sense of vastness. A sky broken by tall, heavy towers diminishes the breadth of the land beneath it by putting it on a human scale. Put perpendiculars on, in, through, or around the prairie and it is no longer the horizontal landscape that can unsettle, reorganize, and ultimately restore us.

Prairie Roots

John Ernest Weaver was a man of open spaces. He was born in Villisca, Iowa, in 1884, a time when there was still plenty of prairie in southwestern Iowa. He arrived in Lincoln in 1905 and spent all but a few of his adult years there, first as a student at the university, where he received his BS in 1909 and his MA in 1911, and later as a professor of plant ecology. During his thirty-five-year tenure at UNL, Weaver directed forty-two doctoral dissertations and over fifty master's theses, and wrote numerous books and articles, as my bookshelves attest. Weaver was remarkable in that he spent his life studying and trying to preserve what most people of his time and place broke up and filled in, with no remorse for what they'd destroyed. Two weeks before his death in 1966, he delivered the manuscript of *Prairie Plants and Their Environment: A Fifty-Year Study in the Midwest* to the University of Nebraska Press. A Lincolnite who knew Weaver says that the old man was buried with prairie dirt beneath his fingernails.

Nine-Mile Prairie was where Weaver tested the botanical philosophy of Frederic E. Clements, his mentor at UNL and at the University of Minnesota, where Weaver received his PhD, and Nine-Mile Prairie was where Weaver was eventually forced to depart from the tenets of Clementsian botany. For Weaver, Nine-Mile was a laboratory and a philosophical testing ground.

Weaver and Clements believed that the prairie formation is a single organism. In the 1929 edition of their widely adopted textbook *Plant Ecology*, they maintain, "Each formation [large unit of vegetation] is a complex and definite organic entity with a characteristic development and structure." And they believed that all plant succession, by which Weaver and Clements meant the series of plant communities that occupy an area as the vegetation develops, is progressive. In other words, plants evolve toward the final or "climax stage" best suited to a climate: pine and hemlock forest near the Great Lakes, basin sagebrush in Nevada and Utah. Before settlement, the relatively flat, open center of the continent was appropriate for wide herds of bison and grasses, but the type of grasses and their associates varied according to climatic factors. From central Indiana to eastern Nebraska was tallgrass prairie, dominated by big bluestem, Indiangrass, and switchgrass. Mixed-grass prairie covered all but the eastern- and westernmost edges of Nebraska, Kansas, and the Dakotas and was comprised mostly of grasses two to four feet tall—needlegrass, prairie dropseed, little bluestem, June grass, side-oats grama, and western wheatgrass. The grasses of the "short-grass disclimax," referred to thus by Weaver because it wasn't a natural stage but one caused by overgrazing, thrived on the High Plains; these grasses were six to eighteen inches tall and were dominated by buffalo grass, blue grama, and triple-awn. Weaver and Clements insist that the dominant climax form of prairie isn't tallgrass but "true" prairie, which once formed a fairly distinct band between tallgrass and mixed-grass prairie. By *true prairie*, they meant a final and stable form of prairie characterized by porcupine grass and tall dropseed. Tallgrass prairie is neither stable nor final since in the absence of fire, it becomes either deciduous forest or true prairie. Weaver and Clements considered tallgrass prairie to be "postclimax," a corruption of sorts that resulted when true prairie was damaged by cultivation and overgrazing. In response, big bluestem moved up the slopes and displaced needlegrass and prairie dropseed as the dominant species. Nine-Mile is within the belt of what was once true prairie.

Weaver and Clements believed that if prairie is damaged or destroyed, it will eventually return to its original state, provided that people don't interfere. The more or less predictable sequence of species that occupy a disturbed site is called "old field" or "secondary" succession. Aerial photographs show that twenty acres at Nine-Mile were cultivated in the early 1940s and probably abandoned shortly thereafter. Aerial photos from the early 1950s show the return of prairie vegetation. After sixty-some years of secondary succession, the edges of "Old Field," as it's now called, are dominated by big bluestem and look like the rest of Nine-Mile. But nearer the center of Old Field are tufts of little bluestem and side-oats grama. Eventually, tall grasses will dominate there, too. This process also occurs on a larger scale. Weaver and Clements believed that short-grass would eventually become mixed-grass prairie, which in turn would eventually become true prairie. Ultimately, secondary succession would triumph. While humans could interfere with this natural process, nothing could destroy the prairie.

Prairie once flourished between southern Manitoba and north-central Texas. Because Lincoln lies near the midpoint, Weaver believed that data from Nine-Mile was representative of conditions over a vast area. There was no better place for him to be. He conducted experiments at what he called the "true prairie station outside of Lincoln," which may refer to Black's, or Belmont, Prairie, 180 upland acres three miles north of the university, probably destroyed for a farm that later became the site of a housing development or stores and parking lots, or to Nine-Mile Prairie, the prairie that Weaver named.

Weaver had various methods for studying the plant communities at these stations. My favorite is the "bisect," in which he and his students dug trenches in the prairie deeper than the deepest roots and excavated the root systems. A photograph in *Prairie Plants* shows a fair, rather young man in a dress shirt and a derby standing in a trench a good three feet taller than him. This man—perhaps he is Weaver—points at something in the trench wall with what appears to be a small bowling pin. Weaver excavated the underground parts of each plant with a hand pick, washed, dried, and measured them, and then plotted the entire root system to scale on coordinate paper. These drawings not only show the form of the root systems of different species but also reveal their relationships to each other and to the different layers of soil. In a bisect drawing from mixed-grass prairie near Hayes, Kansas, one can see that the root system of wild alfalfa, or scurf pea, a legume, plunges eight feet. And diminutive buffalo grass, with only five inches of leaves and stems above ground, sends its roots down five feet.

Two things strike me when I look at Weaver's bisect drawings: the root systems are intricate, beautiful, gracefully branching affairs, and there is more prairie beneath the ground than above it. The roots of the different plants draw nutrients and water from different locations, the tall grasses in the moister lowlands and the shorter grasses on rockier, drier, or hilltop sites, as if they're sharing resources. How could one not have faith that such an organism would persist?

Oceans, Islands, Coasts

The comparison people are most likely to reach for when describing grassland is that of an ocean. Aldo Leopold, who like me was born and raised on a wooded bluff above the Mississippi in Burlington but spent his adult life in a prairie place, uses the metaphor to express his thoughts after watching an Illinois farmer cut down an ancient cottonwood: "Time was when that tree was a buoy in the prairie seas." In *Flowering Earth*, botanist Donald Culross Peattie describes prairie, "There is no close-up here and no detail. Instead, there is horizon like the sea line; there are seas of grass here, running before an unwearied wind, waves of grass winnowing one way to show all silver and dimpling another to darken all green." In *The Prairie World*, a collection of lyrical essays packaged as an ecological textbook, David F. Costello relates, "Whenever I cross the shoreline of the grassland sea I stop and eagerly examine a niche or two of this extraordinarily variable boundary to see what it harbors." When tallgrass prairie stretched from central Indiana to eastern Nebraska, it took weeks to cross and was as dangerous as an ocean passage. When the tall grasses are ripe and head- or shoulder-high at summer's end, walking across the prairie is like trudging through water. Like the ocean, prairie is or was a horizontal landscape that makes people feel small, insignificant, and vulnerable. And unless you know how to see it, prairie, like the ocean, appears flat and monotonous. Years ago when I showed Nine-Mile to my former husband, who had grown up near the lush and vertically crowded rainforest of South America, he said, "This is it? It looks like a cornfield.Sometimes when I walk on, in, through, or around prairie, I try to imagine it as an ocean of grass. Bunches of little bluestem, light green in the spring, purple and coppery in the autumn, are an archipelago. At the bottom of the hill, a swell of big bluestem. As the wind moves across the prairie, the grasses and forbs bounce, quiver, or wave in response: a sea of movement. This is a tide that slows but never recedes. Prairie coasts aren't clean affairs. Borders fluctuate; the size of the islands of grasses and forbs expand and contract according to the moisture level. A fence attempts to part a prairie preserve from the adjacent golf course or pasture or housing subdivision or airport runway, but plants slip beneath it. A little buffalo grass over there, a little leafy spurge over here. Like water, prairie doesn't stop at the property line.

But the prairie-ocean metaphor fails in significant ways. To what do I compare this variegated surface, comprised of blooming milkweeds, gay-feathers, orchids, clovers, leadplant, sageworts, thistles, goldenrods, and the prodigal number of asters? And what of size? The coasts or borders of oceans and prairie are both changing, but one is expanding and one is contracting. As glaciers and ice caps melt in response to rising levels of carbon dioxide in the atmosphere, the seas grow deeper and wider. Wider oceans threaten such major, low-lying American port cities as Boston, New York, Charleston, Miami, and New Orleans, as well as such low-lying or island nations as Bangladesh and the Republic of Maldives. In contrast, the North American prairie is less than one-tenth of 1 percent of its former size. No other North American biome has suffered such destruction. What remains of the once-vast prairie are these little, fenced-off relicts, just a few hundred or a few dozen acres preserved by Audubon and other conservationist groups, each relict in danger of being devoured by sprawling towns, cities, and highways or so invaded by alien species that it's just another weedy plot. Prairie is not an ocean.

Revision

Weaver couldn't imagine that anything could destroy the prairie and enable it to be replaced by some import such as Kentucky bluegrass or smooth brome. What shook his exuberant faith in this stability and his certainty about progressive succession was the Great Drought of 1933–1942. Weaver began studying the effects of the drought in 1934, then the driest summer on record in Nebraska. For thirty-nine days that year, the air temperature in eastern Nebraska was above one hundred degrees. In July of 1934, Weaver observed that no water was available in the soil for plant growth to a depth of four feet. From a distance, the prairie looked normal, but when Weaver studied the basal cover, he found "holes or openings in the prairie carpet." Dead rhizomes of big bluestem and Indian grass. Dead crowns of little bluestem and prairie dropseed. Pale stem-bases of needlegrass and blue grama grass. Weeds flourishing in the once-healthy sod. Where the drought was most severe, the soil was bare. Western wheatgrass, that drought-adapted opportunist, quickly invaded such stretches. Buffalo grass and the invasive six-weeks fescue followed.

Weaver doesn't say that studying the effects of the drought was painful for him, but I can't imagine it being otherwise. "Each prairie studied," he offers in *Prairie Plants*, "was known intimately; hence any changes were readily and clearly observed." For Weaver, Nine-Mile was a graveyard of sorts, both for the true-prairie plants that he loved and for the microparadigm that his research supported.

Within seven years of the beginning of the drought, Weaver watched the true prairie of central Kansas, eastern Nebraska, and eastern South Dakota being replaced by mixed-grass prairie in an area 100 to 150 miles wide. Big bluestem, which thrives in moist lowlands, nearly disappeared. The changes that Weaver and Clements made for the 1938 edition of *Plant Ecology* reveal that their faith in the resilience of the prairie had eroded. The coauthors still maintained that climax communities may display superficial changes "with the season, year, or cycle," but that several years in a row of abnormal rainfall or unusual temperatures would have "little or no permanent effect upon their composition and structure." Yet, Weaver qualified his and Clements's earlier claims about the inevitability of progressive succession and admitted that "man alone can destroy the stability of the climax." Historian Ronald C. Tobey suspects that these revisions were Weaver's rather than Clements's. Indeed, in "The North American Prairie," which appeared in *The American Scholar* in 1944, after Weaver had seen the full effect of the drought and after the rains had returned, Weaver grimly and eloquently concluded, "Prairie is much more than land covered with grass. It is a slowly evolved, highly complex entity, centuries old. It approaches the eternal. Once destroyed it can never be replaced by man." Gone was his faith that true prairie would reclaim the heart of the continent. Perhaps Weaver wanted to revise every present-tense sentence he'd ever written about the prairie, changing "the prairie *is*" to "the prairie *was*."

If Weaver were conducting studies at Nine-Mile today, I suspect that he'd be fencing off square yards of prairie with steel tapes and stakes. In these "list" or "census" quadrats, he'd note the number and ratio of the different plant species from year to year, so that he could quantify the retreat of prairie in the face of global climate disruption. This year, a little less of the moisture-loving tall grasses. Next year, a little less. Each year, a smaller and smaller chance of recovery. The prairie *was*.

Relict

In March 2001, the U.S. Postal Service issued an international postage stamp bearing a photograph of Nine-Mile Prairie taken by Lincolnite Michael Forsberg. This stamp is part of the Scenic American Landmarks Series, which includes photos of the Grand Canyon, Niagara Falls, Yosemite, and the Great Smoky Mountains. In "October in the Tallgrass," one sees tall, ripe big bluestem, thick and sumptuous, shagged and tawny as fur or pelt; in the misty distance, scattered trees; above it all, an unobstructed blue sky with wisps of white clouds. The scene is so pristine that it doesn't seem of this world. Forsberg says that he went to Nine-Mile every morning for seven days in October of 1994 before he shot the photo of the six-foot-tall grass. None of the shots were right. But on the seventh day, "I got there just as the sun came up and the fog was lifting. There was no wind and lots of dew, so the color was really rich." Because he wanted to give people a sense of what the tallgrass prairie would have looked like to someone traveling across Nebraska on horseback or in a covered wagon 150 years ago, he took the photo from a stepladder.

I walk Nine-Mile looking for the spot where Forsberg set his camera. North of Nine-Mile is land owned by the Lincoln Municipal Airport Authority. To the east is the skyline of Lincoln, a city of more than a quarter of a million people. To the southeast is a white and orange checkerboard water tower. To the south is a pole building for farm machinery, a windmill that I've never seen spinning, and an enormous, rather new house. The deck on the house faces east for a view of the city rather than north for a view of the prairie and airport. The land near the house is divided into fields, one gray, one yellow, rather than the blended colors of the prairie. Soon, LES will erect towers and electrical lines along this border. To the southwest of Nine-Mile are towers, ladders, ropes, poles, and a guillotine-like contraption: the university's challenge course. To the west is rather open land, the site of ominous-looking bunkers and a former ammunition dump. Forsberg would have had to position his camera very precisely to keep the shot clear of these obstructions. I read that if LES had erected the towers and lines on the western edge of Nine-Mile, they'd have cut right through the scene that Forsberg shot.

By what accident, by what good fortune or act of will was Nine-Mile saved in a place where so little prairie remains? When Weaver conducted his studies at Nine-Mile, it consisted of eight hundred acres. The western part had been part of the Flader homestead. During the Cold War, the Strategic Air Command (SAC) in Bellevue took over the Lincoln Municipal Airport and the prairie. Just west of Nine-Mile, the government built eighteen bunkers. In the interests of security, SAC strung barbed wire, kept the place brightly lit day and night, and limited the university's access to the prairie. In the 1960s, SAC left and Nine-Mile became surplus government property. The Airport Authority bought the land and the bunkers for one hundred dollars per acre and now rents the bunkers as storage space.

In 1978, Ernest Rousek became interested in preserving the prairie. He was the perfect person for the job. While Rousek has a background in conventional agriculture (he trained as a soil scientist at UNL, was a district manager for a hybrid corn company, and invented planter plates that were used to plant three-quarters of the corn crop in the 1970s), he was passionate about saving the landscape he'd always loved. The one-room school that Rousek had attended in central Nebraska had been surrounded by prairie: the school playground. While herding cattle on the family farm, he passed the time by matching the prairie plants that he saw with those in the Nebraska weed identification book. "Prairie just kind of got infiltrated into my system," he says.

When Rousek became interested in preserving Nine-Mile, he found that part of the 800-acre spread had been overgrazed and part had been cultivated. But the southern 230 acres were native and in good condition, except for the 20 acres that had been cultivated in the 1940s. In the late 1970s, Wachiska Audubon, the chapter to which Rousek belongs, rented the 230 acres. Because paying the $4,600 rent each year was a strain for Wachiska, Rousek cut the grass and sold it as hay to the Omaha Stockyards and other customers. Rousek and A. T. Harrison, a professor of biological sciences at UNL, teamed up and sought more permanent protection for the prairie than a year-to-year lease. Initially, the Airport Authority's board of directors offered to sell the land for fifteen thousand dollars per acre, a steep increase over the one hundred dollars per acre that it had paid in the 1960s. When Rousek asked the board to reduce the price, the directors said that the state constitution forbade them from selling land for less than market value. To reduce the price would be tantamount to making a charitable contribution to the Audubon Society.

Rousek and Harrison went to the state legislature to see if they could change the law. Their request sailed through the unicameral unopposed. In April of 1979, the Airport Authority approved a resolution to preserve 230 acres of airport land, then leased to the Wachiska Audubon Society, and agreed that the uniqueness of the native prairie would be recognized in any future deposition. And it agreed to sell the land for $600 per acre—still too high, Rousek thought. He and Harrison tried to persuade the Nature Conservancy to purchase the land but failed because at the time, the conservancy was more interested in preserving larger tracts. They garnered the support of then University of Nebraska chancellor Martin A. Massengale, an agronomist, and the board of regents, but that wasn't enough to save the prairie. Finally, the University of Nebraska Foundation and Marguerite Hall Metzger, whose late husband, Neil W. Hall, had managed the prairie during World War II, each donated $69,000 toward the $138,000 purchase price. The purchase was transacted in 1983. Since then, the foundation has leased Nine-Mile to the university for one dollar per year.

Near the entrance to Nine-Mile, there is a kiosk that Rousek built and that Wachiska Audubon maintains that provides a map and a brief history of the prairie, several of Weaver's drawings of prairie root systems, and Weaver's words of praise for the prairie: "One is awed by its immensity, its complexity, and the seeming impossibility of understanding and describing it. But after certain principles and facts become clear, one comes not only to know and understand the grasslands, but also to delight in them."

Revision

As always, I begin my walk on a mowed path. On this January day, it's the path along the east fence. Nine-Mile sits two hundred feet above the city, so as I walk, I look down on the Lincoln skyline, a familiar place of routine, compactness, and verticality. At this moment, the distance between the city and the prairie seems slight. My prepositional choice of the moment: I am *up on* the prairie.

I turn and walk along the south fence and into the bowl of the former pond. Because of the current drought, the tall grasses haven't lived up to their name for several years. In the past few summers, I've seen more than one pond go dry. The gray high-water marks on the trunks of the cottonwoods encircling the dry bed are probably from the summer of 1993, the wettest summer I've seen since I became acquainted with prairies. That year the grasses were tall, dense, and lush.

In the ravine, sparrows cheep and twitch in the shrubs. The rusty, eastern red cedars are studded with blue, berrylike cones. The red-orange berries of a bittersweet vine clinging to a bare branch are the brightest things I see at Nine-Mile. Looming in the background is the medieval watchtower at the university's challenge course. Thoreau lamented that sometimes he'd walked a mile into the woods "bodily, without getting there in spirit." I am not yet *in* this demanding landscape. I'm not yet *in* the prairie. As I walk, I adapt. Horizontal. Present tense. Body and spirit.

I stand at the bottom of the hill. My eyes scan the jagged line where grass and sky meet. Here, the prairie seems immense. I leave the path and wade through the dry grasses. Burrs stick to my jeans. If Weaver dug trenches here, I see no evidence of them. From the top of the hill where Meredith took my picture not so long ago, I can't escape the fact that Nine-Mile is a fenced-in relict, so small that I couldn't get lost here if I wanted to. Yet I can lose myself here. A red-tailed hawk soars overhead. Beneath the grasses and forbs are the trails that secretive, nocturnal rodents follow as they gather seeds and seek escape from hawks and coyotes, but I've never noticed the trails or the mice. I can identify some plants by their seed heads alone (the plumed and turkey-footed tall grasses, the thistle's prickly vase, the coneflower's cone, the milkweed's split pod), but to whom do these candelabra, torches, corkscrews, spikes, rattles, whisks, and burrs belong? What is this prairie like after dark, in an icestorm, or during a tornado? More than just nine miles separate the city and the prairie. My prepositional choice of the moment: I am *out in* the prairie.

The slanting afternoon sun lights up the rusty bunches of little bluestem's wire-thin leaves, stems, and fuzzy, white seed heads. At this moment, little bluestem is the grass of my heart. Weaver would have known it as *Andropogon scoparius*. Now botanists call it *Schizachyrium scoparium*. *Scopa*, the indispensable part of the name, is Latin for "broom," which is what the tufts of bronze stems and leaves look like. Soft little brooms that sweep me clean of distractions.

The essence of metaphor, says anthropologist Frederick Barth, is the use of the familiar to grasp the less familiar. What Weaver and Clements were grasping at when they described prairie as a single organism is the living unity they saw there, "each part interdependent upon every other part," as they put it in *Plant Ecology*. If prairie is an organism, for me, it's mammalian. It's competitive and cooperative, hides and flaunts itself, wears different faces, and is pelt-covered. When I see the prairie as a sentient mammal gazing back at me, I feel even more tenderhearted toward it. Yet, the nature of the prairie changes according to the mammal whose characteristics I attribute to it—bison, deer, ferret, coyote, vole.

Many who followed the Great Platte River Road across Nebraska in the nineteenth century saw the prairie as the Great American Desert, a vast emptiness that stood between them and the new home or the fortune to be made in Oregon or Colorado or California. This metaphor persists. In *Dakota*, Kathleen Norris sees the prairie as a desert, specifically that of the Desert Fathers of fourth-century Egypt. In *Great Plains*, Ian Frazier claims that grassland is not desert, yet he conceives of it as desertlike, a blank screen, so to speak, onto which he can project his own desires. This metaphor of prairie as an empty expanse says more about what isn't there than what is. It simply doesn't reach far enough. In a variation on the prairie-ocean metaphor, botanist Peter Bernhardt compares prairies to icebergs, "since most of their mass remains below the soil surface." Like an iceberg, most of the prairie is hidden from my view and it is a vanishing thing. But a prairie is living; an iceberg is not. I reconsider the prairie-ocean metaphor. Despite its limitations, it reveals something essential to me that these other metaphors do not. The closest I can get to the experience of beholding the once-wide, unbroken prairie is at or on or above an ocean, not a perpendicular in sight, nothing but water and sky stretching out farther than the eye or the imagination can follow.

While most explorers, immigrants, and travelers have seen the prairie as something to be crossed as quickly as possible and left behind, for me, it is the end of the journey. *Relict*, which Weaver and Clements defined as "a community or fragment of one that has survived some important change," is close kin to *relic*, the remains, ruins, or vestiges of something now gone or an object venerated because of its association with the sacred. The two words have the same Latin root: *relinquere*, *re* meaning "back" and *linquere* meaning "to leave." To leave back. My pilgrim's journey brings me here to find what was left behind. Though but a shard or splinter of the once-oceanic grasslands, this tiny island of prairie in the vast sea of towns, cities, farms, and highways is the essential piece that can evoke the whole. In the presence of this relic, I'm present, balanced, and spacious.

16

Pawnee Homecoming

The circle of drummers and singers and the slow circle of dancers in turquoise, red, white, and yellow carried on in spite of the light rain. They, in turn, were encircled by at least 2,500 spectators, who, in spite of the rain, stood or sat on bleachers. The crowd was there to watch the 150 members of the Pawnee Nation of Oklahoma, who had returned to their ancestral homeland, the Land of the Platte, hold a powwow at the Great Platte River Road Archway Monument near Kearney. During a break in the dancing, the Pawnee Scouts of Fort Kearny, a reenactment group wearing Union uniforms, fired their rifles, filling the air with smoke. One member portrayed Major Frank North, the leader of the Pawnee soldiers, who assisted the U.S. Army in subduing the Sioux and other tribes. On the front lawn of the monument were demonstrations on flint-knapping and the uses of native plants, and stands selling Indian tacos, fry bread, kettle corn, turkey legs, and powwow T-shirts. North of the 1914 bridge over the north channel of the Platte were white tepees and more exhibitions: hide-scraping, pine-needle-basket weaving, tomahawk throwing, and a garden tour.

The June 20, 2009, powwow was one of several homecomings for the Pawnee people. In 2007, Linda and Roger Welsch donated fifty-eight acres near Dannebrog to the Pawnee Nation. Now tribal members have a place to conduct burial ceremonies for the repatriated skeletal remains of those ancestors of theirs that had been in storage or on display in Nebraska museums. In 2008, the Pawnee were given an ex-officio, nonvoting seat on the Nebraska Indian Commission, which serves as a liaison between the four tribes headquartered in Nebraska (the Omaha, Ponca, Winnebago, and Santee Sioux) and the State. On June 19, 2009, Stan Clouse, the mayor of Kearney, and Roger Welsch, writer, folklorist, and "Tribal Friend" of the Pawnee, gave a key to the city to Pat LeadingFox, head chief of the Pawnee Nation.

It was the garden that I had come to see. Except for the waist-high sunflowers bordering the patch, the corn here was indistinguishable from the vast fields of hybrid corn that I passed on Interstate 80 on my way to the Archway. But if you know what's there, the garden is remarkable. The stalks, strappy fluttering leaves, and ear shoots weren't produced by gold-white seeds of hybrid dent corn but by Pawnee white flour corn, an heirloom corn with large, soft, starchy white kernels.

Before the Pawnee were removed from their homeland near the Platte to Indian Territory in what is now Oklahoma, they planted many varieties of maize, or *Zea mays*—blue, blue-speckled, yellow flint, red-and-white striped, sweet, Osage, as well as eagle corn. But Pawnee corn wouldn't grow in the drier, warmer climate and heavy, clay-based soil of north-central Oklahoma. By the end of the twentieth century, some varieties were almost extinct. One woman, Deb Echo-Hawk, kept the tribe's only remaining eagle-corn seeds in a single Mason jar. This healthy corn crop was yet another Pawnee homecoming.

At some obscure time in the past, the Pawnee migrated northward from some southern place—the Gulf of Mexico, the Southwest, or the southern plains. When Francisco Vásquez de Coronado explored the Great Plains in 1541 in search of the mythical city of Quivira, he found the Pawnee and the Wichita, both Caddoan speakers of the central plains, living together in what is now Kansas. The Pawnee may have arrived in land drained by the Platte, Loup, and Republican rivers by 1600, which means that Nebraska's other American Indian tribes—the Omaha, Ponca, Otoe, and Missouria, who arrived in the eighteenth century; and the Winnebago and the Santee Sioux, or Dakota, who arrived in the nineteenth century—were relative latecomers. Only the Pawnee were true Great Plains dwellers; all of Nebraska's other tribes are linked with northeastern cultures.

The Pawnee lived in circular earth lodges, domes of earth supported by poles and covered with willow branches, in villages built on terraces on the floodplains. Their fields extended for several miles beyond each village. The fields of higher-status farmers were closer to the village, while those of lower-status farmers were farther away. Footpaths linked the fields to the villages. Dr. Edwin James, the scientist for the expedition of Major Stephen Long of the U.S. Army Corps of Engineers, which first visited the Pawnee in 1820, wrote that on June 13 of that year, "As soon as the day dawned we observed the surrounding plain, filled with groups of squaws, with their small children trooping to their cornfields in every direction."

The agricultural cycle began in early April, when the Pawnee returned from the winter hunt. In the sound of thunder, they heard the voice of Tirawa, the supreme deity, a creator-ruler who dwells in the sky and is married to Atira, whose name means "born from corn" or "vault of the sky." In *The Lost Universe: Pawnee Life and Culture,* anthropologist Gene Weltfish describes how Pawnee priests used a rope to "trap the powers of the Heavens" and concentrate them in the holy corn that would be used to replace the old Mother corn in the sacred bundles. During a ritual, three or four holy corn kernels were doled out to those men who kept the sacred bundles so that their wives could plant them in special hills. The sacred corn was reserved for ceremonial purposes and never eaten.

Weltfish identifies the first corn rite of the year as *Awari*, the "Ground-breaking Ceremony." Even though men conducted the ceremony, it was initiated by the vision of a woman, which meant that it was the only Pawnee ceremony in which women played a major role. In the Corn-Planting Ceremony of the Skidi Pawnee, people prayed to the Evening Star, the First Mother, for good crops and hunting, and they celebrated fertility in song and dances that imitated the actions of the women as they hoed and planted. Also around planting time, the Skidi Pawnee sacrificed a girl captured from another tribe to ensure fertility and success in battle. The Skidi Morning Star ceremony was last performed in 1838.

Women worked the ground with digging sticks, elk-antler rakes, and hoes made from bison scapulae. Because these tools weren't suited to working heavy sod, they established their fields in the river valleys, where the soil was fertile and easier to work. There they planted squashes, beans, watermelons, and maize, the descendant of teosinte, the wild grain from Mexico, four kernels to a mound. According to Weltfish, Pawnee women were "skilled horticulturalists": they cultivated ten pure varieties of corn, seven of squash, eight of beans. To maintain the purity of the different strains of corn, they planted squashes between their cornfields, which they bordered with willow fences or earth ridges topped with sunflowers. Within a week, the women had completed a planting. When there were four leaves on the holy corn, Weltfish says that the priests performed a ritual that transformed the corn from an infant to a "mature Mother Corn." The earth mounded around the young plants resembled the earth lodges where the people lived; the stalk rising from the middle of the mound suggested smoke rising from the smoke holes.

The women hoed the corn twice, with the second hoeing in mid-June. Shortly thereafter, the Pawnee left their villages to hunt bison and live on the prairie. When the time came to return to the village and harvest the corn, signs that it was the right moment were all around, from the flowering of the prairie goldenrod on the western prairie to the ripening of milkweed seedpods to the appearance of Canopus in the southern sky.

The harvest was done in stages. First came the harvest of the "green" corn, in late July or early August. The people roasted or boiled, shelled, and dried the immature corn and ate their fill of the soft, milky kernels. When this was done, the women picked and preserved the beans and squashes. Unlike corn, the harvest of these crops wasn't accompanied by elaborate rituals and mythologies. Nor were these vegetables given human attributes, as corn was. Next, the women picked, dried, and processed the mature corn by cutting and hauling wood for the cooking fires, roasting the ears of corn, scraping the kernels from the ears with clamshells, grinding the corn into meal with a pestle, packing the dry kernels and meal in rawhide bags and placing them in deep storage cellars in the earth, and braiding the husks into ropes and hanging them on scaffolds to dry. All of this had to be done before the village left for the winter hunt. Anthropologists describe the corn harvest as a celebratory time, though I don't know when the women would have had the time or energy to feel festive.

The harvest and the harvest ceremony ended with the Making of the New Mother Corn, when priests removed the previous year's corn from the sacred bundle and replaced it with new sacred ears. Weltfish observes that these ears were sewn into a skin cover in the bundle: "the ear for winter in a tanned buffalo skin, and that for summer in a heart skin." When a man led a war party, he wore an ear of sacred corn on his left shoulder so that Mother Corn would lead the party to victory.

This corn-centered way of life continued for centuries. Then, in just a few decades, it ended. By 1800, bison meat had replaced corn as the Pawnee's main food source. The opening of the Overland Trail in the 1830s, now commemorated through multimedia displays at the Great Platte River Road Archway spanning Interstate 80, brought hundreds of thousands of travelers on the long journey west through Pawnee villages and bison-hunting grounds. The travelers shot game birds and animals, trampled the Pawnee's crops, cut what little wood there was, and let their animals overgraze the prairie grasses. The newcomers wanted the Pawnee out of the way; the U.S. government complied.

Another disruption was people from other tribes. To clear land for Euro-American settlements in the early and middle nineteenth century, the federal government arrived at a seemingly logical solution: it would take American Indians' lands in the east and give those tribes "empty" land west of the Mississippi in exchange. But the displaced tribes and their new neighbors fought with each other. The better-armed Sioux raided Pawnee villages, attacked and killed women as they traveled to and from the cornfields, and attacked and killed women, men, and children who were away from the village on the bison-hunting grounds. Feeding the people in one's village became increasingly dangerous work. When their corn crop failed or was destroyed, the Pawnee foraged for food near the river. In the account of his 1820 exploration of the west, Major Stephen Long noted that the Pawnee had stripped the Platte River Valley of vegetation.

During the winter of 1831-1832, smallpox cut the number of Pawnee from ten thousand to five or six thousand, with infants, children, and young adults particularly hard hit. Because so much of the younger generation was gone after smallpox came through, the effects of the epidemic lasted for decades. In the Treaty of 1833, the four bands of the Pawnee, weakened and grief-stricken by loss, traded all of their land south of the Platte, a total of thirteen million acres, for $4,600 in goods to be paid annually for twelve years. The treaty stipulated that the land that the Pawnee had ceded would be a "common hunting ground" that the Pawnee and "other friendly Indians" could use at "the pleasure of the President." Because the Pawnee moved frequently during the 1840s and 1850s in response to the disruptions caused by travelers and settlers and depredations by the Oglala, Dakota, and Ponca, they often were too unsettled to tend a corn crop through to harvest. Though they knew how to forage for prairie turnips, groundnuts, American hog-peanuts, bush morning glories, milkweed, Jerusalem artichokes, wild plums, and chokecherries, and though they knew how to catch turtles, catfish, and bullheads and how to shoot deer and bison, enemy attacks limited their ability to move freely near the river and on the prairie to do these things. Consequently, when the Pawnee came to the council table, they were weakened by disease, malnourishment, and enemy attacks. In the Treaty of 1848, they sold Grand Island and the adjacent Platte River floodplain land, a total of 110,000 acres, and the right to cut "hard timber" on the Wood River, a tributary of the Platte, for $2,000 worth of goods and merchandise.

The Pawnee were surrounded by adversity. Influenza, smallpox, and the deadly cholera epidemic that swept the United States in 1849 killed many and left the survivors too weak to farm and hunt. Because of the drought, their corn plants yielded small ears with little or no grain; clacking, voracious grasshoppers ate whatever green thing they could find. In the 1850s the Pawnee moved east along the Platte River to avoid attacks by other Indians, even though this put them in the way of settlers pouring into the area after the passage of the Nebraska-Kansas Act of 1854. James R. Murie, an anthropologist and a Pawnee, reports that in 1856, the Pawnee performed the corn-planting ceremony for the last time. Two years later, they signed the Table Rock Treaty, which stipulated that in exchange for almost one million acres, the United States would pay them $40,000 per year for five years and thereafter $30,000 per year "as a perpetual annuity," with at least one-half of the annual payments in the form of supplies. The only land that the four bands had left was a 288,000-acre reservation on the Loup River in what is now Nance County, Nebraska. In 1857, the U.S. government prepared the ground where the Pawnee were to plant their corn, a perplexing fact for which I've found no explanation. Was the U.S. government hoping that the Pawnee would produce enough corn to feed themselves? Were the Pawnee so weakened and dispirited that they couldn't even plow the ground?

Or perhaps they found it simply too dangerous to work in the field. On June 23, 1860, a *New York Times* correspondent reported that since their removal to their Nance County reservation, the Pawnee "have been constantly annoyed by bands of Sioux Indians, with whom they are constantly at war and in constant fear of their sudden and fearful attacks." The day before the reporter's arrival a small band of Sioux entered the Pawnee reservation and killed several "herdsmen" and took thirty ponies. "Immediately the Pawnees rallied for a fight, and at a mile from the main village overtook the band of Sioux, who gave them battle, in which five or six of the Pawnees were killed. . . . The Great Spirit, indeed, seemed to favor the Sioux, and although the Pawnees outnumbered their foes in the field, four to one, yet the former returned in haste to their village." The reporter, who showed little understanding of what the Pawnee had been through in the past several decades, judged them to be cowards.

During the summer hunt of 1873, Oglala and Brule warriors attacked and killed between seventy and one hundred Pawnee who were hunting bison near the Republican River. "Massacre Canyon" was the site of this last Pawnee bison hunt and the last war between the Pawnee and the Sioux. Years of drought and grasshopper plagues that left nothing for the horses and cattle to eat made farming particularly difficult in the 1870s. At the same time, white settlers wanted the Pawnee's land and petitioned to have them removed from their reservation. This combination of miseries finally convinced the Pawnee to leave their homeland for a reservation in Indian Territory. In October 1874 most headed south to the Wichita Agency in western Oklahoma. Pawnee land in Nebraska was sold and the proceeds used to buy land and water from the Creek and Cherokee in Oklahoma. In October of 1875, the last Pawnee in Nebraska, a group of about 370, departed from the Land of the Platte in government wagons. In their sacred bundles, they carried pure strains of Pawnee corn.

The story of corn is one of loss. Perhaps as many as several hundred varieties of maize were once grown on this continent. Most are gone. And the loss continues. According to the Food and Agriculture Organization of the United Nations, since 1900 approximately 75 percent of the world's genetic diversity of agricultural crops has been eliminated, resulting in a shallow gene pool. The wide use of high-yielding hybrid corn threatens to further reduce the genetic diversity. At the end of the twentieth century, it appeared that Pawnee corn strains were part of that loss.

But in the early years of the twenty-first century, there is a new and hopeful chapter in the history of Pawnee corn. In 2003, Ronnie O'Brien, the director of educational programs at the Great Platte River Road Archway Monument, sought to plant a native garden at the monument. Through her research, she discovered the work of Deb Echo-Hawk, director of the Pawnee Seeds

Preservation Project in Oklahoma. In 1997, the Pawnee Culture Committee had started the project in an effort to build up the tribe's supply of heritage seeds. Echo-Hawk had successfully grown eagle corn in Colorado in 1980, yet her efforts to grow the heritage corn in Oklahoma had failed. When O'Brien contacted Echo-Hawk about obtaining seeds to plant in Nebraska, Echo-Hawk denied the request since there were so few seeds left. But when O'Brien suggested that the seed would do better on native soil in Nebraska than it had in Oklahoma, Echo-Hawk changed her mind. The soil in north-central Oklahoma is claylike; but in south-central Nebraska, the soil is alluvial, or rich, black chernozem. And, too, the climate in Oklahoma is hotter and drier than that in Nebraska. Since various strains of corn are adapted to different climates and soil types, it seemed likely that the heritage corn would do better in Nebraska. The Pawnee Culture Committee put a notice in the tribal newsletter asking people to donate seeds to the partnership. In 2004, Echo-Hawk sent corn and watermelon seeds from three families, including twenty kernels of eagle corn—half of her own precious supply.

Pawnee eagle corn is exceptionally beautiful. It is a flint corn, with slender ears and hard, thick-shelled kernels. The white kernel is marked with a purple spot that grows as the kernel grows. In the purple splotch, the Pawnee saw an eagle in flight. In this Rorschach test, I see many things: a two-part leaf, a raggedy-edged bow tie, the spread wings of a butterfly, an angel, a vulture, and a phoenix rising.

In accordance with Pawnee tradition, O'Brien soaked the eagle-corn seeds, some of which were eighty to one hundred years old, for twenty-four hours. Then at her home near Shelton, she shaped four hills, each of which she planted with five corn kernels and three watermelon seeds. Because of the cold, wet spring, the seeds rotted in the ground. But Jack Irlmeier, a retired, Kearney-area farmer, produced a good crop with the yellow flint-corn seeds that came from the bundle of the StoneRoad family, and O'Brien's sister, who lives near St. Libory, produced a robust crop of Pawnee watermelon. At summer's end, O'Brien sent Echo-Hawk a thick packet of yellow flint-corn kernels (twenty-three plants had produced about three ears per stalk) and many hundreds of watermelon seeds.

In 2005, O'Brien requested more eagle-corn seeds. After much deliberation, the tribe's culture committee granted her request. Echo-Hawk told the *Omaha World Herald*, "We came to a big conclusion—we may lose it altogether if we don't trust her or trust someone." Echo-Hawk sent twenty-five kernels from the tribe's seed bank. In case the 2005 crop failed, she kept just enough kernels that she could show people what eagle corn had looked like. Knowing that this was her last chance, O'Brien turned to Myron Fougeron, a former professor of biology at the University of Nebraska–Kearney. To increase the likelihood that the seeds would germinate, he wrapped them in paper towels, put them into jars, and sprouted them in his greenhouse. Then O'Brien planted the seedlings in her garden. Of the twenty-five plants, twenty-three survived, yielding seventeen ears and a total of 2,500 kernels of eagle corn. Other gardeners in Kearney grew blue, yellow flint, and red-and-white-striped corn (this gorgeous kernel looks like a piece of peppermint starlight candy), which further increased the stock in the tribe's seed bank.In 2006, O'Brien planted Pawnee watermelon instead of eagle corn, and in 2007, she planted blue-speckled flour corn as well as eagle corn. Since many of the eagle-corn ears were tainted with yellow kernels, O'Brien harvested only five quality ears of pure eagle corn to send to the Pawnee seed bank. O'Brien suspects that moist conditions prevented the pollen from disseminating and storms with winds up to fifty miles per hour may have carried corn pollen from faraway fields to her patch.

In 2008, the eagle-corn crop produced eight good ears, with 110 to 230 kernels per ear, and fourteen smaller ears, with 50 to 80 kernels each. The red-and-white-striped corn that Roger Woolsey of Mason City planted was late and stunted because of cool weather. But the blue-corn harvest was excellent: 135 mature plants produced about eighty-five ears with 125 to 200 kernels per ear. Three ears in the center of the field were nearly a foot long, with 300 to 360 kernels each.

While O'Brien and Echo-Hawk kept some varieties of corn from disappearing, they were too late to save Pawnee blue-speckled flour corn. Of the 151 kernels that Fougeron planted in 2007, none came up because the kernels were too old for the embryos to be viable. While Fougeron believes that it might be possible to harvest genetics from the endosperm of the remaining blue-speckled-corn kernels, those kernels are so precious that they must be saved for cultural purposes.

The white flour corn planted in 2008 failed to pollinate. But the white flour corn that O'Brien planted the following year, ninety-two hills, each containing five kernels, was robust and healthy looking. The sunflowers bordering it were weeks away from blooming.

O'Brien keeps only enough seeds for the next year's crop; the rest she sends to Oklahoma to build up the supply in the tribe's seed bank. Someday, the corn crop may be so abundant that the Pawnee will have plenty of ears to grind for cornbread or to cook in soup, as well as for ceremonial and decorative purposes. Perhaps someday, this ancient corn can be used to bring genetic diversity into the U.S. seed-corn supply. Perhaps someday, there will be enough eagle corn that after I hear the first thunder roll, I will be able to buy a packet of the white and purple kernels at the same greenhouse where I buy heritage tomatoes and plant them four to a hill in my own sunflower-bordered garden.

17

Gone to the Beets

When I moved to Lincoln for graduate school in the summer of 1988, I rented the east half of a duplex in an old neighborhood north of the university and downtown. The North Bottoms, or Russian Bottoms, was filled with small, white clapboard houses, some owned by people who had lived there many decades and who spoke both English and German. As the older residents in the neighborhood died or moved away, investors bought their properties and rented them to students who set couches on the porches, hung floral sheets over the windows, and threw loud parties.

Each evening after supper during my first summer in the Bottoms, my son, Ian, then three, and I walked south on North Ninth Street. We passed Hayward Elementary, which had educated neighborhood children for most of the twentieth century but had recently been turned into condominiums. We passed Faith United Church of Christ at the corner of North Ninth and Charleston, where people had worshipped since 1890. After a few more blocks, we came to the railroad tracks near the Capital Steel Company. My father had instilled the love of trains in my son before he could even walk. So when there was a train coming, Ian stood rapt as the gates closed, the lights flashed, and the bells rang. One evening after we had watched "papa's train" disappear around the bend, a thin, gray-haired woman sitting on the porch of a house not far from the tracks called out to us. I no longer remember what she said or what we talked about when we took a seat on one of her two bright-green porch swings. But it was the first of many evenings in which we visited Lottie after watching a train. While Ian played with a box of toys that Lottie had saved from her own son's childhood, she and I sat in her living room or at the kitchen table or on the front porch, talking about our neighborhood and our families.

Lottie's stories revealed a long, deep history in the neighborhood. She had been born and raised just one block away from where we sat and had attended Hayward Elementary. With the exception of two years during World War II when she and her husband, who was deceased when we met, lived in Chicago, she had fallen asleep each night of her eighty-plus years to the sounds of the trains that ran past the North Bottoms. Over fifty of those years had been in the house with the two green swings. I could point to almost any house on Y Street and Lottie would tell me details about the people who had lived there a few or many decades ago.

Like many of the older residents in the neighborhood, Lottie's parents were Germans from Russia. In the 1760s, the Volga Germans, as they're also called, were suffering in their home country from poverty, heavy taxation, forced labor, and forced military service. At the invitation of Catherine the Great, herself a German, people from Germany and Switzerland immigrated to the provinces of Saratov and Samara near the Volga River in what is now southern Ukraine. Catherine promised them free land, exemption from military service, political autonomy, and the right to speak their own language and practice their own religion for the next hundred years. The czarina even loaned the settlers money. In return, they were to farm the steppes and provide a buffer between Russia and its new acquisitions from the Ottoman Empire. As many as thirty thousand people accepted Catherine's invitation.

Life for the transplanted Germans was relatively uneventful, in a political-cultural sense: they stayed in their German enclaves and were left alone by the Russian people and government. But in the 1870s, Czar Alexander II revoked their privileges and began Russianizing them. This meant forcing the children to speak Russian and conscripting the boys and men into the Russian military. Many of the German Russians looked to immigration to North or South America as their salvation. Because they were already accustomed to living in a relatively treeless, sparsely populated, windy, semiarid grassland prone to grasshopper plagues and great extremes in the temperature and climatic conditions, and because they were hardworking people who knew how to grow sugar beets and winter wheat, U.S. railroad companies found the Germans from Russia to be a group who were particularly open to buying and settling on railroad land in the Great Plains. In 1881, the Burlington and Missouri Railroad published an orange promotional pamphlet written in German that it distributed to prospective immigrants. On the front of the pamphlet were six drawings that showed the transformation of an open prairie with but a few dwellings into a comfortable, idyllic village.

The largest settlement of Volga Germans in the western hemisphere was in Lincoln, Nebraska, where the newcomers lived in little houses on land owned by the Burlington Railroad, the largest employer of "Roosian" men. The German Russians began trickling into Lincoln in 1872; their numbers swelled, peaking in 1913 with 576 new arrivals. Thereafter, migration dropped sharply as the result of World War I, the Russian Revolution, and restrictive U.S. immigration policies. The earliest immigrants to Lincoln settled in the

South Bottoms. So that railroad maintenance workers could live close to the Burlington roundhouse, construction began in the North Bottoms in 1888. The two neighborhoods were bordered on the west side by the Salt, a creek that frequently flooded. In dry weather, alkali appeared on the land. Beyond the creek was the city dump. Despite the undesirability of the area, by 1922 as many as twelve thousand people lived in the North and South Bottoms. Because most Lincolnites thought the German Russians were Russians rather than Germans, the Roosians encountered, in the words of sociologist Hattie Plum Williams, "ignorance, prejudice, and misunderstanding." Their work as migrant field labor only deepened the scorn that they endured.

In the early 1900s, the sugar-beet companies hired German Russians to work in fields near the Platte River in south-central Nebraska and near the North Platte in the Nebraska panhandle, as well as in Minnesota, Michigan, Iowa, Colorado, Wyoming, and the Dakotas. From January to April, the companies advertised in *Die Welt-Post*, a German-language newspaper published in Lincoln; they circulated handbills written in German: "Achtung, Zuckerrüben-Arbeiter!" (Attention, Sugar-Beet Workers!); and they sent agents to Lincoln to recruit the Roosians. The workers signed contracts, the terms of which included transportation, housing from May to November, and wages. Each year before the beet season began, the Burlington parked a train car beneath the Tenth Street viaduct just one block from Lottie's house and one near Fourth Street in the South Bottoms. Families were granted an entire week to load onto the cars the belongings and supplies they would need for their six-month sojourn.

The German Russians were desirable employees. Charles Saylor, the U.S. Department of Agriculture's chief sugar-beet booster, noted that they were "accustomed to the hard work and drudgery incident to growing sugar beet" and that their entire families were willing to work in the beet fields all day long. In the city, only the men could find work, but in the beet fields, even small children could contribute to a family's income by thinning beets. Saylor also believed that in the sugar-beet fields, immigrants would be transformed from "ignorant, vicious, disease-infected classes" into future citizens.

Lottie's family "went to the beets" season after season. I imagine her leaving Lincoln on the "beet-field special" while her classmates were still in school. Perhaps she knew that she'd be missing the relatively carefree summer months when children had time to play outside. Or perhaps many of her friends were also on the train, since most Volga German families went to the beets at least two seasons. As the train headed west, Lottie watched the rolling drift hills and tallgrass and true prairie of southeastern Nebraska become the mixed-grass prairie of the relatively flat center of the state, which in turn became the short-grass prairie in the foothills of the Rockies. In the panhandle, Lottie saw western flora and fauna: magpies, mule deer, pronghorns, prairie dogs, yucca, grama grasses, and prickly-pear cacti. As the train followed the North Platte River through a vast, spare landscape of sometimes violent weather extremes, she saw rocks thrust up into the sky in surprising formations: Courthouse and Jailhouse rocks; the upside-down funnel of Chimney Rock; the rugged cliff of Scotts Bluff. The North Platte River was wide and rushing from snow melt and spring rains.

Six months later, Lottie rode the beet-field special back to Lincoln over a brown, harvested landscape and along a river that was much shallower and skinnier than the one she'd seen in the spring. When she arrived for her first day of classes at Hayward Elementary, the other students had long been settled into the school year. She did not join them. Instead, the three hundred or so "beet-field children" went to classrooms that the school district had set aside for them, where special teachers provided a shorter, condensed term. Between the late start and the early end to their school year, the beet-field children spent three fewer months in school each year than the nonmigratory children. In 1924, the Scottsbluff school district organized a special summer school for beet-field children so they wouldn't fall too far behind. But Lottie's school days were over by then.

At the time that I was becoming acquainted with Lottie and the history of the North Bottoms, I didn't know anything about this twice-removed ethnic group from which my father's paternal grandparents had descended. I hadn't yet seen the North Platte River Valley or a sugar beet. Nor did I know how this sweet and lowly root had changed the river.

Like the deep purple-red beets that you pickle or make into borscht, the sugar beet is a swollen, conical taproot with many treadlike branches and a leafy top. But sugar beets are yellowish white and are many times the size of a table beet. While most plants manufacture sugar, what is so desirable about the sugar beet is that under proper growing and harvesting conditions, the mature root of one beet contains enough sucrose to produce a tablespoon of refined sugar that is indistinguishable from that made from cane.

It was fairly recently in human history that people began to think of sugar beets as a source of sugar. In 1590, the French agronomist Olivier de Serres wrote that, when cooked, "this choice food yields a juice like sugar syrup." But he didn't know what made the roots sweet; nor could his method of extraction be used on a large scale. In 1747, the Prussian chemist Andreas Marggraf discovered that beetroot and sugar-cane crystals are identical. But his method of extracting sugar from beets and carrots wasn't applicable to large-scale production either. In 1784, Marggraf's student, Franz Karl Achard, began selectively breeding sugar beets and developed a more practical method for extracting the sugar. With the support of the Prussian king, Achard opened the world's first beet-sugar factory in Silesia in 1801. Even so, Europeans still relied on expensive colonial sugar cane to sweeten their tea and cakes.

It was the Napoleonic Wars that brought the European beet-sugar industry to maturity. The 1807 British blockade of France prevented Caribbean sugar cane from reaching French markets. Consequently, Napoleon ordered that 32,000 hectares of beets be planted, and he funded the building of new factories. By the end of the wars, there were over three hundred sugar-beet mills operating in France and central Europe. By the 1890s, Germany alone produced more sugar than the entire Caribbean. The U.S. sugar-beet industry got off to a slow and bumpy start in the 1830s, but finally in 1879, a factory opened in Alvarado, California, that was a commercial success.

At the same time that industrialists and scientists were experimenting with beet-sugar production, sugar consumption was rising. Sugar had long been a luxury, a status symbol, enjoyed only by the wealthy. In 1840, sugar extracted from cane grown by slaves was so expensive that Americans consumed, on the average, only fourteen pounds of it per person per year. Corn and maple syrup were cheaper and more available sweeteners. But as sugar prices fell in the latter half of the nineteenth century, sugar consumption rose. By 1860, the per capita consumption of sugar had climbed to thirty pounds. By 1880, it had risen to forty-three pounds. By 1910, it had jumped to eighty pounds. Sugar was no longer a luxury but a staple.

Politicians, USDA officials, investors, university professors, and others saw domestic sugar production as a way not only to reduce the nation's dependence on imported sugar but to diversify agriculture and increase industrial potential. Nebraska joined the sugar-beet craze in the late 1880s. Throughout the 1890s, there was a flurry of promotional activity at the Nebraska State Fair, at various world expositions, and at the state's annual sugar-beet convention. Industry promoters constructed a 200-square-foot palace from sugar beets at Grand Island; the exposition within was devoted to sugar-beet production. From 1891 to 1900, the University of Nebraska Chemistry Department operated the Sugar Beet School, which taught students the best methods for growing sugar beets and producing sugar. Investors built refineries at the Nebraska towns of Grand Island, Ames, and Norfolk.

The real boon came in 1897, when Congress passed the Dingley Act, which increased the tax on foreign sugar imports to 75 percent. This stiff tariff lessened the competition from sugar cane grown in Puerto Rico, the Philippines, and Guam, territories that the United States acquired as spoils of the Spanish-American War. To further advantage the domestic sugar industry, in 1899, the Nebraska legislature created a one-cent-per-pound bounty that it paid to factory owners for the production of refined sugar within the state. That year, 65 percent of the world's sugar came from beets.

Not all Nebraskans championed the sugar-beet industry without reserve. In an editorial published in the *Nebraska City Conservative* in 1908, J. Sterling Morton, a stalwart proponent of Nebraska agriculture and the founder of Arbor Day, criticized the government's subsidy of the sugar-beet industry through the distribution of free seeds, bulletins, and instructions. He was particularly critical of protectionist politicians who, at the mere thought of beet sugar, became free-traders. These double-dealers passed legislation that allowed the machinery for the Nebraska sugar-beet factories to enter the country duty-free, but kept "the plows, harrows, shovels, hoes, rakes and pitch forks of the yeomanry who were to raise the beets . . . on the dutiable list." Morton concluded that efforts to launch the sugar-beet industry in Nebraska in the early years of the twentieth century benefited not the farmers but the "vagarists and promoters."

Early efforts to grow sugar beets in Nebraska were concentrated in the eastern half of the state—a less-than-ideal climate. *Beta vulgaris* requires abundant sunshine, cool nights, and at least twenty-two to twenty-eight inches of summer rainfall during its 140-day growing season. In eastern Nebraska, summer rainfall is not dependable and the fall season is often too wet, causing crown and root rot and harvest problems, since more dirt clings to the beets during damp than dry weather. But semiarid western Nebraska offered cool, dry, sunny autumns, which were ideal for increasing the sucrose content in beet roots. What kept western Nebraska from being the perfect climate for sugar beets was an average annual precipitation of only fourteen inches, but if the late-maturing beets could be watered by the North Platte River, the Nebraska panhandle would be an ideal climate for the crop. Growers, manufacturers, politicians, and the railroads turned their attention westward.

The North Platte River begins as mountain snowmelt in north-central Colorado. As it flows north through Colorado and Wyoming, it is a swift and narrow river enjoyed by trout fishers, canoeists, and kayakers. In central Wyoming, the river takes a turn and flows southeast into Nebraska, past Scottsbluff, Bridgeport, Lewellen, and on to the city of North Platte, where it joins the South Platte to form the Platte River. On the map, the South and North Platte rivers, both of which originate in the Colorado Rockies, look like plow handles; the Platte is the plowshare that stirs the soil. Or rather, the North and South Plattes are the handles and the Platte is the stem on a dowsing rod.

Prior to irrigation, the North Platte, in the eastern Wyoming and Nebraska part of its course, was flat, wide, and shallow, a braided river flowing around alluvial islands in two or more channels, the channels parting and reconnecting again and again. Before irrigation, the North Platte varied widely from season to season, with peak flow in May and June. Sometimes the river ran dry in the late summer.

People began diverting the waters of the North Platte onto their fields in the mid-1800s, when irrigation meant directing river water through hand-dug ditches onto floodplain hayfields and gardens. Since farmers didn't have storage reservoirs to hold the runoff from high spring flows, they didn't have enough water to carry them through the dry summer months. Though the most critical time for sugar beets in terms of reliable moisture is from emergence through thinning and one month after thinning, the greatest volume of water use is from late July to early August, which coincides with the period of greatest growth.

Sugar beets in far western Nebraska need twenty-two inches of irrigation water to meet the crop's consumptive use requirement—the amount of water the plant uses in transpiration, metabolism, and evaporation. One acre-foot, the volume of water necessary to cover an acre to the depth of twelve inches, equals 325,851 gallons. To cover one acre to the depth of twenty-two inches, one needs to draw almost 600,000 gallons of water from the river and the aquifer. In the 1930s, there were 80,000 acres planted with sugar beets in western Nebraska, drawing 48 billion gallons of water from the North Platte River and aquifer per year.

The real boon for sugar-beet cultivation in western Nebraska arrived in 1902, when Congress passed the Newlands Reclamation Act. This legislation funded irrigation projects in seventeen semiarid western states and ultimately led to the damming of every major western river. The North Platte Project was one of the first authorized under the new law. Between 1904 and 1909, thousands of workers poured into the area to build the Pathfinder Dam near Caspar, Wyoming, the Whalen Dam near the confluence of the Laramie and North Platte rivers in Wyoming, and the Interstate Canal and Fort Laramie canals in Nebraska. Impounded river water provided the reliable source of water that farmers needed; the thousands of miles of canals, laterals, and drains that were dug across Wyoming and Nebraska by the mid-1920s carried the water to the fields. In response, farmers planted more acres of beets. In 1905, one year before Lottie was born, there were 250 acres of sugar beets in Scotts Bluff County. By 1924, there were 60,283 acres.

For sugar-beet booster Charles Saylor, converting the river and prairie into beet fields was only part of the dream. "Here is a chance in the sugar industry to see the factory and the farm side by side," he wrote in 1900. He imagined a rural America transformed by "restless volumes of smoke issuing from chimneys early in the morning and late at night." In 1910, the Scottsbluff Sugar Company completed its factory at Scottsbluff. Between 1916 and 1927, sugar refineries were also built in Lyman and Torrington, Wyoming, and the Nebraska panhandle towns of Gering, Bayard, Mitchell, and Minatare. Not only did sugar beets produce sugar to sweeten jellies, cakes, candy, and coffee, but farmers and ranchers fed the molasses, tops, and spent pulp to their cattle. Farmers couldn't grow sugar beets without irrigation; they couldn't afford to irrigate without sugar beets, a cash crop. Between 1914 and 1917, summer flows on the main stem of the North Platte River in Nebraska were overappropriated, meaning that there were more claims on the water in the river than the river could meet. Now the area of the North and South Platte rivers in western Nebraska, eastern Colorado, and eastern Wyoming is the most heavily irrigated area in the country. The lower water volume caused by irrigated farming has changed the appearance of the river. Accounts of vegetation patterns near the North Platte by travelers, residents, and scientists from the late 1800s reveal that prior to the coming of irrigation, scattered shrubs and trees grew on the banks and islands. But now one finds far more woody plants lining the channels and growing on the islands. Because the high June flows that once coincided with seed germination have been regulated by the demands of irrigation, more seedlings survive and so more trees grow near the North Platte.

In *Second Hoeing*, Hope Williams Sykes's novel about German Russian beet farmers in "Valley City" (Fort Collins, Colorado), Hannah Schreissmiller recalls that when she was just four years old, she was left at the edge of a beet field "in the shade of a gunny sack stretched over four upright sticks" to look after her two-year-old sister and her two-month-old brother, while her mother weeded beets with a long-handled hoe. Hannah had cried for her mother, but because the beets had to be thinned, her mother couldn't stop.

Because the heat made Lottie weak and nauseous, she couldn't work in the fields. Instead, she tended her younger siblings. But instead of taking the children to the edge of the fields as the Schreissmillers did, Lottie's parents left them in their shack. Lottie may also have tended other people's children who were too little to go to the beets. With no access to public libraries or parks with swings and merry-go-rounds, with no Tinkertoys, Erector sets or dollhouses meant to quietly engage one for long afternoons, this must have been hot, exhausting, and sometimes boring work.

Though inside the rickety shacks that were provided for seasonal laborers or underneath gunnysack awnings in the Nebraska panhandle were miserable places to spend summer days, if Lottie had been in the fields with her parents, older siblings, and neighbors, her suffering would have been even greater. There she would have had to do the most primitive and labor-intensive of agricultural tasks. Because the beet "seed" is really a cluster of seeds, each the size of a half grain of rice, within a dried fruit, several seedlings may sprout from each fruit. Beets growing this closely produce little sugar. So when the plants are just a few inches above ground, they have to be thinned, or "blocked."

The beet-thinner placed her thumb and forefinger firmly against the healthiest plant in each bunch to hold it in place. Then, with her free hand, she pulled out all of the other beet plants and weeds around it. To do this work at ground level, she either walked stooped over or crawled on her hands and knees. Some workers padded their knees and wore hats, bonnets, or babushkas. Thinning had to be completed speedily, so for three to four weeks, it was fast work from sunup to sundown, with little time left to tend to one's children.

Because weeds grow quickly in the clean spaces between plants, workers had to hoe the beets two or three times during the growing season. During the first hoeing, the worker stooped to use a hoe that was eighteen to twenty-four inches long. In the 1970s, California Rural Legal Assistance would successfully fight to outlaw the short-handled hoe because of the injuries sustained by workers who wielded it for many hours, day after day. The second hoeing was done while standing, with long-handled hoes, since the plants were taller then. Sometimes, there was a third hoeing. Eventually, the robust roseate of large, ruffled beet leaves created a canopy that shaded out the weeds. The various hoeings were completed in early August. Other jobs for the beet-field workers included leveling, plowing, and harrowing the ground before planting, hand-shoveling manure into the spreader, cleaning irrigation ditches, leading water from irrigation laterals to the individual rows of beets, and applying pesticides. Plantings were staggered so that there was time to block all of the young plants and to keep workers busy for as much of the season as possible. Nonetheless, there was idle time between the hoeings and the harvest. Then Lottie's family would have spent more time at the cramped shack. Perhaps there were trips to Scottsbluff to buy supplies from the grocery or drugstore.

Harvesting was also labor-intensive. Beets were kept in the ground as long as possible to achieve the highest sucrose content. If the beets froze, they could only be stacked for ten days or so before they rotted. Consequently, the beets had to be pulled from the ground just before the first frost. Again, one had to work quickly. The mature roots were lifted from the earth by a plowlike, horse-drawn device, also used to lift potatoes. Three types of workers followed, harvesting two rows at a time. The "pickers," equipped with short-handled, short-bladed sickles, hooked the beets to lift them out of the ground and then laid them in rows on the ground facing the same direction: roots to one side, greens to the other. The "toppers" chopped the leaves and crown from the root with a single whack, so that the alkaloids in the crown wouldn't interfere with the sugar-refining process. The "loaders" forked the beets into the back of a cart, wagon, or truck, which then hauled the beets to beet dumps or piling stations. The harvest work was demanding since the air was dusty and the knives were heavy, as were the beets, which weighed as much as five pounds each. From start to finish, the work was repetitive and dangerous, inviting a host of physical ailments: carpal tunnel syndrome, tendonitis, back strain, sore muscles, knife cuts, allergies, asthma, heatstroke, sunburns, skin cancers, and illnesses resulting from exposure to pesticides. And the work was monotonous. How did one occupy one's mind when facing rows of beets as far as the eye could see, from sunup to sundown, day after day?

On display at the Nebraska History Museum in Lincoln is a document entitled "Contract of Hand Labor for Season 19__." Written in the blank in pencil is "20." The legally binding contract was drawn between Craft and Edgerton—either a beet grower or an agent for the American Beet Sugar Company of Grand Island—and a laborer with the last name Franth. The first name isn't clear, but it may be Kolorina, Kolarima, Kalarina, or some variation. The terms of the agreement state that Craft and Edgerton would pay Franth $11 per acre for "bunching and thinning" (that's $116.79 per acre in 2010), $6 per acre for the first hoeing, $3 per acre for the "second hoeing and keeping clean until harvest," and $15 per acre for "pulling and topping and covering piles with beet tops." That's a total of $35 per acre, with the average family working fifteen to thirty acres per season in 1920. If a family worked 22.5 acres, their half year of labor earned them the equivalent of $8,494 in 2010. The contract stated that the Grower would provide the Contractor with "reasonable living accommodations" and "water near at hand for drinking and domestic purposes without expense to him." There was no job protection: if the crop was "destroyed or damaged by the elements or disease, or by insect pests of any kind, to such an extent to make it unprofitable to continue this contract," the Grower could cancel the contract after paying the Contractor for the work he or she had done prior to the date of cancellation. Likewise, there was no provision for workers who were injured so badly that they couldn't work.

In the early years of the beet industry, workers were paid by the day, which meant that at the end of the day, they could leave to work for another grower. To prevent this from happening, farmers began paying workers by the acre. But this, too, presented problems, since there was no incentive for workers to grow and harvest as many beets as possible per acre. Finally, farmers paid contractors by the ton, a system that held workers in place the entire season and encouraged maximum yield. Because the sucrose content of beets is delicate, the mature beets couldn't be sold to faraway markets, so farmers had no choice but to sell their beets to the local factory, where prices had been locked in place far in advance. In turn, the worker was paid according to the price the farmer received from the factory to which he was contracted.

Prior to the arrival of the sugar-beet industry, the agricultural workforce had been comprised of families and local hired hands. But because sugar-beet cultivation and harvesting were so labor-intensive, the local workforce wasn't adequate for the job. So the sugar-beet industry turned to a largely foreign-born supply of workers. For several decades, there was a steady supply of German Russian immigrants to work in the fields. But those who had been in the United States for a while eventually found stable employment and settled in cities and towns. Some even became sugar-beet farmers themselves. World War I disrupted the supply of new immigrants. Increasingly, Great Western Sugar recruited Mexican Americans and Mexican immigrants, advertising their jobs in newspapers, booklets, posters, handbills, and calendars, all written in Spanish. Of the 10,000 migrant workers in the Colorado sugar-beet fields in 1909, 5,900 were German Russians; 2,200 were Japanese; 100 were Hispanic; and the rest were of various ethnicities. But in 1924, 7,600 were German Russians; 175 were Japanese; and 14,300 were Hispanic, primarily Mexican immigrants. While the German Russians and the Japanese were upwardly mobile and only went to the beets for a relatively short period of time, Hispanics and Latinos had fewer opportunities to acculturate, so they went to the beets season after season.

And there were children. A photo from the Office of the Secretary of Agriculture taken in Hall County, Nebraska, on October 17, 1940, shows a boy of about ten in overalls and a girl of about seven in a dress, both filthy from fieldwork. The boy holds a sugar-beet knife and a football-sized beet with the dried leaves still attached. The girl holds a topped beet big enough to cover her belly. A 1915 photograph by child labor reformer Lewis Wilkes Hine in Sugar City, Colorado, shows three children, Mary, six, Lucy, eight, and Ethel, ten, each wearing a big bonnet with ruffles along the edge of the brim, kneeling as they weed young beet plants. Their little hands are dusty from the dry soil. In the background is a kneeling, bonneted woman; a few rows away, a man in a round-brimmed hat is on his hands and knees. In 1920, researchers at the Children's Bureau discovered that by age six, one-tenth of the children of beet-field workers were in the fields; by eight, it was one-half; by ten, all children were working in the fields with their families. In 1923, more than half of all contract laborers in the North Platte River Valley were under sixteen. Until the passage of the Jones-Costigan Act in 1934, child labor in the beet fields was unregulated. This law mandated that children had to be at least fourteen before they could go to the beets. Children between fourteen and sixteen years of age were restricted to no more than eight hours per day. Unfortunately, there was no program in place to enforce the law.

My friendship with Lottie ended when she had a heart attack and was taken to the hospital by ambulance. I knew that she had heart problems. Her diet, which was heavy in meats and sweets and light on fruits, vegetables, and whole grains, surely contributed to this condition. I also knew that she had a Do Not Resuscitate order. When I called the hospital to see how she was doing and when I could visit, the Intensive Care Unit nurse said that since I wasn't family,

I couldn't visit Lottie; nor could the nurse give me information about my friend's condition. At the time, I was newly married and pregnant, and Ian and I were in the process of moving to my husband's house in another part of the city. I knew that Lottie was close-minded about matters of race and would not be receptive to my black husband and his Caribbean accent. And so I didn't call again. But Ian and I missed visiting her and often wondered how she was doing. Several months after her heart attack, we drove past her house, hoping to find her sitting on her porch swing. But the green swings were gone and there was a car in the driveway that I didn't recognize.

Now the North Bottoms is almost entirely student rentals. The old Germans from Russia are gone. A huge apartment complex fills what was once open land near the Salt Creek where Ian and I used to walk and play and watch herons and geese. Faith United Church of Christ held its last service in July of 2009. The trains still run, though one has no access to the tracks, since they are now enclosed by high fences. Lottie's house needs painting, balusters are missing from the front-porch railings, the wooden garage doors hang askance, and the flowerbeds are full of weeds.

Several years after I met Lottie, my brother John showed me the fruits of his genealogical research on our father's father's family. He traced our Knopp ancestry back to Margaretha and Caspar Knopf, who emigrated from the German province of Fulda to Russia with their children in 1766. It was a momentous journey: en route, Caspar died and Margaretha gave birth to Johannes Knopf, one of my great-great-great-great-grandfathers. Margaretha and her children settled in Frank, one of the German enclaves on the western or mountain side of the Volga River. Perhaps Lottie's ancestors were their neighbors. Or perhaps Lottie, too, was descended from Margaretha and Caspar. When my paternal grandfather's family immigrated to the United States in the early 1890s, they first settled in Hastings, Nebraska, but a few years later, during the drought and the depression of that decade, moved to Catfish Bend, with its green hills and more reliable source of water. Perhaps they, too, had gone to the beets for a few seasons before settling on the west bank of the Mississippi.

Sugar-beet production has changed dramatically since Lottie's family and neighbors worked in the fields. The labor shortages of World War II hastened the development of mechanization. Now the seeds are mechanically sown and herbicides, rather than short-handled hoes, control the weeds. Most beets are irrigated by flooding the furrows between the rows; those fields outside of the canal system are watered by center-pivot sprinklers. The harvest is also entirely mechanical: a beet harvester lifts the roots and removes the excess soil in a single pass over the field, covering many rows in one sweep. A many-bladed rotor beater chops the leaf and crown from the root. As the harvester rolls down the field, the beets are dumped into trucks and then delivered to the factory. A conveyor removes soil. If the beets are scheduled for a later delivery, they are left at piling stations.

One October, when Ian and Meredith had a few days off from school, we drove to the Nebraska panhandle to visit Chimney Rock National Historical Site, Scottsbluff National Monument, and the point near the city of North Platte where the North and South Plattes meet to form the Platte. In the midst of a long drought, the river was but a thin trickle. Even so, we saw enormous piles of sugar beets: mountains made from sun and seeds, soil and river water.

Because of various irrigation projects, the North Platte River is but a shadow of its former self. Now the peak and mean flows at North Platte, Nebraska, are but one-fourth to one-half of what they were at the start of the twentieth century. In 2004, the Nebraska Department of Natural Resources designated the North Platte River Basin, which includes both surface water and groundwater, as overappropriated, which means that existing uses are unsustainable and will deplete the long-term supply. As a result of that designation, the Natural Resources Districts of that area must enforce a stay prohibiting the expansion of irrigated acres and the construction of new water wells with a capacity of more than fifty gallons per minute, and they must develop an Integrated Management Plan for water use in the basin.

As we climbed Scotts Bluff, high, keening winds pulled in a cold front. We wished that we'd brought hats and gloves. Tumbleweeds bounced past. Mule deer bounded over rocks and brush. From the top of the bluff, we could see yellow-brown fields, rough and rocky terrain, and the scrawny North Platte. I imagined the fields full of stooping workers and a cluster of shacks and tents nearby. On a day like this, Lottie's family and friends would have put in long hours in the fields, since the beets had to be pulled and topped before the ground froze. When that job was done, Lottie's family would have loaded their belongings into a boxcar and boarded the train for Lincoln, where she would have returned to school and a more carefree lifestyle. But in the meantime, she and her younger siblings would have walked beneath the big, gray sky along the banks of a river that was wider and more free-flowing than the one that we saw, though not as wide and full as it had been before it went to the beets.

18

Meanderings

The morning after a heavy spring rain, I started my car but only drove a few feet before a raking sound and a dragging pull stopped me. I looked under my car to see a mass of sticks: a sloppy bird's nest. I removed what I could and drove away. When I got an oil change and travel check the next day, the mechanic said that he "cleaned out lots of sticks and leaves" from the grill and underneath my car. "Were you in a flood?" he asked. An interesting question since I was getting my car serviced so I could drive to my hometown on the Mississippi River and help sandbag during a flood, the Iowa Flood of 2008.

"I park it on the street in front of my house," I said. "No floods." Then I remembered that in the heavy rains of the night before, a wide, deep, and fast stream of water, a flood of sorts, had rushed down the sloping street in front of my house.

A few weeks later, my son, Ian, told me that his landlord, who lives near me, said that our street used to be a creek. So that the creek bed could be paved, the waters were diverted east into Antelope Park and now flow north into Antelope Creek. Suddenly, I could see it. Seven-block-long Jefferson Avenue sweeps down an incline, making three wide and graceful curves. The avenue ends in Antelope Park at Memorial Drive, which makes a broad turn before ending at A Street. I named the creek bed and the water that once flowed there Phantom Creek, since I could feel its presence, even though it's no longer physically there.

Jefferson Avenue is an anomaly in the older part of Lincoln, where the numbered and lettered streets run, for the most part, in straight, flat lines. But Antelope Park near the center of the city and its creeks, Phantom, Antelope, and the unnamed tributary of the latter, make a mess of the grid. Jefferson Avenue is also an anomaly in a city where most houses and yards are level with the street. Because my house is located atop the outer curve of a meander, I climb five steps up a terrace, "the creek bank," and another seven steps to my porch. Yet to be in my backyard, I go down only six steps. In a heavy rain, the water remembers where to go and flows down the sloping, meandering bed of Phantom Creek, leaving behind sticks, leaves, and food wrappers.

On summer evenings, I sit on my porch high above the street and read, write, converse with company, watch my neighbors, and wait for the bats that cut sharp turns in the night air. And I think about meanders: where they come from and what they're good for.

The shortest distance between the top and bottom of an incline is a straight line. Yet water rarely flows in such a logical path. When water flows down a slope and encounters an obstacle in the streambed, say, a fallen tree, a big rock, or an irregularity in the substrate, it flows around it. The water runs deeper and faster at the outer, or concave, portion of the bend created by the water's change in direction; it runs slower and shallower at the inner, or convex, portion of the bend. The faster, diverted current collides into the opposite bank, gradually wearing it away, and deposits the eroded silt at the convex curve of the next bend, forming a point bar. This meandering pattern repeats again and again as the current crosses at the point of inflection, the relatively straight area between two bends, and bounces off the opposite bank on its way downstream.

But curiously, a meander, one of the loops in a sinuous stream of water, also develops in the absence of obstacles. For instance, rainwater meanders down a clean windshield. Nor does the obstacle theory account for the predictable pattern one sees in meandering streams. Theoretically, a stream could wander all over the floodplain in a string of cursive *m*'s, *r*'s, lowercase *e*'s, zigzags, or a more random form. But it doesn't. For the most part, it flows in irregular waves. Luna Leopold, a geomorphologist (and son of ecologist Aldo Leopold) who refers to this shape as a "sine-generated curve," concludes that the meander is "the most probable geometry for a river."

What initiates the turning that results in a meander seems to be a mystery, but there are parts of the phenomenon that can be explained. Geographer Peter P. Sakalowsky says that meandering is "dependent not only on stream flow," but on a whole host of variables, including "the rate of stream discharge, sediment load, size and type of sediment, channel roughness, depth, width, velocity of flow, and [the] quality of water itself." Sakalowsky believes that the best explanation as to why meanders develop is found in the very nature of helicoidal flow. The spiraling or corkscrew-like motion of water as it flows in a channel is caused by the tendency of the thalweg, the fastest, deepest part of a channel, to transfer momentum from one bank to the opposite bank and back, creating a sinuous channel in the process. A meandering river may seem kind of aimless and in no hurry to reach its destination. But because this shape minimizes such variables as the angle of deflection of the current, the water-surface slope, and the total work of turning done by the river, the meander is the shape by which the stream does the least amount of work with the least expenditure of energy. A meandering river is, in Henry David Thoreau's words, "sedulously seeking the shortest course to the sea."

Most meanders have a characteristic scale, proportional to the width of a river. After sampling fifty typical meanders, Leopold found that the average length of a meander is ten to fourteen times the full-bank channel width, with eleven times being average, and that the distance a river flows in a more or less straight line between two bends doesn't exceed ten times its average width at that point. Leopold also found that the ratio between the distance along the ground separating two successive bends in the same direction (the wavelength of the curve) and the radius of the arc that bend makes (radius of curvature) averages 4.7:1, and the ratio of the radius of curvature to the width of the stream is 2:1. Leopold refers to these proportions as "the nearly geometric regularity of river meanders."

When I drive, bike, or walk down Phantom Creek's smooth and sweeping shifts of direction, it's not the remarkable predictability of the loops in the creek and the distance between them that I'm thinking of, but that I don't know what danger or delight, what marvel or mundanity, awaits me around the next bend until I get there.

A few blocks east of my house near the bike and pedestrian paths in Antelope Park is a creek that flows north for about eight blocks. "Flows," I say, even though it is dry most of the year. If my son's landlord is correct, the waters that once flowed in Phantom Creek were diverted there so that my house and others could be built along its lovely banks eighty-some years ago. Perhaps the waters were diverted into a creek bed that was already there in the park or perhaps someone made a channel in what seemed like a good place for a creek. Diversion Creek, as I call it, disappears through an iron gate into a graffiti-filled tunnel beneath Memorial Drive at what would have been Phantom Creek's widest and lowest point.

While Diversion Creek is dry most of the year, heavy rains cause flash floods around it. Over the years, the flooding has created steep banks and a clogged channel. In 2006 as part of a storm water project, the City of Lincoln corrected the problems with Diversion Creek not by straightening the channel, but by making it meander. J. J. Yost, construction manager for the Lincoln Parks and Recreation Department, says that a meandering channel slows the water flow and reduces erosion; and during big floods the channels convey water without backing up. To further slow erosion, workers gave the creek gently sloping banks, piled big white rocks on some bends, and planted purple-flowered legumes, yellow composites, red clover, and other vegetation that doesn't have to be mowed. For the most part, the southern part of Diversion Creek runs straight and the northern part moves in one tight, human-made loop after another. With its close meanders, Diversion Creek fails to evoke the wonder and mystery that I feel when rounding one of the wide and gentle contours of Phantom Creek.

We humans have a deep preference for single-thread, meandering streams. In *The Analysis of Beauty,* William Hogarth, an eighteenth-century British painter, social critic, and philosopher, explained the importance of the serpentine line to our perception of beauty. "The eye hath this sort of enjoyment in winding walks, and serpentine rivers, and all sorts of objects, whose forms . . . are composed principally of what I call waving and serpentine lines . . . that lead the eye in a wanton kind of chase, and from the pleasure that gives the mind, entitles it to the name of 'beautiful.'" Hogarth admired the elongated *S*, the line of grace and beauty that he saw in many places, including candleholders, country dancing, curly hair, women's corsets (indeed, a woman's form can also meander!), and even the worm gears on fireplace controls. Hogarth's notions of beauty were put into practice by such landscape designers as Capability Brown, who fashioned serpentine forms on the estates of his wealthy clients so that they had the pleasure of expectation and revelation as they strolled along sinuous rills and paths.

To see the meandering process and pattern writ large, look at a map of Nebraska. At the city of North Platte, the North and South Platte rivers meet. East of that point, a single river begins its southeastern descent, swinging low like a hammock, a swayed back, or a catenary curve, as it flows through the Big Bend in south-central Nebraska. The Platte rises in a wide meander known as the North Bend; then it descends again and flows through a small crook of a meander, the South Bend, before rising to meet the Missouri. Along the way, the Platte gathers water from the Birdwood and Salt creeks and from the Wood, Loup, and Elk Horn rivers.

And there are loops within these loops. "Across this plain the Platte River meanders side to side, like a man who has lost a hubcap and is looking for it in the high grass on both sides of the road," muses Nebraska essayist and poet Ted Kooser. Dams, reservoirs, and irrigation have restricted the Platte, replacing many with fewer channels and reducing the water volume. But these unnatural acts haven't straightened the river's gentle, serpentine turns as it flows down from the Rockies, across the High Plains, toward the center of the continent.

As I sit on my front porch on summer evenings, my thoughts meander. My house and others should have been built where Diversion Creek now flows. Antelope Park should be here, on the banks of the meandering Phantom Creek, with trails, benches, and picnic tables nearby, with people fishing in the creek or ruminating as they watch the crinkled, light-filled water flow past. Instead of pin oaks and ornamental fruit trees, cottonwoods and willows should grow on the creek's brushy banks.

As I sit here, I imagine the pavement dissolving and water flowing again in Phantom Creek. During spring rains, the creek overflows its banks and my son stops by to throw out a fishing line from my front porch. The waters draw down and I gather mussel shells. Kingfishers rattle and dive. Muskrats carry reeds in their mouths from this bank to that one. In the evenings, deer come to the creek to drink and raccoons patrol the banks.

I imagine following Phantom Creek northwest to its confluence with Antelope Creek. There, I follow Antelope Creek west, past outcroppings of Dakota sandstone and then north, through a new and costly, Armorflex-lined channel to the point where the Antelope enters the Salt Creek near the former Nebraska State Fairgrounds. I follow the Salt northeasterly to its confluence with the Platte at Ashland in Saunders County, what Alfred T. Andreas in his 1882 history of Nebraska called the "best watered county in the state." I follow the Platte east, past the low Interstate 80 bridge, past the wooded bluffs of Schramm and Platte River state parks to the river's confluence with the Missouri River at the appropriately named Plattsmouth. I follow those waters south, where they draw the borders between Nebraska and Iowa, then Nebraska and Missouri, then Kansas and Missouri. In Kansas City, the Kansas flows into the Missouri and the combined waters hook and meander past the north edge of the city before angling across the state of Missouri; past the sites of Civil War battles and slave auctions; past Missouri wine country and the lovely hills of Hermann; past Fort Belle Fontaine, where Lewis and Clark and the Corps of Discovery spent the first night of their epic journey; to the confluence with the waters of the Mississippi, born in northern woods and flowing past big northern cities, ancient bird- and bear-shaped effigy mounds, little river cities and towns that once milled lumber, cut mussel-shell buttons, and made trains, but now are known as the hosts of steamboat or catfish or eagle-watching festivals; and past Hannibal, where a boy with wanderlust once watched the boats dock. I follow the river past its confluence with the Mississippi, past St. Louis, once a little fur-trading post but now a city that bills itself as the Gateway to the West. I follow the river past Kaskaskia Island, past the forested hills of southern Illinois, past that spit of land where the blue waters of the Ohio pour into the brown waters of the Mississippi. I pass the mouths of the White, the Arkansas, the Yazoo, and the Red rivers, on to the Gulf of Mexico, where the waters of Phantom Creek, with its beautiful, graceful, and geometrically regular meanders, join the waters of many other rivers and the Atlantic Ocean.

Works Cited and Consulted

I divide my references into sections by essay, and I include some works that I have not cited directly but that contributed to my understanding of the topics I explore in my essays. All citations of articles from the *Burlington Hawk Eye* are from the online editions of that newspaper.

PART I. THE MISSISSIPPI

1. Catfish Bend

Andreas, Alfred T. *Andreas Illustrated Historical Atlas of the State of Iowa, 1875.* Chicago: Andreas Atlas Co., 1875.

Bergin, Nicholas. "Two Years after the Flood, Life Is Starting to Look Normal." *Burlington Hawk Eye,* June 13, 2010.

Courtney, Thomas. Iowa State Senate, District 44. E-mail communication with author, January 26, 2009.

Crippes, Christina. "Gulfport's Flood of '65 Mirrors 2008 Event: Villagers Face Many of the Same Woes Decades Later." *Burlington Hawk Eye,* June 8, 2009.

———. "Challenges Confront Henderson County." *Burlington Hawk Eye,* March 1, 2009.

"DOA Catfish Swimming with the Fishes: 'Sad Footnote to a Great Story' after Record Catch in Mississippi." May 26, 2005. MSNBC. http://www.msnbc.msn.com/id/7978360/ns/us_news/.

"Effort Underway to Hook Channel Cat as State Fish." *Radio Iowa,* February 15, 2005.

Grant, Miles. "Climate Crisis Fuels Mississippi River Flooding." May 11, 2011. Grist. http://www.grist.org/climate-change/2011–05–11-climate-crisis-fueling-Mississippi-rivers-historic-floods.

Iowa Legislature. House. House Joint Resolution 2, General Assembly 83 (1/12/2009–1/9/2011), House Joint Resolution Listing (0000–0099).

http://www.legis.iowa.gov/Legislation/BillTracking/directoryListing. asp x?billType=HJR&min=O&max=99&ga=83.

Jolliet, Louis. *The Jesuit Relations and Allied Documents: Travels and Explorations of the Jesuit Missionaries in New France, 1610–1791.* Ed. Reuben Gold Thwaites. Vol. 11. Cleveland: Burrows Brothers, 1899.

Knopp, Patricia. Interview by author. January 3, 2009.

Leopold, Aldo. *A Sand County Almanac and Sketches Here and There.* New York: Oxford University Press, USA, 1949.

Murray, Gene. "Big Flathead Catfish: Local Legend Still Swims the Waters of the Mississippi River." *Burlington Hawk Eye,* June 23, 1998.

Pond, Peter. Quoted in Cyrenus Cole, *A History of the People of Iowa.* Cedar Rapids, IA: Torch Press, 1921.

"Since 1960s: West Burlington's George Marzeck Pushes Lawmakers to Officially Recognize Channel Catfish." *Burlington Hawk Eye,* February 8, 2000.

Smith, William. "A Tragedy of Two Towns: Oakville and Gulfport Present Remarkably Similar, Yet Surprisingly Different Recovery Stories." *Burlington Hawk Eye,* June 7, 2009.

Twain, Mark. *Life on the Mississippi.* Mineola, NY: Dover, 2000.

"West Burlington Man's Dream of State Fish May Come True." *Keokuk (IA) Gate City,* March 19, 2007.

"Western Forest Doomed: Minnesota, Wisconsin, and Northern Michigan Will Soon Be Depleted of Their Timber." *New York Times,* November 29, 1897.

Wilson, Mike. "And the Council Is Jumpin'." *Burlington Hawk Eye,* February 13, 2001.

2. Painting the River

Arrington, Joseph Earl. "Henry Lewis' Moving Panorama of the Mississippi River." *Louisiana History: The Journal of the Louisiana Historical Association* 6, no. 3 (Summer 1965): 239–72.

Lewis, Henry. "Making a Motion Picture in 1848: Henry Lewis's Journal of a Canoe Voyage from the Falls of St. Anthony to St. Louis." Introduction and notes by Bertha L. Heilbron. *Minnesota History* 17, no. 2 (June 1936).

———. *The Valley of the Mississippi Illustrated.* Ed. Bertha L. Heilbron. Trans. Hermina Poatgieter. St. Paul: Minnesota Historical Society, 1967.

Missouri Republican. Excerpted in John Francis McDermott, *The Lost Panoramas of the Mississippi,* 85. Chicago: University of Chicago Press, 1958.

Robb, John S. Letter, July 24–25, 1848. *Weekly Reveille,* August 7, 1848, p. 1785.

Smith, Thomas Ruys. *River of Dreams: Imagining the Mississippi before Mark Twain.* Baton Rouge: Louisiana State University Press, 2007.

3. Mississippi Harvest

Alexander, Melanie K. *Muscatine's Pearl Button Industry*. Charleston, SC: Arcadia, 2007.

Anfinson, John O. *The River We Have Wrought: A History of the Upper Mississippi*. Minneapolis: University of Minnesota Press, 2005.

"Barry Name Is Linked with Industrial Life for Four Generations." *Muscatine Journal*, May 31, 1940. Iowa Old Press—An IAGenWeb Special Project. http://www.iowaoldpress.com/IA/Muscatine/1940/MAY.html.

Boepple, John. Quoted in Jeffrey J. Kurtz, "The Old Pioneer: The Journey of John F. Boepple, Founder of the Freshwater Pearl Button Industry." Muscatine: Pearl Button Museum, 2003. http://69.49.80.78/museum/Update%20Web/Boepple.htm.

Brady, Tony. Quoted in U.S. Fish and Wildlife Service, Freshwater Mussels of the Upper Mississippi River System: "History of Mussel Harvest on the River." http://www.fws.gov/midwest/mussel/harvest.html.

"Button Workers Indicted: Muscatine Grand Jury Holds Labor Officials Responsible for Workers." *New York Times*, December 31, 1912. http://www.nytimes.com/.

Davis, Mike. Quoted in Mike Brunker, "Mile 640: Gambling, Shellfish and a Nuclear Reactor: Survival and Development on Ancestral Homelands." MSNBC. http://www.msnbc.msn.com/id/5591511/ns/news_The_Mighty_Miss/t/gambling_Shellfish_nuclear_reactor/#.Trk9W65mBQ.

Federal Writers' Project, Works Progress Administration for the State of Iowa. *Iowa: A Guide to the Hawkeye State*. New York: Viking, 1938.

Iowa Public Television. "The Pearl Button Story." Iowa Pathways 2005–2008. http://www.iptv.org/iowapathways/mypath.cfm?ounid=ob_000031.

Kurtz, Jeffrey J. "Resentment Ran High . . . : The Button Worker Strike of 1911." Pearl Button Museum, 2003. (No longer available online.)

"Pearl Clamming and Pearl Button Clamming on the Upper Mississippi River." Kari Pearls. http://www.karipearls.com/pearl-clamming.html.

Regennitter, Melissa. "Engineers Show Off Their Mussels." *Muscatine Journal*, October 3, 2007. http://www.muscatinejournal.com/news/local/article_8dac5c50–385d-5285–9066-cdf9d2be74e5.html.

University of Iowa College of Engineering. "UI Engineer to Help Release Endangered Mussels into Mississippi River Oct. 2." October 1, 2008. http://www.engineering.uiowa.edu/news/newsDetail.php?newsID=88.

Twain, Mark. *Life on the Mississippi*. Mineola, NY: Dover, 2000.

4. Nauvoo, the Beautiful Place

Baxter's Vineyards. "Baxter's History." http://www.nauvoowinery.com/.

Berry, Orville F. "The Deserted City." In Inez Smith Davis, *The Story of the Church: A History of the Church of Jesus Christ of Latter-day Saints and of Its Legal Successor, the Reorganized Church of Jesus Christ of Latter-day Saints*. 3rd ed. Independence, MO: Heritage, 1943.

Black, Susan Easton. "Isaac Galland: Both Sides of the River." *Nauvoo Journal* 8, no. 2 (Fall 1996): 3–9.

Brunker, Mike. "Animosity Simmers in a River Town: Mormon Roots and Mormon Resentment." August 9, 2004. MSNBC. http://www.latam.msnbc.com/id/5625277.

Carroll, Dennis J. "Fear of a Mormon Return: Illinois Town's Fundamentalists Feel Threatened by Giant Temple." *San Francisco Chronicle*, April 29, 2002. http://www.sfgate.com/cgi-bin/article.cgi?f=/c/a/2002/04/29/MN113880.DTL.

City-Data.com. "Stats about All US Cities." http://www.city-data.com/.

Dennis, Jan. "Mormon Temple a Tourism Draw for Tiny Nauvoo." *USA Today*, August 22, 2006. http://www.usatoday.com/travel/destinations/2006–08–22-mormon-temple-tourism_x.htm.

Krakauer, Jon. *Under the Banner of Heaven: A Story of Violent Faith*. New York: Random House, 2004.

Lippincott, Rustin. Interview by author. January 16, 2006.

Logan, Brenda. Interview by author. January 20, 2006.

Nauvoo Tourism Office. Our History: "Exploration and Settlement." Beautiful Nauvoo. http://www.beautifulnauvoo.com/history.html.

———. Our History: "German/Icarian Era: The Most German-Speaking Town in Illinois." Beautiful Nauvoo. http://www.beautifulnauvoo.com/germanera.html.

———. Our History: "Industry/Prohibition." Beautiful Nauvoo. http://www.beautifulnauvoo.com/industry.html.

———. Our History: "Restoration." Beautiful Nauvoo. http://www.beautifulnauvoo.com/restoration.html.

Pinney, Thomas. *History of Wine in America: From the Beginnings to Prohibition*. Berkeley: University of California Press, 1989.

Public Broadcasting Service. *American Prophet: The Story of Joseph Smith.* "Timeline." PBS. http://www.pbs.org/americanprophet/timeline.html.

Quincy, Josiah. "Joseph Smith at Nauvoo." In *Figures of the Past from the Leaves of Old Journals*, 376–400. Boston: Roberts Brothers, 1883.

Sharp, Thomas C. "The Time Is Come!" *Warsaw Signal*, June 11, 1844. In *Uncle Dale's Old Mormon Articles*. www.sidneyrigdon.com/abraodhu/IL/sign1844.htm#0611.

Thomas, Janet. "Nauvoo: On the Banks of the Mississippi." *New Era,* May 2005. http://lds.org/new-era/2005/05/nauvoo-on-the-banks-of-the-mississippi? lang=eng.

Van Biema, David. "The Invasion of the Latter-day Saints." *Time,* July 10, 2000. http://www.time.com/time/reports/mississippi/nauvoo.html.

5. Mound Builders

Birmingham, Robert A., and Leslie E. Eisenberg. *Indian Mounds of Wisconsin.* Madison: University of Wisconsin Press, 2000.

Cockrell, Ron, and HRA Gray and Pape, LLC. *Figures on the Landscape: Effigy Mounds National Monument Historic Resource Study.* Omaha: National Park Service, Midwest Regional Office, 2003. http://www.nps.gov/archive/ efmo/web/hrs/hrs.htm.

Hall, Robert L. "Red Banks, Oneonta, and the Winnebago: Views from a Distant Rock." *Wisconsin Archeologist* 74, nos. 1–4 (1993): 10–79.

Mallam, R. Clark. "Birds, Bears, Panthers, 'Elephants,' and Archeologists." *Wisconsin Archeologist* 61, no. 3 (1980): 375–84.

"National NAGPRA (Native American Graves Protection and Repatriation Act)." Federal Register 66, no. 47 (March 9, 2001): 14201–3.

O'Bright, Jill York. *The Perpetual March: An Administrative History of Effigy Mounds National Monument.* Omaha: National Park Service, Midwest Regional Office, 1989.

Taylor, Richard C. "Notes Respecting Certain Indian Mounds and Earthworks in the Form of Animal Effigies, Chiefly in Wisconsin Territory, U.S." *American Journal of Science and Art* 34 (1838): 88–104.

Thomas, Cyrus. *Report on the Mound Explorations of the Bureau of Ethnology.* Washington, DC: Smithsonian Institution Press, 1985.

6. What the River Carries

State Lines

Allen, Michael R. "Kaskaskia Remains." Ecology of Absence: The Preservation Research Office Blog. March 11, 2008. http://preservationresearch.com/ 2008/03/kaskaskia- remains/.

Handwerk, Brian. National Geographic News: "Steamboat Wreck Sheds Light on Bygone Era." November 18, 2002. *National Geographic.* http://news. nationalgeographic.com/news/2002/11/1118_021118_steamboat.html.

State of Iowa v. State of Illinois, 147 U.S. 1 (1893). Justia.com: U.S. Supreme

Court Center. http://supreme.justia.com/us/147/1/case.html.

Weeks, John A., III. "Keokuk Municipal Bridge, Keokuk, Iowa." July 17, 2009. http://www.johnweeks.com/river_mississippi/pagesB/umissBR04.html.

Oxygen

Beaver, Chaimongkon. "Respiratory Rate of Mayfly Nymphs in Water with Differing Oxygen and Ionic Concentrations." In I. C. Campbell, ed., *Mayflies and Stoneflies: Life Histories and Biology,* 105–7. Boston: Klaver Academic Publishers, 1990.

Francis-Floyd, Ruth. "Dissolved Oxygen for Fish Reproduction." University of Florida IFAS Extension, Fact Sheet FA 27, September 1992 (rev. February 2003).

Commodities

Mangalonzo, John. "Pigs Perish on Submerged Farmland." *Burlington Hawk Eye,* June 19, 2008.

Evidence

Twain, Mark. *Life on the Mississippi*. Mineola, NY: Dover, 2000.

Welvaert, Todd. "Klindt a Free Man Today." March 11, 2004. Quad-Cities Online. http://qconline.com/archives/qco/display.php?id=187492.

Sediment

"*Micropterus dolomieu*. Smallmouth Bass." Texas Freshwater Fishes. http://www.bio.txstate.edu/~tbonner/txfishes/micropterus%20dolomieu.htm.

"Smallmouth Bass." Iowa DNR Fish and Fishing. The Iowa Department of Natural Resources. http://www.iowadnr.gov/fish/iafish/sm-bass.html.

Sunken Treasures

"Destructive Fire in La Crosse: Steamer War Eagle Burned." *La Crosse Evening Democrat,* May 16, 1870, 4.

Jalbert, Andrew J. "The Wreck of the Steamship War Eagle." *Big River Magazine,* July 27, 2007.

Politics

AXYS Analytical Services Ltd. "Emerging Contaminants: Perfluorinated Carboxylates and Sulfonates (including PFOS and PFOA)." AXYS Analytical Advantage. http://www.axysanalytical.com/services/emerging_contaminants/pfos_pfoa_perfluorinated_carboxylates_and_sulfonates/.

"Conflict of Interest: Minn. Official Tied to 3M Drags Feet on Teflon Testing." EWG Home Environmental Working Group. http://www.ewg.org/node/8752.

Edgerly, Mike, and Sasha Aslanian. "Toxic Traces." 5 pts. Minnesota Public Radio, February 22, 2005

————. "The Long Reach of Perfluorochemicals." Minnesota Public Radio. February 22, 2005.

"Hazardous Sites and Substances in Minnesota: 3M Woodbury Site." *St. Paul Pioneer Press,* February 2007.

Lien, Dennis. "Scientist Issues PFC Report: Former MPCA Employee Details Research into 3M Chemical." *St. Paul Pioneer Press,* February 28, 2006.

————. "Down-River Tests Show More PFCs: But State Won't Alter Fish-Consumption Advisories." *St. Paul Pioneer Press,* June 3, 2006.

Oliaei, Fardin, Don Kriens, and Katrina Kessler. "Investigation of Perfluorochemical (PFC) Contamination in Minnesota, Phase One." *Report to Senate Environment Committee.* February 2006.

Philosophies

Marx, Leo. "Mr. Eliot, Mr. Trilling, and Huckleberry Finn." *The American Scholar* 22 (Autumn 1953): 34–39.

Metcalf, Ben. "American Heartworm." *Harper's Magazine,* December 1998, 26–30.

Twain, Mark. *The Adventures of Huckleberry Finn.* New York: Penguin, 1986.

PART II. THE MISSOURI

7. Point of Departure

Brown, Stuart. "Old Kaskaskia Days and Ways." *Transactions of the Illinois State Historical Society,* 1905.

Fitch, George. "The Missouri River: Its Habits and Eccentricities Described by a Personal Friend." *American Magazine* 53, no. 6 (April 1907): 637–40.

"Fort Belle Fontaine." http://www.usgennet.org/usa/mo/county/stlouis/bellefontaine/fort.htm.

Fremling, Calvin R. *Immortal River: The Upper Mississippi in Ancient and Modern Times.* Madison: University of Wisconsin Press, 2005.

Galat, David L., and Robin Lipkin. "Characterizing the Natural Flow Regime of the Missouri River Using Historical Variability in Hydrology." Missouri Cooperative Fish and Wildlife Research Unit, University of Missouri, Columbia, 1999.

Latka, Douglas, John Nestler, and Larry Hesse. "Restoring Physical Habitat in the Missouri River: A Historical Perspective." In *Biological Report 19*, National Biological Survey, Proceedings of the Symposium on Restoration Planning for the Rivers of the Mississippi River Ecosystem, 1993.

Least Heat-Moon, William. *River Horse: A Voyage across America.* New York: Houghton Mifflin, 1999.

"Missouri National Recreational River Nebraska/–South Dakota Water Resources Information and Issues Overview Report." U.S. Fish and Wildlife Service, 2005.

Mussulman, Joseph. "The Missouri Meets the Mississippi." Discovering Lewis & Clark. http://lewis-clark.org/content/content-article.asp?ArticleID=2952.

———. "Mouth of the Missouri: Confluence of the Missouri and Mississippi Rivers, 1880–1890." Discovering Lewis & Clark. http://lewis-clark.org/content/content-article.asp?ArticleID=1411#.

Riddler, Rory. "Rivers Out of Time: Names of State's Two Major Rivers Got Lost in the Translation." *First Capitol News of St. Charles, Missouri,* June 9, 2007.

Schneiders, Robert Kelly. *Unruly River: Two Centuries of Change along the Missouri.* Lawrence: University Press of Kansas, 1999.

St. Louis County Parks and Recreation. "Fort Belle Fontaine Park." St. Louis County, Missouri. http://ww5.stlouisco.com/parks/ftbellefontaine.html.

Thwaites, Reuben Gold. *The Jesuit Relations and Allied Document: Travels and Explorations of the Jesuit Missionaries in New France, 1610–1791; the Original French, Latin and Italian texts, with English Translations and Notes; Illustrated by Portraits, Maps, and Facsimiles.* Cleveland: Burrows Brothers, 1896–1901.

8. Little Dixie

"The Battle of Lexington/Hemp Bales, September 13–20, 1861 in Lexington, Missouri." n2genealogy.com. Last Modified: November 13, 2010. http://

www.civilwar.n2genealogy.com/battles/610913.html.

Croy, Homer. *Jesse James Was My Neighbor.* New York: Duell, Sloan and Pearce, 1949.

Davis, Richard M. "USA Hemp Agriculture Room." 2009. http://www.hempmuseum.org/ROOMS/ARM%20AGRICULTURE.htm.

Fuenfhausen, Gary Gene. "Missouri's Little Dixie: Missouri's 'Slave Belt,' or 'Black Belt,' Also Historically 'Little Dixie.'" 2009. http://littledixie.net/.

Geiger, Mark W. *Missouri's Hidden Civil War: Financial Conspiracy and the Decline of the Planter Elite, 1861–1865.* PhD diss., University of Missouri, 2006.

Hartshorne, Henry. *Household Cyclopedia.* New York: Thomas Kelly, 1881.

"Jesse James's Mother Dead." *Holden (MO) Enterprise,* February 16, 1911. Return to Civil War St. Louis. http://www.civilwarstlouis.com/history/jameszereldasamueldeath.htm.

"Secession at Lexington, MO." *New York Times,* May 5, 1861. http://query.nytimes.com/gst/abstract.html?res=F10812F8395E14768FDDAC0894DD405B818AF0D3.

Stiles, T. J. *Jesse James: Last Rebel of the Civil War.* New York: Vintage, 2003.

Stone, Jeffrey C. *Slavery, Southern Culture, and Education in Little Dixie, 1820–1860.* New York: Routledge, 2006.

9. The Overlook

Andreas, Alfred T. *History of the State of Nebraska.* Chicago: Western Historical Co., 1882.

Bucko. "A River Runs Right Past It; or, Landing in Nebraska City." March 27, 2009. Cowboylands. http://cowboylands.net/blog/2009/03/a-river-runs-right-past-it-or-landing-in-nebraska-city/.

Cooper, T. R. *Nebraska City: The Most Beautiful City of Nebraska; As It Is Today in Story and Pictures.* Nebraska City: Leidigh and Cooper, N.d.

"1804 Journal Entry Archives July 14–21, 1804." The Lewis and Clark Trail. http://www.lewisandclarktrail.com/section1/necities/missouribasin/history1.htm.

Olson, James C. *J. Sterling Morton.* Lincoln: University of Nebraska Press, 1942.

Nebraska State Historical Society. "Nebraska City's Pontoon Bridge Featured in New Book." October 1999. Historical Newsletter. http://www.nebraskahistory.org/publish/publicat/newsletr/oct99.htm.

———. "Nebraska City's Pontoon Bridge." January 2000. Nebraska Timeline. http://www.nebraskahistory.org/publish/publicat/timeline/nebraska_city_pontoon_br.htm.

10. Missouri River Music

Warble (River Mile 2,341, the Headwaters, to River Mile 700)

Gatliff, Robert. "Anatomy of the Plains Flute and What Goes on Inside Them." November 20, 2009. Flutetree. http://www.flutetree.com/nature/InsideNAPF.html.

Hofman, Charles. "Frances Densmore and the Music of the American Indian." *Journal of American Folklore* 59 (January–March 1946): 45–50.

Paulson, Marcy. "Varying Styles of American Indian Wooden Flutes: The History of Making Native American Flute Music." October 26, 2008. Musical Instruments @ Suite 101. http://flute.suite101.com/article.cfm/varying_styles_of_native_american_flutes.

Powers, Maria N. *Oglala Women: Myth, Ritual, and Reality*. Chicago: University of Chicago Press, 1988.

Riggs, Alfred Longley. *Tah-koo Wah-kan: The Gospel among the Dakotas*. Boston: Congregational Sabbath-School and Publishing Society, 1869.

Turkey Legs. Recording on "A Brief Native American Flute History" (website). http://wildhorsemtnflutes.com/.

Another Golden Age (River Mile 617)

Binelli, Mark. "King of Indie Rock: From the Badlands of Omaha Comes Conor Oberst of Bright Eyes—the Best Young Songwriter in America." *Rolling Stone,* January 12, 2001. http://www.rollingstone.com/news/story/6822956/king_of_indie_rock.

Decurtis, Anthony. "Best Songwriter: Conor Oberst." *Rolling Stone's Best of Rock 2008,* May 1, 2008. http://www.rollingstone.com/news/story/20274062/best_songwriter_conor_oberst.

Gulla, Bob. "Blazing Saddle: The Improbable Story of Saddle Creek Records." Posted August 8, 2008. Shock Hound. (No longer available online.)

Hermes, Will. "Next Stop Nowhere." Posted June 29, 2003. Spin. http://www.spin.com/articles/next-stop-nowhere.

McMahan, Tim. "Bright Eyes: It Is Certain." *Omaha Reader.* Posted on Lazy-i, April 5, 2007. http://www.lazy-i.com/Welsch, Casey. "Awesome Alums: Class Assignment Spawns Saddle Creek Records." Posted September 18, 2008; updated December 14, 2008. Daily Nebraskan. http://www.dailynebraskan.com/news/class-assignment-spawns-saddle-creek-records-1.1128468.

Osage Orange (River Mile 465)

Faurot, Charlie. *Three Fiddlers from the Show-Me State: Lyman Enloe, Casey Jones, Cyril Stinnett,* liner notes. CD. County Records, 2005.

Lansford, Kim. Review of *Now That's a Good Tune. The Ozarks Mountaineer,* July/August 2009. Posted in "What the Reviewers Say: *Now That's a Good Tune.*" Voyager Recordings and Publications. http://www.voyagerrecords. com/RVGT.htm.

Ramsay, Meredith. Interview by author. October 2, 2009.

Roberts, Paul. Review: "Cyril Stinnett, 'Grey Eagle'; Lonnie Robertson, 'Lonnie's Breakdown'; Fred Stoneking, 'Saddle Old Spike.'" September 22, 1997. Musical Traditions. http://www.mustrad.org.uk/reviews/us_fiddl.htm.

———. Review of *Joseph Won a Coated Fiddle and Other Fiddle and Accordion Tunes from the Great Plains,* by Dwight Lamb. November 2, 2000. Musical Traditions. http://www.mustrad.org.uk/reviews/lamb.htm.

Walden, Charlie. "Missouri Valley Fiddling." Missouri Old-Time Fiddling Traditions. http://www.missourifiddling.com/MO_FID_TRADITIONS. htm.

Jamming (River Mile 365)

Daniels, Douglas Henry. *Lester Leaps In: The Life and Times of Lester 'Pres' Young.* Boston: Beacon Press, 2005.

Driggs, Frank. *Kansas City Jazz: From Ragtime to Bebop.* New York: Oxford University Press, USA, 2005.

Public Broadcasting Service. *Jazz: A Film By Ken Burns:* Places, Spaces and Changing Faces: "Kansas City: A Wide Open Town." PBS. http://www. pbs.org/jazz/places/places_kansas_city.htm.

Russell, Ross. *Jazz Style in Kansas City and the Southwest.* New York: De Capo Press, 1973.

Vitale, Tom. "Lester Young: 'The Prez' Still Rules at 100." "Morning Edition." National Public Radio, August 27, 2009.

Weinstock, Len. "Coleman Hawkins, Father of the Tenor Sax." The Red Hot Jazz Archive. http://www.redhotjazz.com/hawkinsaticle.html.

Harmony (River Mile 97)

Averett, Nanci. Title not available (Ehren Oncken article). *Columbia Tribune,* October 17, 1996. http://archive.columbiatribune.com/1996/Oct/ 19961017Enteindex.htm.

Burnett, Robyn, and Ken Luebbering. *German Settlement in Missouri: New*

Land, Old Ways. Columbia: University of Missouri Press, 1996.

Conard, Howard Louis. "Gasconade County." In *Encyclopedia of the History of Missouri: A Compendium of History and Biography.* New York: Southern History Co., 1901.

Herman Hill Vineyard and Inn. Hermann Area Performing Artists: "Loehnig German Band." Hermann Hill. http://www.hermannhill.com/.

The Bowman (River Mile 1)

Boyden, David D. "The Violin and Its Technique in the 18th Century." *The Musical Quarterly* 36, no. 1 (January 1950): 9–38.

Lewis, Meriwether. Quoted in "Dance Excerpts." Pierre Cruzatte. http://www.cruzatte.com/resources/danceexcerpts.html.

Mussulman, Joseph. The Corps: Music on the Trail: "Cruzatte's Fiddlin'." Discovering Lewis & Clark. http://www.lewis-clark.org.

Ramsay, Meredith. Interview by author. January 7, 2009.

Slosberg, Daniel. "Lewis and Clarke Dance Party." 2006. Pierre Cruzatte. http://www.cruzatte.com/.

Stowell, Robin. *Violin Technique and Practice in the Late 18th and Early 19th Centuries.* Cambridge: Cambridge University Press, 1985.

"What the Reviewers Say: VRCD 358 *The New Columbia Fiddlers: Fiddle Tunes of the Lewis & Clark Era.*" Seattle, WA: Voyager Records, 2003. Voyager Recordings and Publications. *http://www.voyagerrecords.com/RV358.htm.*

11. The Taking

Brokaw, Tom. *A Long Way from Home: Growing Up in the American Heartland in the Forties and Fifties.* New York: Random House, 2003.

Dunn, Robert A. *Fever, Fire Power, and Flood: The Transformation of the Missouri River Bottomlands in the Dakotas, 1804–2005.* PhD diss., Louisiana State University and Agricultural and Mechanical College, May 2007.

"Floods." *Time,* May 31, 1943. http://www.time.com/time/magazine/article/0,9171,851697–2,00.html.

Melmer, David. "Judge Rules against Yankton Sioux Tribe; Sacred Ground to Become Campground." *Indian Country Today,* April 30, 2003.

Reybold, Eugene. Quoted in Michael L. Lawson, *Dammed Indians Revisited: The Continuing History of the Pick-Sloan Plan and the Missouri River Sioux,* 40. Pierre: South Dakota State Historical Society Press, 2009.

Ritter, Beth R. *Dispossession to Diminishment: The Yankton Sioux Reservation, 1858–1998.* PhD diss., University of Nebraska, 1999.

United States v. North American Transportation and Trading Co., 253 U.S. 330 (1920). http://caselaw.lp.findlaw.com/scripts/getcase.pl?court=us&vol=253&invol=330.

"U.S. Masters the Big Muddy." *Life*, August 22, 1955.

12. Restorations

Beasley, Conger, Jr. *Sundancers and River Demons: Essays on Landscape and Ritual.* Fayetteville: University of Arkansas Press, 1990.

Gross, Stephen P. *The Missouri River Ecosystem: Exploring the Prospects for Recovery.* Washington, DC: National Academy Press, 2002.

The Journals of the Lewis and Clark Expedition. Lincoln: University of Nebraska Press, 2005. University of Nebraska–Lincoln Libraries, Electronic Text Center. http://lewisandclarkjournals.unl.edu.

National Research Council. *Restoration of Aquatic Ecosystems: Science, Technology and Public Policy.* Washington, DC: National Academy Press, 1992. http://books.nap.edu/openbook.php?isbn=0309045347.

U.S. Fish and Wildlife Service. "Boyer Chute National Wildlife Refuge." Last updated August 4, 2008. hppt://www.fws.gov/Midwest/boyerchute/.

PART III. THE PLATTE

13. The Middle Ground

Dillard, Annie. Introduction to *The Best American Essays 1988,* ed. Annie Dillard and Robert Atwan. Boston: Houghton Mifflin, 1988.

Ehrlich, Gretel. *The Solace of Open Spaces.* New York: Penguin, 1985.

Kromm, David E. "Ogallala Aquifer." Water Encyclopedia: Science and Issues. http://www.waterencyclopedia.com/Oc-Po/Ogallala-Aquifer.html.

Laukaitus, Algis J. "DNR: Platte Has Hit Its Limit for Irrigation." *Lincoln Journal Star,* December 16, 2008.

Mitrofanova, Yelena. "Lincoln Is Gathering Place for Refugees from Around the World." University of Nebraska–Lincoln Extension in Lancaster County. http://lancaster.unl.edu/community/articles/lincolnrefugees.shtml.

Tuan, Yi-Fu. *Topophilia: A Study of Environmental Perception, Attitudes, and Values.* Englewood Cliffs, NJ: Prentice-Hall, 1974.

14. No Other River

Barbour, Erwin Hinckley. "Wells and Windmills of Nebraska." *Water-supply and Irrigation Papers of the United States Geological Survey* 29 (1899): 6–82.

Bent, Arthur Cleveland. "Sandhill Crane." Familiar Birds: Life Histories of Familiar North American Birds. http://www.birdsbybent.com/ch61–70/shcrane.html.

Dobesh, Mike. "The Platte River Boondoggle." *Lincoln Journal Star,* May 8, 2008. http://www.journalstar.com/articles/2007/04/06/opinion/columns/doc46157b133c d48852994662.txt.

Eiseley, Loren. *The Immense Journey.* New York: Vintage Books, 1957.

Goeke, James. "Surface Water and Groundwater Relationships in Nebraska." http://watercenter.edu/WRRI/WaterResearch/GoekeLegislatorsBriefing MaterialsOct10pdf.

Grooms, Steve. *The Cry of the Sandhill Crane.* Minocqua, WI: NorthWord Press, 1992.

Hendee, David. "Trees along the Platte River Using Less Water." *Omaha World-Herald.* Posted on Farm and Ranch, October 8, 2009. http://www.myfarmandranch.com/90/nws/3676.

Johnsgard, Paul A. *Cranes of the World.* Bloomington: Indiana University Press, 1983.

———. *Cry of the Sandhill Cranes.* Lincoln: University of Nebraska Press, 1991.

Krapu, Gary L. "Sandhill Cranes and the Platte River." In *A Gathering of Angels: Ecology and Conservation of Migratory Birds,* ed. K. P. Able. Ithaca: Cornell University Press, 1999.

McGuire, V. L. "Water Level Changes in the High Plains Aquifer, Predevelopment to 2005 and 2003 to 2005. Revised, September 2007." USGS Scientific Investigation Report 2006–5324. http://pubs.usgs.gov/sir/2006/5324.

Moore, Martha Missouri. Quoted in Merrill J. Mattes, *The Great Platte River Road.* Lincoln: Nebraska State Historical Society, 1969.

National Audubon Society, Inc. "Sandhill Crane." Audubon. http://web1.audubon.org/waterbirds/species.php?speciesCode=sancra.

Nebraskans First. September 1, 2008. http://www.nebraskansfirst.com/.

Olson, James C., and Ronald C. Naugle. *History of Nebraska.* 3rd ed. Lincoln: University of Nebraska Press, 1997.

U.S. Fish and Wildlife Service. Species Profile: "Whooping Crane (*Grus Americana*)." http://ecos.fws.gov/speciesProfile/profile/speciesProfile. action?spcode=B003.

15. Nine-Mile Prairie

Barth, Frederick. *Ritual and Knowledge among the Baktaman of New Guinea.* New Haven, CT: Yale University Press, 1975.

Bernhardt, Peter. *Wily Violets and Underground Orchids.* Chicago: University of Chicago Press, 1989.

Costello, David F. *The Prairie World.* Minneapolis: University of Minnesota Press, 1969.

Frazier, Ian. *Great Plains.* New York: Penguin, 1989.

Hachiya, Kim. "Teaching Geography with a Camera." *Scarlet,* March 8, 2001. http://www.unl.edu/scarlet/v11n08/v11n08features.html.

Leopold, Aldo. *A Sand County Almanac with Essays on Conservation from Round River.* New York: Ballantine Books, 1991.

Merton, Thomas. *A Year with Thomas Merton: Daily Meditations from His Journals.* New York: HarperCollins, 2004.

Norris, Kathleen. *Dakota: A Spiritual Geography.* New York: Ticknor and Fields, 1993.

Peattie, Donald Culross. *Flowering Earth.* Bloomington: Indiana University Press, 1991.

Rousek, Ernest. Interview by author. December 19, 2006.

Tobey, Ronald C. *Saving the Prairies: The Life Cycle of the Founding School of American Plant Ecology, 1895–1955.* Berkeley: University of California Press, 1981.

Weaver, John Ernest. *Prairie Plants and Their Environment: A Fifty-Year Study in the Midwest.* Lincoln: University of Nebraska Press, 1968.

———. "The North American Prairie." *The American Scholar* 13 (1944).

Weaver, John Ernest, and Frederic E. Clements. *Plant Ecology.* 1st ed. New York: McGraw-Hill, 1929.

———. *Plant Ecology.* 2nd ed. New York: McGraw-Hill, 1938.

16. Pawnee Homecoming

Bouc, Ken. "Pawnee Corn: New Hope for Old Crops." *NEBRASKAland,* June 2007.

Burke, Paul. "Treaty with the Pawnee: October 9, 1833." First People. http://www.firstpeople.us/FP-Html-Treaties/TreatyWithThePawnee1833.html.

Dunbar, John B. "The Plains Indians: Their History and Ethnology." *Magazine of American History* 4, no. 4 (1880): 242–79.

Fine-Dare, Kathleen S. *Grave Injustice: The American Indian and Repatriation Movement and NAGPRA.* Lincoln: University of Nebraska Press, 2002.

"Interesting [*sic*] from Nebraska and the Pawnee Reservation; Sioux Indians Attacking Pawnees Upon Their Reservation; A Day Among the Pawnees and at the Agency; Sunday in a Mormon Hand-cart Train Returning Miners from Pike's Peak General News." *New York Times,* July 9, 1860.

James, Edwin. Quoted in George Francis Will and George E. Hyde, *Corn among the Indians of the Upper Missouri.* St. Louis: William Harvey Miner Co., 1917.

KOLN. "Students Help Shell Sacred Pawnee Corn in Kearney." October 26, 2010. 1011Now. http://www.1011now.com/gieveryday/headlines/Students_Help_Shell_Sacred_Pawnee_Corn_in_Kearney_105732783.html.

Long, Stephen. Quoted in George Francis Will and George E. Hyde, *Corn among the Indians of the Upper Missouri.* St. Louis: William Harvey Miner Co., 1917.

Lowrie, Robert H. *Indians of the Plains.* Garden City, NY: American Science Museum Books, 1954.

Murie, James R. *Ceremonies of the Pawnee.* Ed. Douglas Parks. Lincoln: University of Nebraska Press, 1989.

Potter, Lori. "Historic Crop: A Corn Crop that Yielded Just Five Undersized Ears of Corn Small Success for Ronnie O'Brien." August 25, 2007. Kearney Hub. http://www.kearneyhub.com/news/local/article_52d194ae-e211-5cf2-ad16-ac45806c291b.html.

Reed, Leslie. "Pawnee Heritage: Tribe's Corn Grows Anew in 'Original Homeland.'" *Omaha World Herald,* May 26, 2009.

Weltfish, Gene. *The Lost Universe: Pawnee Life and Culture.* Lincoln: University of Nebraska Press, 1977.

Wishart, David. *An Unspeakable Sadness: The Dispossession of the Nebraska Indians.* Lincoln: University of Nebraska Press, 1994.

17. Gone to the Beets

Biennial Report of the State Board of Irrigation to the Governor of Nebraska. Issue 1. Lincoln: Nebraska State Board of Irrigation, 1914.

Eschner, T. R., R. F. Hadley, and K. D. Crowley. "Hydrologic and Morphologic Changes in Channels of the Platte River Basin in Colorado, Wyoming, and Nebraska: A Historic Perspective." United States Geological Survey Professional Paper 12-A, 1983.

Harmon, L. C. "Children and Sugar Beets." October 17, 1940. U.S. National Archives, Hall County, NE. Records of the Office of the Secretary of Agriculture (16-G-159-AAA-6437W). http://fr.wikipedia.org/Wiki/Fichier:Children_and_Sugar_beets_Nebraska_1940.jpg.

Hine, Lewis Wickes. "Sugar Beet Workers, Sugar City, Colorado. Mary, Six Years . . ." Lewis Hine Photographs. www.lewishinephotographs.com/content/sugar-beet-workers-sugar-city-colorado-mary-six-years-lucy-eight-ethel-ten-family-has-been-h.

Johnson, W. Carter. "Woodland Expansions in the Platte River, Nebraska: Patterns and Causes." *Ecological Monographs* 64, no. 1 (1994): 45–84.

Mapes, Kathleen. *Sweet Tyranny: Migrant Labor, Industrial Agriculture, and Imperial Politics*. Urbana and Chicago: University of Illinois Press, 2009.

Morton, J. Sterling. "New Things Which Are Very Old." *Nebraska City Conservative*, July 19, 1908.

Preston, Jack R. "Heyward G. Leavitt's Influence on Sugar Beets and Irrigation in Nebraska." *Agricultural History* 76 (2002): 381–92.

Rundin, Walter C. Scotts Bluff County: Nebraska's Garden Spot: The Valley of the North Platte. N.d. http://www.wnfrhc.org/~scottsbluff/booklet/booklet.html.

Saylor, Charles. *Progress of the Beet-Sugar Industry in the United States in 1899*. Washington, DC: Government Printing Office, 1900.

———. *Progress of the Beet-Sugar Industry in the United States in 1901*. Washington, DC: Government Printing Office, 1902.

———. "The Present Status of the American Beet Sugar Industry." *American Sugar Industry and Beet Sugar Gazette* 7 (February 1905): 76.

Sykes, Hope Williams. *Second Hoeing*. 1935. Reprint, Lincoln: University of Nebraska Press, 1982.

TCD Economic Development. "History of the Valley—Twin Cities Development Association, Inc.—Nebraska: Scottsbluff, Terrytown, Mitchell, Bayard." 2002–2003. Twin Cities Development Association., Inc. http://www.tcdne.org/.

Twitty, Eric. "Silver Wedge: The Sugar Beet Industry in Fort Collins: A Historical Context." August 2003. SWCA Environmental Consultants. http://www.fcgov.com/historicpreservation/pdf/sugar-beet-industry-doc.pdf.

U.S. Department of Agriculture. "Additional Net Irrigation to Raise a Maximum Sugar Beet Crop 10 out of 20 Years (Median Year)." http://efotg.sc.egov.usda.gov//references/public/NE/Irrig_Guide_maps_pdf.

U.S. Department of Agriculture Natural Resources Conservation Service. "National Irrigation Guide, Part 652, Nebraska Supplements to NIG." http://efotg.sc.egov.usda.gov//references/public/NE/NE_Irrig_Guide_Index.pdf.

U.S. Geological Survey. "Platte River Ecosystem Resources and Management, with Emphasis on the Big Bend Reach in Nebraska." 2006. USGS Northern Prairie Wildlife Research Center. www.npwrc.usgs.gov/resource/habitat/plrivmgt/factors.htm.

Williams, Hattie Plum. "A Social Study of the Russian Germans." *University of Nebraska University Studies* 16, no. 3 (1916).

18. Meanderings

Andreas, Alfred T. *History of the State of Nebraska.* Chicago: Western Historical Co., 1882.

Hayes, Brian. "Up a Lazy River: Meandering through a Classic Theory of Why Rivers Meander." *American Scientist,* November–December 2006. http://www.americanscientist.org/issues/num2/up-a-lazy-river/1.

Hogarth, William. *The Analysis of Beauty.* New Haven, CT: Yale University Press, 1997.

Kooser, Ted. *Local Wonders: Seasons in the Bohemian Alps.* Lincoln: University of Nebraska Press, 2002.

Laukaitis, Algs J. "Creek in Antelope Park Gets Facelift." *Lincoln Journal-Star,* March 20, 2006.

Leopold, Luna, and W. B. Langbein. "River Meanders." *Scientific American,* June 1966.

Sakalowsky, Peter P. "Theories of Stream Meander Causation: A Review and Analysis." *Earth Sciences Reviews* 10, no. 2 (1974): 121–38.

Thoreau, Henry David. *Henry David Thoreau: Collected Essays and Poems.* New York: Library of America, 2001.

Twain, Mark. *Life on the Mississippi.* Mineola, NY: Dover, 2000.

About the Author

Lisa Knopp is Associate Professor of English at the University of Nebraska–Omaha and the author of four previous books, including most recently *Interior Places*. She lives in Lincoln, Nebraska.

PHOTO BY WYN WILEY